FATIH AKIN'S CINEMA AND THE NEW SOUND OF EUROPE

NEW DIRECTIONS IN NATIONAL CINEMAS

Robert Rushing, editor

FATIH AKIN'S CINEMA AND THE NEW SOUND OF EUROPE

Berna Gueneli

INDIANA UNIVERSITY PRESS

This book is a publication of

Indiana University Press
Office of Scholarly Publishing
Herman B Wells Library 350
1320 East 10th Street
Bloomington, Indiana 47405 USA

iupress.indiana.edu

 The paper used in this publication meets the minimum requirements of the American National Standard for Information Sciences—Permanence of Paper for Printed Library Materials, ANSI Z39.48-1992.

Manufactured in the United States of America

Cataloging information is available from the Library of Congress.

ISBN 978-0-253-03788-6 (hdbk.)
ISBN 978-0-253-02445-9 (pbk.)
ISBN 978-0-253-03789-3 (web PDF)

1 2 3 4 5 24 23 22 21 20 19

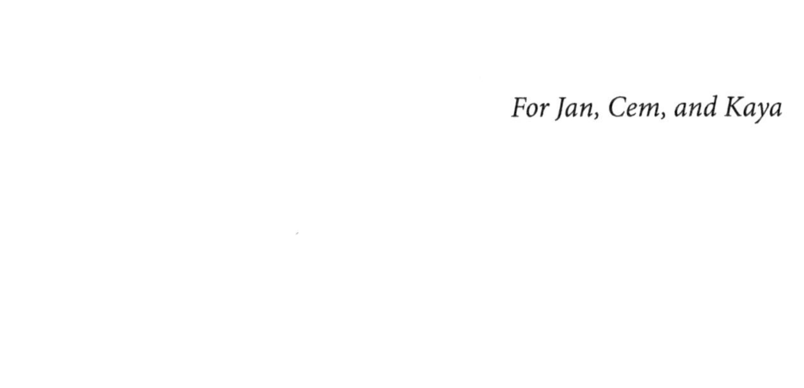

For Jan, Cem, and Kaya

Contents

Acknowledgments

SEVERAL PEOPLE HAVE generously provided academic mentorship during the intellectual journey that eventually led to this book. I would particularly like to thank Sabine Hake, Katherine Arens, and Janet Swaffar at the University of Texas for their guidance. I was able to begin writing *Fatih Akın's Cinema and the New Sound of Europe* after being awarded a Harris Fellowship research leave from Grinnell College in 2015–2016, and the manuscript gradually took shape in an office provided by the Georgia Institute of Technology during my fellowship year. I would like to thank my colleagues at both Grinnell College and Georgia Tech for these resources, which were enormously helpful in bringing this project to fruition. It was also during this time that I initiated contact with the Indiana University Press. I especially thank my acquisitions editor, Janice Frisch, and the New Directions in National Cinemas series editor, Robert Rushing, for their early interest in my project and their continuous support throughout the review process. I would also like to express my thanks to the anonymous reviewers for their detailed and constructive criticism that I believe improved the book immensely. I further thank Ann-Kristin Homann and Nurhan Şekerci from Bombero International, Marine Dorville from Pyramide Distribution, Anja Padge from Wüste Film, and Richard Reitinger from the Hamburg Media School for their friendly support and for providing the images for this book. I would like to thank them particularly for their kindness, despite the quite excessive number of emails I sent. I also thank my new colleagues at the University of Georgia, where this manuscript received its finishing touches, for warmly welcoming me into the department and for giving me a new academic home. I am grateful for the University of Georgia's First-Book Subvention Program of the Franklin College of the Arts and Sciences, which provided generous financial support for this book. Ultimately, I would like to express my gratitude to many dear colleagues from across the country for their invaluable support and good humor. I would particularly like to thank Bradley Boovy, Gwenola Caradec, Ela Gezen, Mariana Ivanova, Werner Krauss, Matthias Rothe, Gemma Sala, and Per Urlaub for their friendship throughout the years, and for reminding me to laugh sometimes. None of my endeavors would have been possible without the unwavering support of my family: my mom and dad and my siblings, Ali and Nur, who have been so supportive in countless ways during my lifelong studies, travels, and explorations! I thank Jan Uelzmann for sharing his intellect, wit, and humor with me. And finally I would like to thank Jan, Cem, and Kaya for their unconditional love and for simply being with me, anytime and anywhere.

FATIH AKIN'S CINEMA AND THE NEW SOUND OF EUROPE

Introduction

FATIH AKIN: A CONTEMPORARY FILMMAKER FROM GERMANY

And the Winner Is: Fatih Akın[1]

Winner of the Golden Bear at the Berlin International Film Festival for *Gegen die Wand* (*Head-On*) in 2004, thirty-year-old Turkish German filmmaker Fatih Akın quickly became one of the most prominent European directors of the new millennium. Shortly after, his international success reached new heights with *Auf der anderen Seite* (*The Edge of Heaven*, 2007), which brought him the Best Screenplay Prize at the Cannes Film Festival, the European Film Award, and the LUX Prize of the European Parliament, to name but a few of his honors. In 2008, claimed by two nations, Akın was selected with two films in Turkey and Germany as a candidate for Academy Award nominations.[2] Perceived as a migrant, Turkish, German, and European filmmaker, Akın is hard to pin down to a single category. He has multiple, fluid affiliations. The Douglas Sirk Award, announced at the 2014 Film Fest Hamburg in Akın's hometown in northern Germany, highlighted the transnational aspect of Akın's cinema. He was particularly praised for putting the city of Hamburg onto the global screen and for inspiring filmmakers in Germany and Turkey with his work as a director and producer. Akın received the 2014 award after completing his trilogy "Liebe, Tod, und Teufel" ("Love, Death, and the Devil"), with *The Cut* (2014), joining previous award winners such as Tilda Swinton in 2013 and Andreas Dresen and Peter Rommel in 2011.

An essential aim of my book is to show that through Akın's films, an aesthetically orchestrated multiethnicity within the context of a transnational Europe becomes increasingly audible and visible and reshapes notions of Europe, European cinema, and cinematic history. That is, *Fatih Akın's Cinema and the*

New Sound of Europe analyzes the aesthetic and thematic composition of Akın's Turkey-engaged cinema, as much as it clarifies the audiovisual understanding of the changing configurations of European cinema. Through close readings of *Im Juli* (*In July*, 2000), *Head-On*, and *The Edge of Heaven* in chapters 1 through 3, I untangle the sonic and visual composition of multiethnicity and polyphony in Akın's films. In so doing, I argue that Akın audiovisually aestheticizes European diversity and complicates existing notions of the continent, its history, and its cinema. I place these inquiries into a European context by discussing European-auteur cinema in chapter 4. The analysis of Akın's cinematic narrative, mise-en-scène, and sound foregrounds his "aesthetic of heterogeneity"—a productive and creative interplay of diverse, transnational, and often intertextual audiovisual elements manifest in his choice of music, dialogue, setting, and cast.

Hence, I assert that with Akın's cinema, a new and innovative diversity in terms of plot and story, aesthetics, and intertextualities has begun in German filmmaking. Additionally, a new transnational aspect of his cinema, reaching across geographical, temporal, and generic boundaries, has taken center stage. His production, method, and aesthetics reflect diversity and interact with each other. More precisely, this means that the production of Akın's films is transnational, his method is intertextual, and the resulting aesthetics are heterogeneous.[3]

As a participant and winner in festivals and award ceremonies, Akın certainly continues in a particular German film tradition, although with a fresh twist. German cinema has been a long-standing participant in the international film circuits, be it in art house cinemas or in international film festivals and competitions in Europe and around the globe. Known especially for its so-called art house cinema of the past and present—ranging from expressionist film of the early Weimar Republic, to the New German Cinema of the 1970s and 1980s, to contemporary Berlin School directors such as the prolific Christian Petzold—and the more popular, historically engaged films of the early 2000s,[4] German cinema has made its mark internationally throughout film history, although with varying intensity, especially considering the hiatus after the decline of New German Cinema.[5]

Young and up-and-coming German filmmakers, including Akın, have once more revived and increased German participation in the international film circuits. This new generation has shown the breadth and new directions of contemporary German film either by participating in alternative webfests for internet films–which defy the limitations of conventional capital- and profit-driven film production and distribution—or by participating in the more conventional film festivals that provide visibility for more traditionally produced and distributed films.

At the Melbourne Web Series Festival, for example, the Grand Jury Prize 2013 went to *Mission Backup Earth*, a German sci-fi production by Alexander

Pfander, who uses crowd sourcing for his films. At the Webfest Berlin 2015, official selections included the locally colored Bavarian comedy *Positive Sinking* by Thomas Heinemann, but also *Polyglot*, a multilingual web series by self-taught Rwandan German director Amelia Umuhire and Turkish German cameraman Ferhat Yunus Topraklar, to name just a few of the aesthetically, thematically, and stylistically divergent productions.

At the more traditional Student Academy Awards in 2015, for example, all three Student Oscars in the category "foreign," went to German and Austrian film schools. İlker Çatak from the Hamburg Media School, already a Turkish German finalist in 2014, was the 2015 Gold winner for his short film *Sadakat* (*Fidelity*, 2014), a film that reminds viewers of the 2013 Gezi protests in Istanbul. Through the international platform of festivals and award ceremonies, these young German/European filmmakers bring a variety of topics, aesthetics, and genres/genre mixes, related in one way or another to European sensibilities and inquiries, to an ever-growing international audience.

Despite the transnational and global aspirations and conditions of most contemporary cinematic productions, such festival entrees and international distribution often frame a particular film in a national context—additionally, there has always been a (governmental) interest and agenda in the nationalizing of cinema for the purposes of self-definition and presentation inside and outside the nation.[6] Already in its early days, however, European cinema featured an international crew, cast, and production.[7] Today, with globalization's effect on film, most of European cinema operates in a transnational and "Europeanizing" context of film production, and Randall Halle even suggests that the films he studies in *German Film after Germany: Toward a Transnational Aesthetic* indicate that "transnational cinema is often synonymous with European cinema."[8]

Surely the widely used critical term "transnational" has several definitions. The notion of transnational cinema captures the effects of globalization on the production, distribution, and aesthetic composition of film, and it foregrounds diasporic, exilic, and postcolonial themes, focusing almost exclusively on non-Western filmmakers working "within the West," as discussed most prominently in Hamid Naficy's seminal *An Accented Cinema*.[9] Most of the different approaches advocate a transnational cinema because of the limitations of the category "national" for many films produced in today's globalized film industry. While global financing and distribution structures certainly have an effect on the filmic products themselves, I suggest that the transnational ties and lifestyles of young filmmakers producing in Germany (and Europe) have a vast impact on the products as well.

With award-winning filmmakers such as the winner of the 2015 Student Academy Awards, Çatak, and webfest awardee Umuhire, as well as Fatih Akın, international attention is now shifting to filmmakers with a transnational background and to the stories they tell set in a heterogeneous and diverse society. Increasingly, they provide for a multiethnic and polyphonic disposition of a national "German" cinema and transform it into a transnational European cinema. This vision of society and cinema is precisely what sets Akın and his contemporaries apart from the "accented cinema" that Hamid Naficy locates in 2001 at the margins of Western filmmaking, but they are also different from Naficy's more recent "multiplex cinema," which generally seems to be credited with less artistic merit.[10]

Ultimately, I argue that these present-day European filmmakers' cinematic productions, aesthetics, and narratives represent important interventions into the new millennial filmic landscape of Germany, Turkey, and Europe. That is, I claim that, on the one hand, their films recall the transnational makeup of the contemporary European film industry that Anna Jäckel, Katrin Sieg, Mike Wayne, and Randall Halle discuss and analyze in their work, and, on the other hand, I maintain that these directors and their films also occupy a creative space representing the transnational composition of Germany's and Europe's past and present. Not only does their work reach far beyond the national and even supranational boundaries of Germany and Europe in terms of production and setting, but by entering, as for example in the case of Akın and Çatak, into Turkish territories and aesthetically and thematically incorporating Turkish texts and contexts into their work, their films extend, redefine, and shift hegemonic narratives about German (European) film and film history.

In the field of literature, Leslie Adelson makes a similar point. In her groundbreaking work *The Turkish Turn in Contemporary German Literature*, Adelson analyzes the "literature of Turkish migration" from the 1990s and focuses on "the reconfigurations of the German national archive" through these texts.[11] Adelson detects "new modes of orientation in German literature."[12] She continues, "These literary narratives provoke us to ponder the historical intelligibility of our time, to become more historically literate by reading against the grain of existing categories, concepts, and statistics of migration in order to ask what worlds we inhabit as the millennium turns."[13]

Adding to this mode of reading, I propose including Turkish archives, texts, and contexts in the analyses of the Turkish German cinema of Akın.[14] For I argue that these Turkish entanglements are highly significant in Akın's oeuvre, and that they carry a different weight as compared to Adelson's observations in her study of the literature of the 1990s. Adelson states that "While individual texts may allude to greater and lesser degree to the Republic of Turkey, the national culture of Turkey is not a necessary or primary frame of reference for the literature in question."[15] Analyzing the work of directors such as Akın and Çatak, I argue that both "national" cultures serve, among other cultures, as frames of references for the filmic products. Here, the creative process is multidirectional.

That is, just as Ela Gezen, Kader Konuk, Mert Bahadır Reisoğlu, Karen Yeşilada, and others in the field of literature productively expand the field of inquiry and scholarship into the Turkish archive,[16] I claim that the Turkish intertextualities in Akın's work equally intervene in our understanding of film and film history and urge us to include an inquiry of the Turkish archive.

Ultimately, the filmmakers' multiperspectival look at a multiethnic world reflects the complexities of the twenty-first century. With their films, they help to envision and normalize—in a popular format—a pluralistic, diverse demography in Germany and Europe, as in the case of Akın's cinema. Adelson sees the literature of migration to be more than a mere contemplation of the demographically transformed landscape of Germany.[17] I agree that also in the field of cinema, there are certainly additional dimensions to the heterogeneity of Turkish German film than a mere demographic one, but at the same time, I also believe in the importance of the dissemination of images and sounds of multiethnicity and polyphony in the audiovisual medium of film, in addition to whatever else their thematic and artistic foci might be. Such cinematic imaginings of diversity across a multitude of thematically, stylistically, and aesthetically divergent productions are the more important in a European society that persistently displays xenophobia and racism well into the twenty-first century.

In the second half of the twentieth century, economic, educational, and political im/migration to Europe has resulted in an ever more multiethnic citizenry. Yet xenophobic events, such as the Pegida[18] rallies, an increase in support for ultraright political parties, such as the AfD, the killing of refugees and assaults on refugee camps in Germany (1992, 2014/15), the Brussels attacks in Belgium (2016), the Paris attacks and the Charlie Hebdo attacks in France (2015), and the London bombings (2005), to mention but a few, reveal complicated relationships between race, ethnicity, religion, citizenship, and belonging in contemporary Europe. My work engages with these complications through a scholarly analysis of the artistic perspectives.

By no means do I suggest that Akın's films are an essentializing ethnographic representation of a certain minority. However, the way the fictional stories and figures are put into scene, with their particular aesthetics, foreground to the spectator and scholar alike a meticulous choreography of European heterogeneity. By analyzing the audiovisual aesthetics, combined with the narrative structures, casting, and mise-en-scène, of each cinematic production, I show how the films in my study subtly reveal filmic imaginings of a diverse Europe that in some way want to—and manage to—productively engage with, and in some cases overcome, these complications.

Fatih Akın's Cinema and the New Sound of Europe is the first comprehensive book-length study in English on Turkish German filmmaker Fatih Akın.[19] The son of Turkish migrants in Germany, Akın is arguably one of the most critically acclaimed directors in Germany and Europe today. As stated above, his transnational films are celebrated at film festivals and in the press worldwide. He is the first minority director in Germany to receive numerous awards, including the Order of Merit of the Federal Republic of Germany (for depicting the problems of minorities). Often seen as a poster child for Turkish German migration, Akın is particularly relevant due to the subtle treatment of European integration and diversity that has crystallized in much of his work and to the artistic merits in his filmography. In several of his films made during what I call the "Turkish German entanglement period" (1995–2014), which includes the completion of his Turkey-engaged trilogy "Love, Death, and the Devil" (2004–2014), Akın gives a voice and face to the contemporary fabric of and discourses on German and European society. These include Europe's often underrepresented multiethnic and multilingual citizenry.

Many of the films from Akın's first period—the period in focus in this book—develop a particular filmic aesthetic and style that in one way or another engage with Turkey, Turkish musical and filmic traditions, or history, all of which merge and become an important part of Akın's filmmaking.[20] Certainly, periods are never clear cut and include overlaps and incongruities. The Turkish German entanglement period also includes films that have a different geographical context such as Akın's segment in the multidirector work *New York, I Love You* (2009), or a different historical setting, as in *The Cut*. Likewise, later films that were produced after the completion of his trilogy, such as his road movie *Tschick* (2016), an adaptation of Wolfgang Herrendorf's novel of the same title that Akın cowrote with Hark Bohm, revisit genres and themes from his early period (road movie, multiethnic characters).

By repeatedly including characters of Turkish and Turkish German backgrounds as well as other so-called hyphenated identities in his Turkey-engaged films, such as in *In July*, *Head-On*, and *The Edge of Heaven*, Akın foregrounds a normalization of ethnic minorities in Europe and in European cinema, which has wide-reaching implications. Akın's films from the early period include his first shorts *Sensin- Du bist es* (Sensin, you are the one, 1995) and *Getürkt* (Turkified, 1996); his documentaries *Wir haben vergessen zurückzukehren* (We forgot to return, 2001), *Crossing the Bridge: The Sound of Istanbul* (2005), and *Müll im Garten Eden* (*Polluting Paradise*, 2012); and his features *Kurz und schmerzlos* (*Short Sharp Shock*, 1998), *In July*, *Head-On*, *The Edge of Heaven*, and *The Cut* (2014).

The production of these transnational films coincided with the expanding of the European Union in the 2000s, in which the prime concerns were, and continue to be, the EU's economy; eastern enlargement and integration; issues of race, ethnicity, and illegal immigration; and the questions related to the increase of non-European refugees. Akın's audiovisual aesthetics and the sociopolitical relevance therein are of utmost importance for an analysis of his work of that time. Taking the Turkish German setting of these films as an example, I argue that the sound and mise-en-scène (composition of setting, actors, props, and so on) in his films often provide insights into more general questions of European society and politics. On the one hand, Akın's audiovisual imaginings of a New Europe challenge traditional (EU) perspectives on Turkey. For example, Akın adds Istanbul to the ranks of classic cosmopolitan European urban spaces (e.g., London, Paris, Berlin), despite Turkey's long tenure as the only Muslim candidate country to the EU. In terms of history, Akın adds new dimensions, from a Turkish German perspective, into complicated historical debates between Europe and Turkey by portraying a narrative about the violent Armenian expulsion in the Ottoman Empire and the resulting Armenian global migration. Akın's filmic Europe thus includes intertwined global histories, such as Ottoman-Armenian history. *The Cut* therefore participates in creating a "multidirectional memory" discourse, to use Michael Rothberg's term.[21] In Akın's films, places do not exist side by side in isolation, but are placed in dynamic relationships. Through tensions of aural and visual displays of multiethnicity—subverting monolingual, homogenous fantasies—and through different converging histories, the films construct a vision of a complex, cosmopolitan, and mobile Europe of both the past and present.

Akın's cinematic evaluations of Europe's and Turkey's role in this New Europe are relevant, especially considering the protests (2013, 2014) in Turkey against former Prime Minister Recep Tayyip Erdoğan (president of Turkey since 2014) and his government, and the solidarity that was shown across Europe in 2013—including Akın's YouTube video and open letter in support of the Turkish Gezi Park protesters.[22] The media discourse surrounding the Turkish president and his government continued in 2016 and 2017 in Germany and throughout Europe. In 2017, for example, President Erdoğan received much international news coverage for his outspoken criticism of European countries that prevented Turkish politicians from campaigning on their soil for a planned constitutional referendum in Turkey.[23] Already in 2016, global media attention turned to President Erdoğan with coverage on Turkey's internal political instabilities after the attempted coup in the summer of 2016. Even earlier that year, Erdoğan's personal denouncing of German comedians such as Jan Böhmermann ("the Böhmermann affair") and other German TV hosts for their direct criticism of his presidency and person had received extensive media attention. Lastly, the media in 2016 had covered Turkey's opposition to the online text of the Aghet concert—an EU-funded project based on the events of 1915—performed by the Dresden Symphony.[24] At the same time, the Turkish government continued negotiations concerning its position in the EU, where such freedom of expression—artistic and political—is a basic right.

Akın's cinema participates in the creation of the new sound and visuality of European cinema, a move that also carries a decidedly political dimension.

Through in-depth analyses of the films, my book reveals the political nature of soundscapes, settings, and cast decisions, thereby interweaving aesthetics and politics. Such analyses employ Akın's audiovisual aesthetics as a lens to examine questions of migration and citizenship in the New Europe and the filmic representations of a diverse and modern Turkey, with its ambiguous position therein.

Competing Narratives about Europe: Discourse, Experience, Imagination

Examining the mythological origins of Europe's name from the perspective of the twenty-first century invokes a sense of bitter irony. Europa was a Phoenician noblewoman, whose origins would be located in today's Middle East along the eastern Mediterranean coast (reaching into today's Gaza, Israel, Jordan, Lebanon, and Syria), and who was abducted by the Greek god Zeus. Greece, considered one of the ancient centers for European philosophy and civilization, was close to "exiting" the EU (in the short-lived "Grexit" movement) due to its financial crisis in 2015. And contemporary Syria, a war-torn region in the Middle East, beyond the geopolitical borders of Europe, is a country whose refugees, desperate to reach Europe for survival, are not embraced by all of Europe, in contrast to the beautiful kidnapped maiden who gave Europe her name.

Europe defies a simplistic definition. It both does not exist and yet is multiple. Taking Akın's settings, characters, and soundtrack into account, we might find a similarly flexible, diverse version of Europe that is equally hard to define as a single homogenous unity. Scholars from a variety of fields have tried to pinpoint the phenomenon of Europe. "Europe as such does not exist," states Gerard Delanty, and Halle, like others, believes that Europe is "not a place or culture," but a discourse.[25] Discussing "cultures" and "people" in flux, Akhil Gupta and James Ferguson acknowledge shifting borders and intermingling cultures, and add that cultures and people are not necessarily "identifiable spots on a map."[26] Yet there do exist realities of multiple competing narratives about Europe and its people, as reiterated by popular imaginings of a European community (UEFA, Eurovision Song Contest), or by geopolitical imaginations of the EU, or in historic definitions from the Judeo-Christian tradition.[27] "Europe" as a geopolitical and historical entity has evolved through multiple centuries, and the space it has occupied has frequently changed throughout its history.[28] In this context, Halle observes, "Europe is filled with imaginative communities that compete with each other, motivate collectives, establish complex connectivities, and unsettle the simplest experience of neighborliness with the people next door." With reference to the fairly recent development of nation-states, which "are [often] the result of forcibly tethering together a patchwork quilt of tribes, clans, of culturally and linguistically distinct groupings," Thomas Elsaesser adds, "there is no-one in Europe who is not diasporic or displaced."[29]

In Akın's films, the protagonists are from a variety of regional and national backgrounds, the settings often alternate between neighborhoods or regions in Germany and Turkey, and the soundtrack mixes various global styles and traditions. Akın's cinema becomes an example of positive representations of multiethnicity in Europe and Europeanness in a globalizing world, notwithstanding tragic developments in the films' narratives. It becomes an artistic counter voice to xenophobic, Islamophobic discourses in Europe that have resurfaced and risen since 9/11, and intensified again in 2015 after the European refugee crisis and the IS attacks in Europe and across the globe.[30]

Fatih Akın's Cinema and the New Sound of Europe illustrates that Akın's imagining of Europe echoes the fluidities of a post-1989 Europe in featuring a connected and expanding European space, a space that was formerly divided politically into a western and eastern Europe, especially during the Cold War years, and economically into a northern and southern Europe, reflecting economic inequalities. Today, to a certain extent, it continues to be divided along those lines in times of crisis. I nevertheless argue that in Akın's cinematic Europe, especially in his features from the 2000s—*In July*, *Head-On* and *The Edge of Heaven*—eastern and southern states and states beyond the EU become integrated into Europe through the depiction of local sights and sounds of settings in Hamburg, Budapest, and Istanbul that are informed by a dynamic heterogeneity. This is an important filmic addition to and comment on the EU's existing enlargement projects of the time that clearly stipulated who could and who could not participate in the integration of Europe. I claim that by using a variety of linguistic sounds (e.g., English, Turkish, Serbo-Croatian, *Hamburgisch*, and Bavarian), these films aurally diversify Europe. Transnational European films, like Akın's, become a projection screen for networks of European city-, land-, and soundscapes that are informed by links to places seen traditionally as the "Others" of western Europe, such as Turkey or eastern Europe.[31]

Ultimately, Akın's imagined filmic Europe emerges through the tensions created between the existing concepts of "Fortress Europe" and "New Europe" that, in fact, are two sides of the same coin. Fortress Europe, for example, insists on borders and the exclusivity of access—a topic that resurfaced in European public discourse within the context of the European refugee crisis and which led to the resurrection of physical inner European borders in 2015—while the imagining of a New Europe focuses on mobility and integration within Europe, as enjoyed by European Union member states. Akın employs and undermines images of these existing notions of Europe, which include national paradigms such as borders and political or cultural boundaries, but also transnational networks that reach well beyond such established borders.

Challenging existing ideas of Europe, Akın's cinematic Europe features Turkey taking center stage. Turkey figures prominently not so much as a governmental entity, but as a cultural space that becomes part and parcel of Akın's cinema in terms of music, languages, characters, settings, and also film history. Akın's display of Turkey as an integral part of Europe emphatically defies concepts of a Fortress Europe and thus takes opposition to persisting ideas about cultural and political borders between the "Occident" and the "Orient."

In contrast to Akın's films, conservative political discourse, xenophobic rallies across Europe, and the administrative and legislative sphere of the EU all demonstrate that Turkey has not been fully accepted as a part of Europe. As Fatima El-Tayeb observes, Turkey often represents what Europe is not.[32] Even though Chancellor Merkel restarted negotiations with Turkey about its status within the EU in 2015 in order to find a legal solution for controlling migratory movements of refugees from Syria and Iraq to central and northern Europe via Turkey,[33] Turkey, an official candidate country to the EU, remains a nation that is perceived as the "Other" in relation to western European countries. The idea of Turkey as an extended part of Europe has been heatedly disputed by a variety of politicians, journalists, and other conservative and ultraconservative public voices. This dispute intensified substantially after the Turkish government's reaction to the 2016 coup attempt and even more so after the tensions increased between Turkey and Europe in 2017.

In 2007, the year *The Edge of Heaven* was released, former French President Nicolas Sarkozy made his stance clear: "I want to say that Europe must give itself borders, that not all countries have a vocation to become members of Europe, beginning with Turkey which has no place inside the European Union. . . . Enlarging Europe with no limits risks destroying European political union, and that I do not accept."[34] Former German chancellor and *Die Zeit* contributor the late Helmut Schmidt had already announced similar sentiments about Turkey's possible EU entry in the 1990s, when he said, "We Europeans are strongly influenced by our culture, which is grounded on the Judeo-Christian tradition. The Turks, mainly part of a Muslim nation, belong to a very different cultural sphere, whose home is in Asia and Africa, but not in Europe."[35] And fellow *Die Zeit* journalist Theo Sommer has early on also written critically about the EU membership of Turkey, "If the Turks want to become a part of the European community, they have to get rid of anything that is Asian."[36]

These public statements are embedded in a discourse of "culture clash," which assumes the existence of intrinsically different and mutually exclusive cultures. In its most extreme form, these types of statements merge "Turkish," "Islamic," and "Asian" cultures that are understood as essentially different from "German," "Christian," or "European" cultures. The dissemination of these views on cultures results in a fixture of cultural borders.[37] The above quotes by European politicians and commentators combined with the news footage of thousands of asylum seekers and immigrants trying to reach European shores in overloaded boats, for example, drowning and dying in the Mediterranean by the hundreds, underline the idea of a Fortress Europe, a Europe that has restricted access not only for Turkish, but also for other non-EU, nonwhite, non-Christian migrants.

There are a variety of European films that increasingly adopt the theme of (illegal) migration and human trafficking to European countries. In this context Yosefa Loshitzky observes: "Until recently the term 'European' has retained in the popular imagination its associative affinity with Christianity and whiteness despite the fact that Europe's population has been 'hybridized,' 'creolized,' and 'colored' by waves of nonwhite, non-Christian migrants throughout its history."[38] Loshitzky further reminds us that "Fortress Europe increasingly erects racial, ethnic, and religious boundaries" and that by "encouraging the expansion of the EU, it is also defining and closing its borders to the 'others.'"[39]

The reversal, or better, the other side of the coin, of Fortress Europe, is the concept of a New Europe, which—beginning with the formation of the new EU in 1992 and reaching a height in the first decade of the 2000s with its enlargement projects—enjoys and promotes a freedom of movement granted especially to the EU countries and other countries traditionally considered a part of Europe, such as Norway and Switzerland. Most important for the construction of this New Europe has been the EU's emphasis on disseminating a sense of unity and "Europeanness" through its institutionalized body. In this mission of European unity and identity construction, film plays a particularly important role, as is manifested through European film funding structures, award committees, and prizes.[40]

Akın, winner of such a European cinema prize, has officially been accepted and promoted as a European filmmaker whose films are read in accordance with the European Union's visions about integration and diversity in Europe. However, a close analysis of his films shows that Akın goes beyond a purely EU vision of such a New Europe. He even undermines its Schengen freedom of movement, for example, by extending the spheres of Europe well into northeastern Turkey, and by displaying already-integrated musical and linguistic soundscapes, including sounds associated with the peripheries of a geopolitical Europe.

Akın's films are informed by Europe's past and provide cinematic imaginings about its present and future. Migration to or within Europe, with particular peaks in the periods after 1945 (displaced people in eastern Europe), 1989/90 (post–Cold War crisis in former Soviet states and the Balkans), and 2011/2014 (Arab Spring and war in Syria), have shaped and continue to shape European diversity, especially within urban areas. The resulting demographic diversity—often associated with migration from non-Western European countries—challenges fantasies of homogenous and monolingual nation-states within the

European Union. While such migrations have often resulted in xenophobia and racism in Western Europe, the continuous migratory practices of the twentieth and twenty-first centuries have simultaneously led to critical renegotiations of ethnic, racial, and regional identifications in the public spheres. Cinema, and the arts in general, negotiating at the nexus of experiences of multiethnicity, polyphony, and diversity in all of its forms, provide new ways of reimagining concepts of Europe that challenge existing, preconceived ideas thereof.

It is mainly, but not exclusively, the work of minorities such as Akın that normalizes today's hybrid, diverse, transnational communities. Such artistic productions carefully shape our understanding of a changing, complex European space that is ever more exposed as multiethnic and polyphonic. This is achieved by telling stories about love, reconciliation, and mourning that carefully visualize an optimistic imagination of multiethnicity on the screen. In Akın's case, such imaginations are subtly invited through the filmic soundscapes, his cast, and mise-en-scène.

Akın—whose multiethnic films include a variety of stories including lesbian love; prostitution; the local music scenes in Hamburg, Istanbul, and the Black Sea; and the Armenian Ottoman relations in the Ottoman Empire—becomes an *au courant* filmmaker of European discourses on inclusion, race, ethnicity, religion, and history, but also of local issues such as gentrification in Hamburg. His influence on European discourses has been recognized and has garnered awards early on by European institutions. Akın was the first recipient of the aforementioned LUX Prize that was established by the European Parliament in 2007 to recognize a film that addresses European issues. Former EP President Hans-Gert Pöttering said that the EP "want[s] to award annually a film that raises attention to current social questions that affect our continent and highlights European integration especially. Furthermore, the award is supposed to highlight the richness of linguistic diversity within the European Union and to support the artistic production of the cinema sector."[41] With the LUX Prize, Akın and his production team received global distribution support for the film. In cooperation with the Goethe Institute, the EP provided the means for the subtitling of *The Edge of Heaven* into the twenty-three official languages of the European Union and into seven additional languages such as Arabic, Chinese, Russian, and Turkish. This endeavor emphasizes the attention that is given to cinema in general and to this specific film and its director in particular.

Film helps to create a variety of imaginings about Europe. European film awards and funding structures in combination with a new "freedom of movement" for EU citizens create a new form of cosmopolitanism and promote and mobilize a "supranational audience" for film.[42] European programs such as Eurimages and MEDIA subsidize, fund, and promote European filmic production and thereby acknowledge the importance film has in the "cosmopolitan" imagining of and positive identification with today's Europe through film.[43] Thus, cinema becomes a projection screen for fantasies, visions, and utopias of Europe. With the LUX Prize, Akın became officially such a representative of European visionaries.

On a local level, Akın's work often showcases his native port city, putting "Hamburg on the world map."[44] Recognized for his local and global sensibilities, Akın received the aforementioned Douglas Sirk Award in 2014. Through this award, Akın is linked to an international exile filmmaker, a fellow Hamburg director, who became known for his work within genre cinema. Films from Sirk's career in exile in Hollywood are well known for being visually lush and thematically subversive melodramas that inspired Rainer W. Fassbinder,[45] and later Akın. This link to Sirk, Fassbinder, and the city of Hamburg invites reconsiderations of Akın's cinema from new angles. That is, in addition to inquiries about Akın's films that in one way or another engage with questions of minorities, integration, and identity politics in Germany and Europe, it is also important to scrutinize the audiovisual aesthetics of his cinema, his engagement with film history, and the cinematic interplay of aesthetics and politics in his work.

Akın: A Transnational European Auteur

From the beginning of his career, Akın has been called, in the broadest sense of the term, an auteur. The term, however, has undergone many changes through the history of film and still provides for a variety of understandings. I will provide a brief overview of the genealogy of the term that is so readily assigned to Akın. As early as 1921, Jean Epstein referred to the film director as auteur and in 1948, Alexander Astruc wrote about the "camera-pen," indicating the author quality of the filmmaker.[46] But it was not until the mid-1950s in Paris that the auteur discourse began in its initial form with André Bazin, François Truffaut, and others in the *Cahiers du cinéma* group.[47] The group's initial concern was to critique "quality in cinema" in France, which since the 1940s had shown a preference for literary adaptations over more popular genre films and tried to establish a cinematic high art form through first-rate literary adaptations. The *Cahiers* group's early auteur criticism resisted such exclusive notions of cinematic art. They were invested in elevating popular cinema—that is, classical Hollywood cinema—to the realm of art. With Truffaut's "*la politique des auteurs*," looking at films through their authors became ever more important. The critics focused on the mise-en-scène to identify the thematic preoccupations of auteurs and to designate the film's overall style. Later formalists criticized the *Cahiers* group's visions of the auteur for being overtly romantic, much in line with a nineteenth-century model of creative genius.

In the late 1960s, there was a transformation in the *Cahiers* group: the contributors became more critical, intellectual, and theoretical in their approaches, in part because of the student movements in 1968 and influences of the philosophical and psychological theoretical approaches of Jacques Lacan and Louis Althusser. Authorship became conceptualized as an unconscious process: as Wright Wexman states, "In place of knowing transcendental genius enshrined by the Romantic auteurists, the new generation of French critics theorized the author as a force-field of libidinous energies whose presence could subvert the surface meaning of a given filmic text."[48] Other major influences for the auteur concept in the late 1960s and 1970s were Roland Barthes's essay "Death of the Author" and Michel Foucault's lecture "What Is an Author?"[49]

Barthes principally equated the author with a "scriptor" rather than a creator. According to Barthes, the "modern scriptor is born simultaneously with the text" instead of existing a priori.[50] Foucault examined the evolution of the term and concept of author to conclude that the modern-day author is the result of a certain concept of Western individualism, an ideology that supports individual expression. Thus, the auteur concept became disentangled from the Romantic idea of genius. The director became a construct that was born together with his or her film.

The concept was further used and developed in the United States and in Great Britain. Andrew Sarris introduced the author/auteur concept—the Romantic notion of auteur—to the American audience in the 1960s. He continued with the *Cahiers* group's praise of Hollywood films in the United States. The British cinema journals *Screen* and *Movie* were very influential in further developing notions of auteurist readings and appreciations of films. *Movie*, for example, was dedicated to lengthy auteurist analyses of Hollywood films and interviews with directors. Close readings of films were particularly prominent. The 1960s and 1970s in Britain were more theoretically inspired. The British Film Institute worked with the ambitious auteur-structuralism, which distinguished it from Romantic auteurism, such as in the work of Peter Wollen, who focused on the structure of film rather than the director. Despite such ambitions for a more theoretically founded reading and analysis of films, *Screen*, another British cinematic journal, dedicated a great deal of space for lengthy interviews with directors such as Douglas Sirk and Luc Godard.[51]

In Germany of the 1970s, German cinema appropriated the auteur concept for its New German Cinema (NGC). Rainer W. Fassbinder and Werner Herzog were among the directors grouped together under the term "Autorenkino."[52] Influenced by the *Cahiers* group, following the Oberhausen Manifesto in 1962, where twenty-six directors, writers, and other filmmakers were present, a proclamation for the *Autor* in filmmaking was introduced in Germany. Filmmakers needed liberation from constraints of the industry and commercial exploitation.

Sheila Johnston notes, "The concept of the *Autor* film implied both that it should clearly convey the vision of its creator and that the director should retain overall control without having any financial obligations."[53]

However, in contrast to the auteur theory of Andrew Sarris, for example, the German *Autor* was not necessarily a director whose oeuvre one had to look at retrospectively in order to find its quality or individual style. In fact, a German *Autor* could have been a young first-time filmmaker, someone who would "convey and reflect on ideas."[54] Johnston states that whereas authorship was a critical tool for the auteur theorists, the "idea of the *Autor* was . . . a programmatic principle which was to be achieved not just by arguing for a particular relation of director to film, but by setting up new legal, contractual, and institutional relations and special forms of training."[55] That is, state subsidies and film schools were providing a platform for artistic education, production, and criticism. Additionally, as Ulrike Sieglohr stresses, NGC functioned as a "public sphere—as a forum for debating contemporary issues—rather than within the realm of entertainment."[56]

The term auteur has become contested for some, and is still a productive term for others in today's scholarly use. According to film scholar Rosanna Maule, with the advent of structuralism, poststructuralism, and deconstruction, and, finally, cultural studies in film discourse, the antiauthorial enterprise began.[57] Scholars often focus on multiauthorship, collaboration, and the sociology of production.[58] Yet, despite these criticisms, authorial cinema is still alive and well. Seung-hoon Jeong and Jeremi Szaniawski, for example, have conceptualized a "global auteur" for twenty-first-century cinema. They state that "Cinema is now the most vulnerably attentive, yet active respondent to global capitalism and digital convergence, but unlike other media, it also generates (sufficient attention to) auteurs who can sustain critically meaningful or artistically transformative stances. This potential enables us to better understand the immanent plane of political positions and ideologies around cinema, which might not be effectively accessible when only looking at films under other, apparently more trendy rubrics such as art cinema, film festivals, transnational media, etc."[59] In a different context, Mary Wood claims, "Authorial cinema survives as a category because it is enshrined in institutional practice and in public discourse. Auteurs have a cultural and commercial function, licensed by virtue of their skills and aims to explore areas outside the mainstream and existing as a commercial performance of 'the business of being an auteur.'"[60]

In the media, Akın is singled out and celebrated as an auteur-filmmaker—even as a global auteur.[61] He has attracted categorizations within German, Turkish, European, and global cinema.[62] Since his early successes, many scholars and critics have labeled Akın an auteur, linking him particularly to the New German Cinema of Rainer Werner Fassbinder in the German context,[63] even though the term auteur has been contested in much of today's academic discourse. Although I agree that directors are collaborators, for the most part, I nevertheless claim that European filmmakers such as Akın, Michael Haneke, and Nuri Bilge Ceylan are still key figures in European filmmaking, arranging the content, style, and form of their films in distinctive and significant ways.

Acknowledging the directors' differences, Russian film critic Andrej Plachow was one of the first to make the connection between Fassbinder and Akın. In a radio interview following Akın's Moscow retrospective in 2009, Plachow pointed out that both directors brought new energy to German cinema. While Fassbinder brought the energy of the marginal, Akın demonstrated that the nationally marginal could be the main subject of German cinema, of German culture even. Plachow concluded that Akın and Fassbinder are both "engines" that pull others along with them.[64]

Akın himself has been eager to create references to auteurs from Germany, Turkey, Italy, and the United States. He does so, for example, by using actors such as Hannah Schygulla and Tuncel Kurtiz (who represent national cinemas made by auteurs such as R. W. Fassbinder and Yılmaz Güney) in *The Edge of Heaven*, by referencing Michelangelo Antonioni discussing the establishing shot in *The Edge of Heaven*, by talking about the Grandes Dames of Italian Cinema when discussing his casting of Nursel Köse in the same film, and by thanking Martin Scorsese and Francis Ford Coppola in the credits of his first features *Short Sharp Shock* and *In July*. Through such gestures, Akın creates links to national and international auteurs and film legends and constructs himself as the auteur-director of his films. Even if Akın himself stresses in interviews that his filmmaking is not directly connected to Fassbinder,[65] his casting and genre choices certainly resonate with the legacy of the famous German director and his cinema.

In extra features on home video releases and in interviews, Akın also emphasizes that he works on many aspects of his films either by himself or in close collaboration with others. These aspects include music, script, editing, and directing, as well as acting. With the founding of his production company Corazón International in 2004, together with Klaus Maeck and the late Andreas Thiel, Akın has also become the producer of his films. Additionally, the production company Bombero International, headed by Monique Akın as managing director, was founded in 2012. Akın, thereby, even fits certain criteria of the traditional German *Autor*, a concept referring mainly to the New German Cinema of the 1970s and 1980s as discussed above.

Akın is a contemporary European filmmaker who is the product of state education and the cinematic institutions of Germany. He has considerable artistic control over his product, and, as discussed by Sieglohr in the context of NGC, through his films, Akın, too, inspires discussion about contemporary issues within Germany, Turkey, and about European and world history, especially in the case of *The Cut*, his 2014 film about an Armenian family's displacement, set during World War I in the Ottoman Empire. However, in contrast to most NGC filmmakers, Akın does not exclude the aspect of entertainment from his films. He states in an interview that he seeks to combine popular entertainment cinema with so-called critically acclaimed cinema.[66] As discussed in chapter 4, this is also true to some extent for filmmakers Emir Kusturica and Stephen Frears.

Understanding Akın as a transnational auteur-filmmaker facilitates an analysis of him, as well as the other European directors in this book, as directors that have authorial control over their films, both aesthetically and thematically. Other film personnel, such as cameramen, sound designers, and editors—with whom Akın collaborates closely—certainly also contribute to the final product and its reception. Indeed, such collaborations would perhaps allow us to call Akın an auteur-collaborator. Yet, with the self-presentation as auteur through interviews and documentaries, Akın creates a particular form of authorial power over his filmic product.[67] In addition, I read Akın as the main designer of the filmic structures in his films—in writing, directing, and producing most of his films, Akın clearly invites such a reading. Ultimately, I argue that there is a binding thematic and stylistic continuity in Akın's films—especially if we consider the period of the 2000s—and my goal in chapters 1 to 3 is to reveal patterns and interconnections in Akın's oeuvre through close textual readings of his work.

Akın and Transnational Europe, Cinema, and History

Although Akın is such an important contemporary European filmmaker, it is astonishing that to date, there is no in-depth book-length study in English on his cinema, with the exception of Daniela Berghahn's book on *Head-On*, which offers a detailed reading and contextualization of the film. Generally, Akın scholarship has focused on individual films, primarily in shorter studies. While for many years, these focused on social-realist readings of Akın's films,[68] by now scholars are also exploring aesthetic and formal questions of his cinema, beyond a Turkish German minority narrative.[69] Additionally, Göktürk, Gueneli, Ezli, Berghahn, Gemünden, and Suner have made initial connections to other filmmakers of global art house cinema.[70] Books such as Isolina Ballersteros's *Immigration Cinema in the New Europe* and Berghahn's *Far-Flung Families in Film* further offer insightful surveys of a variety of European films, including some of Akın's films. These engage with the topic of immigration and the diasporic family respectively, creating a particular framework for their study within minority studies.[71] Including discussions of art installations along with film, Nilgün Bayraktar's *Mobility and Migration in Film and Moving Image Art: Cinema Beyond Europe*, which includes a chapter on Akın's *The Edge of Heaven*, offers an interdisciplinary approach to a variety of artists and filmmakers that mark today's mobile Europe.[72] Taking an innovative and critical approach, Ipek A. Çelik's *In Permanent Crisis: Ethnicity in Contemporary European Media and Cinema* analyzes how the European media discourse as well as established cinematic auteur filmmakers across Europe such as Alfonso Cuarón, Michael Haneke, Constantinos Giannaris, and Fatih Akın, ultimately frame immigrants, refugees, and other migrants and minorities within the trope of victimhood who experience violence or are a cause for it. That is, despite the directors' complex engagement with the topic of ethnicity, they have difficulties completely freeing themselves from a link to medial discourses on victimhood.[73] Within the context of Akın scholarship, Çelik's chapter on *Head-On* and the film's "multisensory relationship with its audience," in which she discusses the film at the intersection of melodrama, affect, and ethnicity, is particularly intriguing.[74] However, within the larger Akın scholarship, a comprehensive analysis of Akın's work remains a necessity, especially in the context of European and Turkish cinema, within and outside of minority cinema. That is a need my book addresses.

Moreover, *Fatih Akın's Cinema and the New Sound of Europe* demonstrates that Akın's elaborate soundtrack becomes an aesthetic strategy that makes subtle suggestions about a new, transnational Europe and its visualization on the screen. Additionally, my book's particular focus on the aural components in Akın's cinema makes an important contribution to a long-neglected area of film studies: the sound and music of cinema. Interest in film sound as a point of departure for film analyses has begun to surface as an important new subfield in film scholarship, as the work of Jeremy Barham and Holly Rogers, Michel Chion, Mervyn Cooke, Helen Hanson, Kathryn Kalinak, David Neumeyer, Gianluca Sergi, and James Wierzbicki demonstrates.[75] Also, within Turkish German cinema studies, film sound is slowly receiving more attention, as seen, for example, in the work of Deniz Göktürk, Roger Hillman and Vivien Silvey, Barbara Kosta, and Senta Siewert.[76] In combination with my work, these offer different, yet related, responses to the sonic dimension of Akın's cinema. In discussing the soundscapes in Akın's films, my research aligns itself with existing scholarship on film sound in general, and with Akın and film music in particular. It extends this innovative discussion about Akın's cinema into a broader argument about the aural experience of a European polyphony in Akın's films.

An essential aim of my project is to show that through transnational films, such as Akın's, an artistically staged multiethnicity in a transnational Europe gradually becomes perceptible, and that such films are capable of restructuring notions of Europe, European cinema, and the history of cinema. Linguistic and musical diversity, for example, not only punctuate the vivid acoustics of Akın's films, but have also become a common soundtrack of European cinema. European directors such as Yamina Benguigui, Michael Haneke, Emir Kusturica, and Stephen Frears capture the changing perceptions about the sights and sounds of

Europe in their imaginings of a new diversity in Europe; this invites the films' audiences to experience aesthetically a European polyphony coupled with a visualized multiethnicity.

From a cultural studies perspective, the audiovisual study of Akın's cinema contributes to the discussions of anti-Islamic sentiments, long-standing debates about integration of immigrants in Germany/Europe, and the ambiguous position of Turkey and its history in Europe. Venkat Mani admits to "Turkey's intellectual presence in Europe" and explores through literary voices "aesthetic and political claims that unsettle concepts of home, belonging, and cultural citizenship."[77] The films central to my project do the same by introducing a new, transnational Europe and its multiethnic citizenry to a wider audience through an engaging and affective cinema.[78]

Aspects of transnational cinema have been influencing the dominant cinemas of Europe, which increasingly display a multiethnic Europe on cinema screens. Looking into the transnational context of films reveals a variety of studies. Some film scholars have put a focus on so-called European diasporic films such as *beur* (North African–French) or Black/Asian–British cinema.[79] Seminal works, such as the anthology *European Cinema in Motion: Migrant and Diasporic Film in Contemporary Europe*, span a geographical focus from western to eastern and southern Europe, and primarily look at the work of minorities. Other important work in the field, such as Yosefa Loshitzky's *Screening Strangers: Migration and Diaspora in Contemporary European Cinema*, mainly focuses on the theme and representation of migrants and refugees. That is, Loshitzky specifically pays attention to nondiasporic films to decipher the dominant discourse about migrants.[80]

While my book is primarily on Akın and his work, it nonetheless scrutinizes minority cinema in a comparative context. It includes chapters that juxtapose Akın's work with filmmakers who have a migratory background, who are part of an "accented cinema," that is, a cinema of migration, exile, and diaspora,[81] and with others who do not have a minority background or a directly minority-related theme in their work. Additionally, by including the neglected Turkish cinema in my discussions, my book extends the fields of transnational cinema studies.

Finally, *Fatih Akın's Cinema and the New Sound of Europe* aims to contribute to a growing movement toward a transnational understanding of film history by discussing Akın's cinema's elaborate intertextualities with Turkish, German, and other European and non-European film histories. Ultimately, my book argues for a transnational cinema and history alongside national cinemas and histories. National categories seem to have become too narrow for filmmakers with a transnational focus, like Akın. This study gives insight into Akın's thematic preoccupations and his use of ethnicity in his films, but I also scrutinize heretofore insufficiently analyzed aesthetic and film-historical components that in my analysis lay bare transnational ties, intersections of different film histories, and connections between contemporary cinemas.

Within and Beyond Turkish German Cinema

Throughout the book, I use the term Turkish German without a hyphen. The hyphen can be perceived as a limiting factor that enforces binary models, suggesting that two mutually exclusive categories combine to form a hybridized new, different entity, or other combinations thereof.[82] In omitting the hyphen for such terms within film studies, as has been practiced in other disciplines, I agree with and follow Sabine Hake and Barbara Mennel's elaborations on the issue in their introduction to *Turkish German Cinema in the New Millennium: Sites, Sounds, Screens*.[83] They state, "Our decision to leave out the hyphen signifies our unwillingness to reduce the remarkable productivity of Turkish German filmmakers to the easy logics of compatibility and commensurability implied by it."[84]

Akın's cinema can simultaneously be read in the context of Turkish German cinema, German or Turkish national cinemas, and European, European diasporic, or transnational cinemas. Critics have often read Akın's work in the context of Turkish German cinema, despite frequent objections by Akın himself to being classified within the niche category of migrant cinema.[85] Yet categories such as "Turkish German" need not be limiting but can offer useful paradigms to discuss and frame a particular cinema. Certainly, as scholars we should be cautious not to overgeneralize and ask what exactly is being analyzed within the category of Turkish German cinema. This is especially important if we consider that films that have often been analyzed under the umbrella term "Turkish German cinema" include the works of Kurdish[86] (e.g., Yüksel Yavuz and Züli Aladağ) and Azerbaijani (Cüneyt Kaya) filmmakers, and films that incorporate actors and figures from different nationalities (e.g., Moroccan actor El Hedi ben Salem is cast as Moroccan Ali in *Angst Essen Seele Auf* [*Ali: Fear Eats the Soul*], Turkish actor Burak Yiğit plays the Arab-German Jamal in *Ummah unter Freunden* [Ummah among friends]). Ultimately, cinematic categories do not have to be considered as mutually exclusive, since categories in a multidisciplinary field such as film are inherently permeable, and any attempt to fixate or contain them would impose limitations on film analysis.

Films can have multiple identities and entanglements. These offer multiple entry points for analysis. That is, each of the categories above (ethnic, national, transnational, and so on) have their validity and offer different, productive points of reference and comparison for film analyses. On the one hand, it is vital to analyze Akın's stylistic and thematic concerns within German, Turkish, European, or transnational contexts to move beyond niche categories, and see their relevance in the broader field of nationally, European-wide, or globally organized film studies. On the other hand, it is equally vital to compare and contrast Akın's filmmaking with prior Turkish German cinema in order to scrutinize ruptures and continuities within this particular film history that has shaped and continues to shape the discourse on minorities in Germany. Therefore, it is informative for this study to discuss Turkish German cinema history and Akın's position within and beyond it.

Akın's cinema, in large parts characterized by the motif of travel and migration, the use of an international cast and setting, and a diverse musical and linguistic soundtrack, provides a new reflection on twenty-first-century Europe and highlights the shifting roles Turkey and Germany play in this new Europe. The cosmopolitan subjects in Akın's films move in various geographical directions, switch languages, and cease, or actively refuse to be, either "Turks" or "Germans," but perform instead a version of "Europeanness," which allows for an aesthetic appreciation of heterogeneity and diversity in his cinema. While migration, movement, and foreign languages were present in earlier Turkish German films, Akın's images and soundscapes offer a new take on these aspects of Turkish German cinema. Earlier films often focused on the differences between cultures and languages in the narrative and in the formal language of the film.[87] Akın's films narrate stories about interpersonal relationships and display integrated sounds and sights that are in mutual exchange. That is, his films reflect on the level of form the heterogeneity of Europe and its inhabitants that dominates the content level. I will discuss this more in depth in the upcoming chapters.

After almost five decades of Turkish German cinema, it is crucial to revisit and rethink the films as well as the changing discourses on the subject matter that should be considered a part of Akın's filmic background. Much has happened between Fassbinder's 1969 film *Katzelmacher*, which brought fame to the director and introduced the figure of the Mediterranean *Gastarbeiter* (guest worker) onto the cinema screens, and Akın's 2004 film *Head-On*, in which the Turkish German offspring of guest workers evoke Turkey as much as Germany in a transnational setting. In Turkish German cinema, the mute, victimized guest worker who lived in enclosed, peripheral spaces in the Germany of the 1970s has been transformed into the multilingual, mobile subject of the twenty-first century, who travels the wide and complicated transnational space of Europe and beyond.

I divide Turkish German cinema into four different phases, with a fifth phase still emerging at the time of writing. There might be films that do not allow for easy categorization or periodization. My four-phase periodization relies on a general overview of Turkish German cinema focused on the work of its most prominent directors. While there are also other possibilities for periodizations, in which films from the 1960s, 1970s, and 1980s are merged, as in Göktürk's or

Ezli's work, I choose to distinguish these decades to highlight their minute thematic differences.[88] Thus I locate phase one between the late 1960s and the late 1970s. These films were directed by German filmmakers and often depict the life experiences of guest workers. The films of phase two stem mainly from the 1980s. These films, made by German and Turkish German directors, were about first- and second-generation Turkish Germans living in Germany, focusing on female suffering. The films of phase three are from the 1990s. They are characterized by a broader array of themes and aesthetics and include directors who are second-generation Turkish Germans. The 2000s represent the fourth phase of Turkish German cinema, which is characterized by a fundamentally changed vision of Germany, Turkey, and Europe with an influx of mobility and transnational connections. I read Akın as the initiator and most prolific director of this fourth phase of Turkish German cinema, which includes about a dozen Turkish German directors of fame such as Züli Aladağ, Buket Alakuş, Thomas Arslan, Hussi Kutlucan, and Ayşe Polat.[89] Finally, I perceive a new development on the horizon. This includes, for example, the work of internationally praised and award-winning filmmaker İlker Çatak, a graduate of the Hamburg Media School. Çatak, whose short film *Fidelity* depicting Istanbul during the Gezi protests won the 2015 Student Oscars in Los Angeles and the 2014 German Nachwuchspreis, mentions Akın as an inspiration and role model.[90] Çatak and his contemporaries might be the voices of a transition stage for Turkish German cinema building on what Akın has started, moving into new territories.

The directors of the first phase raised awareness about guest workers and made a discourse on things Turkish German possible, at a time when guest workers were not seen as active members of contemporary German social life.[91] This initial phase of Turkish German cinema includes films such as Fassbinder's *Katzelmacher* (1969) and *Ali: Fear Eats the Soul*, or Helma Sanders-Brahms's *Shirins Hochzeit* (*Shirin's Wedding*, 1976). Much of the early and recent scholarship has criticized the depiction of guest workers in these films for being stereotypical and clichéd. [92] Often the ethnically other guest worker does not receive a positive conflict-solving treatment but is banned. The only "solution" is to die, become hospitalized, or cease to exist as a meaningful component in contemporary German society.[93] However, despite their limitations, these films provided a forum for discussion of the guest worker issue. Although the topics of the first phase were often depressing and focused only on a few limited aspects of guest workers' lived experiences, the films made the topic of guest workers more public in Germany and abroad.[94]

In the course of the feminist movement of the 1970s, feminist filmmaker Helma Sanders-Brahms introduced the first female protagonist in the series of guest worker depictions. After all, Rita Chin informs us, by 1973, 30 percent of the foreign work force was female.[95] *Shirin's Wedding* tells the story of a courageous

Turkish guest worker who follows her fiancé to Cologne but fails in society, loses her job, is confronted with the harsh realities of exclusion as a "foreigner," and, finally, is killed as a prostitute. That is, although *Shirin's Wedding* is progressive in terms of depicting a female Turkish protagonist, the film remains trapped in the depiction of victimized Turkish Germans, as is frequently featured in the "cinema of duty."[96]

The content and focus of Turkish German cinema in the 1980s gradually changed from stories about exploited Turkish men and their masculinity to stories about threatened Turkish women and their femininity. The focus on female suffering dovetailed with the increasing numbers of migrants from Turkey to Germany, often wives and children of male guest workers, due to the family reunification law (1973–1979).[97] Prominent examples include films by Turkish German director Tevfik Başer, *40qm Deutschland* (*40 Square Meters of Germany*, 1986), *Abschied vom falschen Paradies* (*Farewell to a False Paradise*, 1989), and by Hark Bohm, who focused on a second-generation Turkish German daughter figure in his celebrated *Yasemin* (1988). Although praised and critically acclaimed in earlier years, later scholarship aligns these films with the 1970s agenda of victimizing and with stereotypical portrayals of guest workers and their families.

Intensifying the sympathetic portrayal of Turkish Germans, core themes of this period were the disillusionment and "imprisonment" of immigrants in Germany and a cultural segregation between "German" societies and "Turkish" exile societies. Both of Başer's films, for example, use tropes of imprisonment, which, according to Hamid Naficy, occur frequently in films about exile and migration.[98] A prominent theme in the characterization of second-generation Turkish Germans was the "two-world" model, the portrayal of a life in between two cultures.[99] This phenomenon of in-betweenness in the Turkish German community, being torn between the "Turkish" culture of the parents and the "German" culture of the "host" country, as staged in *Yasemin*, was considered a main social problem.[100] In such films, the Turkish "other" needs to be completely assimilated into German society by breaking with things Turkish. That is, through these films, German society confirms its superior status, which the second-generation immigrants still have a chance to enter, if they radically break with the first generation—a viewpoint that also affirms the assimilation politics of the 1980s in Germany.[101]

Whereas the 1980s seemed to offer a new form of assimilation as a solution to the *Ausländerproblem* (foreigner problem), the 1990s, marked by demographic and geopolitical changes, once again took a new shift in terms of cultural approaches. The second and third generations of minority youth were reaching adolescence during the context of post–Cold War Europe, which was affecting all areas of European life. In the wake of German-German reunification, German public discourse was confronted with new questions pertaining to its contemporary identity and its relationship to its history, both to World War II and, more recently, to the German Democratic Republic's history and perpetration. At the same time, borders in central and eastern Europe were shifting, and resulting political uncertainties and war in post-Soviet states, especially in the former Yugoslavia, resulted in new international flows of people, including refugees, who migrated to Germany and Europe. Due to Germany's comparatively "generous" refugee law, numbers of global applicants increased considerably between 1987 and 1992, which was quickly lowered by more restrictive updates to refugee law in Germany in 1993.[102] This was also the time when neo-Nazi violence became more visible.

In this time of change, social workers, educators, and cultural studies scholars supported and advocated a multicultural turn on different platforms, replacing the assimilationist approach in the treatment of migrants. According to this multicultural approach, the expectation was no longer the erasure of ethnic traits and an adaptation to German lifestyle and culture, but rather the acceptance of a diverse cultural simultaneity by German and non-German citizens living in Germany.[103] This multicultural tolerance effort dovetailed with the outbreak of xenophobia in various right-wing subcultures in the early 1990s, which culminated with the racially motivated arson attacks in Rostock (1992), Mölln (1992), and Solingen (1993) that killed several foreigners, including children and women, in their homes.

In cinematic terms, Turkish German cinema of the 1990s provided more diversified representations of Turkish Germanness than earlier portrayals. Whereas the early 1990s still adhered to a thematic reliance on the "two-world" model, exemplified through film titles such as Serap Berrakkarasu's 1991 film *Töchter zweier Welten* (*Daughters of Two Worlds*), there are also refreshing turns and twists and shifting perspectives on minorities, which begin with Turkish director Sinan Çetin's 1993 film *Berlin in Berlin*.[104] Toward the end of the 1990s, a newer, younger generation of Turkish German directors emerged whose films engaged with a diversity of genres such as satire, comedy, gangster, and documentation films. A new appreciation of hybridity, which evolved within various discourses, but which was also visible in the real-world experiences in urban public spaces, could be observed in new urban films.[105]

That is, the 1990s brought a new Turkish German tone onto the movie screens.[106] This younger generation of filmmakers started to portray new cinematic visions of specific neighborhoods in urban spaces. Hamburg, Berlin, and Kiel suddenly became venues for a new diversity.[107] Akın is one of these new directors. With him, a new aesthetically oriented filmmaking has been on the rise since the late 1990s. Akın's first feature film, *Short Sharp Shock*, resulted in prizes and fame for the director and brought gangster aesthetics onto the screen. The language, style, and lifestyle of a multiethnic, petty-criminal circle of friends seemed not to focus much on the cliché pictures of foreignness in Germany. The director carefully adopted a Scorsese-esque gangster style for his Turkish German film, combining it with narratives of urban hip-hop culture.[108] In telling a story about the contemporary urban experiences of three ethnically diverse friends, Akın shifted, once and for all, the focus from the oppression and victimhood of guest workers and their families to the adventures of his young and energetic characters. Turkish German cinema changed after Akın's *Short Sharp Shock*. The year 1998 marked a boom in Turkish German film production, since next to Akın's *Short Sharp Shock*, there have been several other productions, such as Yüksel Yavuz' *Aprilkinder* (*April Children*), Yilmaz Arslan's *Yara* (*Wound*), Kultuğ Ataman's *Lola & Bilidikid*, and the TV coproduction *Ich Chef, Du Turnschuh* (*Me Boss, You Sneakers!*) by Hussi Kutlucan that focused on urban experiences of diversity.[109] Such Turkish German films have brought new political and aesthetic demands to German cinema. This is remarkable, since German film from the 1990s has been famously called a "cinema of consensus."[110] Certainly, in such discussions, the focus was on (popular) mainstream German film, and not on Turkish German cinema, art films, gay and lesbian films, and any other nonmainstream films of that time.

This new Turkish German cinema, including works by Arslan, Ataman, and Akın, brings about two relevant issues. First, young Turkish German directors in general, and Akın in particular, are recognized as a post–guest worker generation who moved beyond the victim discourses that centered on their parents' generation. Their depictions of second- and third-generation immigrants, the new German citizens, vary drastically from earlier versions of the often othered guest-worker depictions. Their subjects are part of a local cultural space in Germany. They participate and identify with the urban space. Second, their films suggest an artistic turn in Turkish German filmmaking, including innovative uses of genre, style, narrative, and other aspects of cinema that are not solely read in social-realist terms.[111] While social realism is still a common mode of producing and interpreting Turkish German film—as can be seen in the public discourse on Muslim male aggression surrounding the 2006 WDR TV production *WUT*[112] —the late 1990s experienced a surge of artistic production and reception of Turkish German cinema that continues today. The screening of such Turkish German films at festivals marked the transition to a new phase. In the new millennium, this shift became prominent and introduced what I call the fourth phase of Turkish German cinema. First and foremost this reflects a normalization of ethnicity in German cinema. This normalization is most prominently established within Akın's oeuvre.

This fourth phase of Turkish German cinema dovetails with a fundamentally changed Europe and Germany in the new millennium. The European Union has been expanding its borders since the Maastricht Treaty, in effect since 1993, and the Treaty of Amsterdam in 1999; several countries such as Turkey and Serbia made it to the list of candidate countries and are waiting to join the EU. Since 1993 more and more countries have been joining the European Union. With Croatia becoming a member in 2015, the EU member states reached a total number of twenty-eight. More and more borders have opened due to the Schengen-Protokoll, in effect in the EU since May 1999.[113] The Schengen-Protokoll has made European regions more accessible from various directions; rules about movement, travel, and work have become more flexible than ever before in Europe's long history.

However, the lifting of these borders also began the creation of new borders within Europe. Halle observes, "The lifting of state borders in the EU has resulted in the proliferation of mental borders. The free flow of people, goods, and services fostered by a Europe without borders has actually resulted in the dynamic production of distinctions based on class, region, ethnicity, religion, education, loyalty, dialect, and so on."[114] The EU-envisioned free movement of people and goods was, of course, already restricted from the beginning to people inside the EU: EU mobility largely remains a privilege for EU citizens. Border crossings for citizens from non-EU nation-states at the fortified edges of the political Europe have remained more difficult.[115]

The image of the rather unrestricted, borderless movement (for EU citizens) of the first decade of 2000 has been visually (and physically) interrupted early on with images of often non-European refugees trying to escape war and economic hardships. This is especially true for refugee movements after 2015. Across Europe the high number of refugees from war-torn places like Syria migrating through eastern into central Europe has received increased media attention since 2015. Much opposed to the Schengen utopia of borderless Europe, EU member countries like Hungary, for example, reacted to the transit of refugees by building fences and starting to guard their borders with heightened military patrols.[116] Germany, too, momentarily installed border patrols in Bavaria when the number of refugees entering Germany reached beyond the initially allowed eight hundred thousand within a few days in the late summer of 2015.

However, earlier in the new millennium, selective border enforcements of this sort were not yet anticipated in public and political discourse. It was the time of a new and positive imagining of Europe, of envisioning a united, post–Cold War Europe that allowed for transnational mobility, economically and culturally.[117] It was in the early 2000s that a move beyond the nation-state as an organizing principle for artistic and cultural production was becoming more and more popular in academic discourse.[118] Discourses on the transnational, cosmopolitan, and even postnational are among trends in Turkish German studies. In the first decade of the unifying "Schengen-Europe," literary, filmic, and other artistic productions such as theater, cabaret, and satire have been woven into the scrutiny of things Turkish German. An increasing number of anthologies discussing themes of transnationalism within the film sector were published in the early twenty-first century, paying particular attention to the German cinema landscape.[119] European cinema, like German cinema, has developed into a transnational cinema. German cinema is more and more woven into networks of trans-European financial, contracting, filming, and production ties.[120]

Well into the twenty-first century, an increasing number of films illustrate alternative depictions of a diverse Europe. There are gangster films (*Chiko*, 2008), ever more comical and satirical versions of "culture clash" topics (*Süperseks*, 2004; *Kebab Connection*, 2005; *Almanya—Willkommen in Deutschland* [*Almanya: Welcome to Germany*], 2011; *300 Worte Deutsch* [300 words of German], 2013, *Einmal Hans mit scharfer Soße* [Hans in hot sauce], 2014), universal themes such as love, death, and friendship (*The Edge of Heaven*, 2008), environmental concerns (*Müll im Garten Eden* [*Polluting Paradise*], 2012), genre mixes such as a suspense tragicomedy critical of German national security (*Ummah unter Freunden* [Ummah among friends], 2013), episodes of the quintessential German TV crime show *Tatort* (Crime scene) directed by Turkish Germans (e.g. *Feuerteufel*, [Pyromaniac], 2013), or new feature-length comedic TV crime shows depicting a mix of regional (Bavarian) and ethnic (Turkish) traits, such as the Turkish Bavarian detective in *Kommissar Pascha* (*Inspector Pascha*, 2016–present).

These films take center stage in the thematic diversity among Turkish German film productions. Turkish German cinema no longer simply refers to victimized, mute Turkish men of the 1970s, nor to oppressed Turkish wives or daughters of guest workers of the 1980s, nor to marginalized, criminalized Turkish aggressors of the 1990s. While the early films from the 1970s, in fact up until the late 1990s, were often seen as an "authentic" documentary of the state of the Turks living in Germany, the later productions force the audience to read the depictions of a diverse cultural setting as a backdrop for different narratives in addition to or beyond an ethnicity-framed one. However, there are still films that often invite ethnovoyeurism, as the media coverage of films such as *Die Fremde* (*When We Leave*, 2010) and *Wut* suggests; the initial screening of these films was framed with TV and newspaper discussions on honor killings and minority aggressions, respectively.[121]

Yet the transnational aesthetics, or, as I call it, the aesthetics of heterogeneity in Akın's films, for example, help to normalize ethnicity and bring minority cinema into film history. Thereby, Turkish German cinema is discussed in a variety of platforms, addressing issues related to minorities, but also film genres and schools, and themes such as the environment, state criticism, and so forth. Göktürk's repeated demands for an aesthetic production and reception of Turkish German film instead of a narrow look at cultures in between "two worlds" seem to have been finally accepted. Productions of the twenty-first century also prove that her well-observed criticism of a lack of humor in Turkish German film is finally no longer justified.[122]

A new style, confidence, and tone of Turkish German cinema surfaces in the films of Cüneyt Kaya and İlker Çatak. As they engage confidently with sociopolitical discourses of their time, whether in Turkey (Gezi protests in 2013) or in Germany (secret police and NSA criticism; refugee situation in Europe), their work opens up an innovative set of questions regarding contemporary Germany, Turkey, and Europe. Çatak, a promising director, cinematically refers to Akın, who has pioneered such inquiries, especially bringing to the European screen topics that are less represented within much of Turkey's mainstream media (Kurdish protagonists, homoeroticism, and the Armenian-Ottoman relations). A brief look at Çatak's and Akın's work reveals visual and thematic similarities.

New questions within Turkish German cinema that need to be addressed in more depth, which have only recently appeared in research, are, for example, the changes in visual and aesthetic representations of Turkey, its past and recent history, and its local cultures. To what extent did Turkey in general, and Istanbul and other Turkish urban and rural places, change from a non-European, threatening space to a metropolitan urban space in the light of an expanding Europe (as in Akın's trilogy) and to a politically active space foregrounding young, urban Turkish femininity (in Akın's *The Edge of Heaven* and Çatak's *Fidelity*)? What do belonging, *Heimat,* Germany, or Turkey mean for the new generation of Turkish German filmmakers and their subjects? Such questions were inspired and initiated by the groundbreaking work of Göktürk, Halle, Konuk, and several other scholars in the field of Turkish German studies, and variations of these questions have been addressed in platforms that support and promote interdisciplinary Turkish German scholarship—crossing disciplinary, geographical, and temporal boundaries—such as the first anthology of its kind, *Turkish German Cinema in the New Millennium: Sites, Sounds, and Screens,* or *Transnational Hi/Stories: Turkish German Texts and Contexts*, a special issue of the journal *Colloquia Germanica* (2014), and the annual international anthology *Jahrbuch türkisch-deutsche Studien,* in particular its special volume on *Turkish German Studies: Past, Present, and Future* (2015).[123] These and similar collections of shorter studies within literary, filmic, anthropological, historical, and other fields have tackled Turkish archives, Turkish texts and contexts, to inquire about Turkish German discourse, and about artistic, cultural, and sociopolitical productions from new perspectives.

My questions in this book that will accompany and help guide the sequence and thematic analyses of the individual films and chapters pertain to the filmmaker and public figure of Akın and to the cinematic specificities of his oeuvre from his beginnings in 1995 to the end of his trilogy in 2014. Through my analyses and discussions of Akın's cinema, I aim to add to existing Akın scholarship

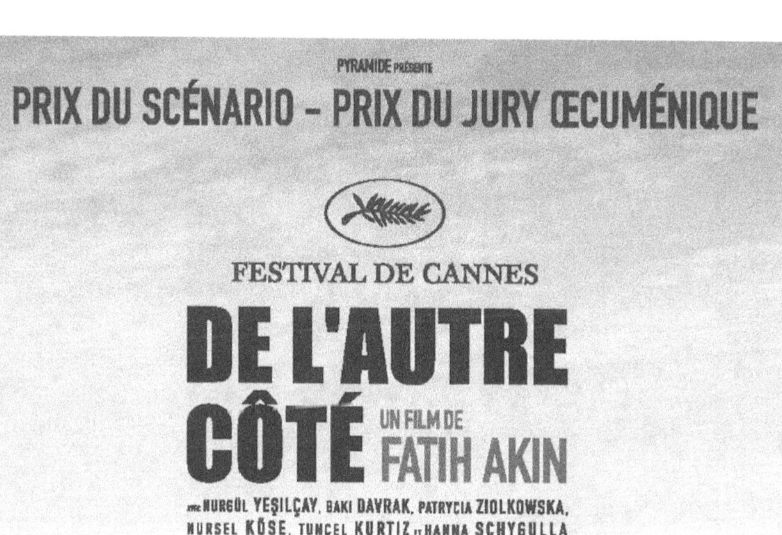

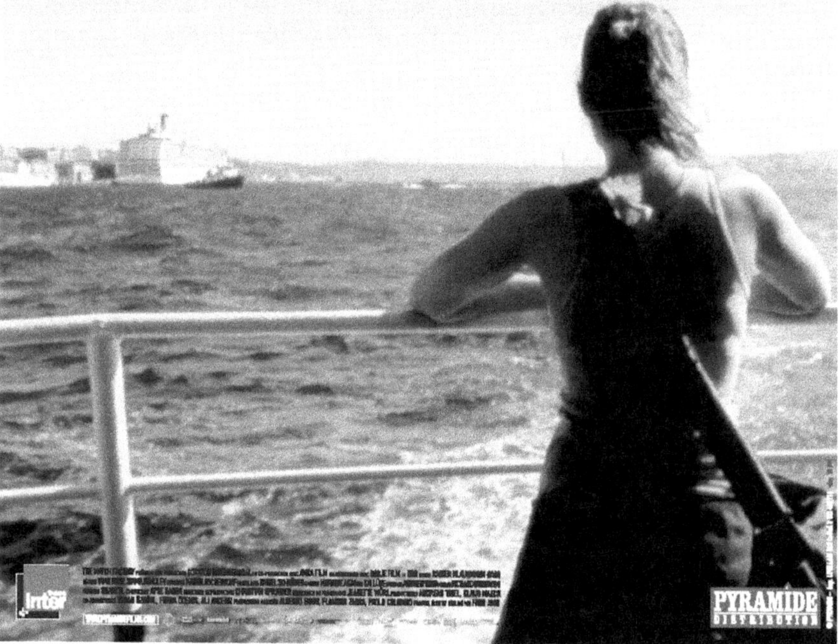

Figure 0.1. Ayten (Nurgül Yeşilçay)—a strong female figure who fights for "100 percent human rights"—commutes on the Bosporus. Scene shown on French film poster, *The Edge of Heaven* (2007). With kind permission of Pyramide Distribution.

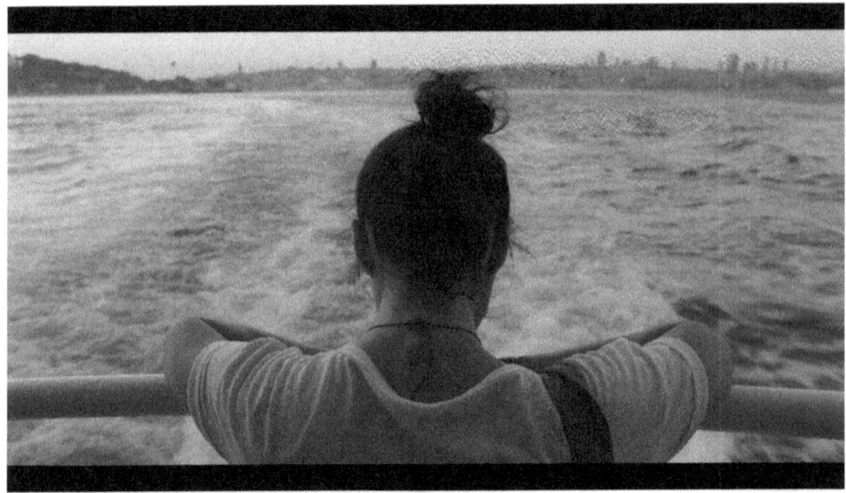

Figure 0.2. Aslı (Sanem Öge)—a strong female figure, who helps a protester during the protests in Istanbul—commutes on the Bosporus. *Fidelity* (2014). With kind permission of Hamburg Media School.

within Turkish German, German, European, and transnational cinema studies. His work has been informed in one way or another by past and present Turkish German and German film, most prominently by Rainer Werner Fassbinder, as much as by international film, including directors and stars such as Michelangelo Antonioni, Alejandro González Iñárritu, Martin Scorsese, Krzysztof Kieślowski, Yılmaz Güney, and Tuncel Kurtiz, to name a few.[124] My close reading of Akın's cinema will clarify that the transnationalism of his filmmaking is intertwined with the aesthetics, politics, and even with his engagement with the history of film. That is, the aesthetics of heterogeneity in his filmmaking strategies reflect his engagement with film history. Akın thereby transnationalizes the category of film history, as I hope to show in chapters 3 and 4, and in the conclusion of this book. As such, Akın's cinema loosens any singular category such as German or Turkish national cinemas, or Turkish German, or any other minority niche category.

Chapter Outline

Focusing on Akın's distinctive imagining of Europe, I argue that his transnational films of his Turkish German entanglement period challenge existing notions of Europe and Europeanness. Through an aesthetic of heterogeneity, Akın's cinematic Europe particularly questions notions of a clear-cut and nationally organized Europe. In developing this argument, chapters 1 to 3 analyze the specificities of sound and mise-en-scène (setting, actors, props, and décor) in three films from the 2000s. The films are the early and light-hearted road movie *In July*, in which the protagonists travel from Hamburg to south Turkey; Akın's first internationally acclaimed multiethnic drama about an unconventional love story, *Head-On* (2004), which is set in Hamburg and Istanbul; and *The Edge of Heaven* (2007), his award-winning film about three transnational parent-child relationships across Turkish, Kurdish, and German lines. These films—as products of the 2000s—are especially relevant for imaginations and negotiations of things European as they became cinematic interlocutors of the EU and its project of enlargement and integration in the new millennium.

Chapter 1, "Mapping Europe: The Road Movie Genre and Transnational European Space in Film," begins by positioning Akın and his films in a wider European context. This chapter uses *In July* as an example to showcase how Akın, already with a very early feature film, began to map Europe as a transnational space that goes beyond EU borders. A combination of transnational sounds, casting, and mise-en-scène constructs a fluid, almost borderless imagination of European space, including of a pre-EU eastern Europe. In this context, the next two chapters give a more detailed analysis of the aural aesthetics by discussing the transnational sound of Akın's cinema of the 2000s.

Chapter 2, "The Sound of Polyphony: Multilingualism, Multiethnicity, and Linguistic Empowerment in *Head-On*" primarily scrutinizes language use in *Head-On* to map out the changing sounds and demographics in the filmic European urban and rural spaces. The range of multilingualism and the linguistic polyphony on European screens not only subtly depicts the diversity of accents and languages as integral elements of today's European spaces—and as such unsettles nationalistic ideas about language, identity, and belonging—but, more than that, it transforms Akın's Turkish German characters by default into "models" for the EU's education program of trilingual citizenry. Furthermore, language use in *Head-On* helps to reverse preconceived ideas about Turkish/Turkish German gender roles.

Chapter 3, "The Sound of Music: Transnational Soundscapes," takes *The Edge of Heaven* as an example and emphasizes the musical sound of Akın's cinema. Looking particularly at music and music lyrics in the film, I argue that Akın's use of dubbed and remixed music (especially by the artist Shantel) underscores Akın's filmic challenges to national European borders. By foregrounding the mixed styles of music, where an "original" becomes hard to decipher, the director shows, on an aural level, that blurring boundaries and multidirectional movement are the predominant components of today's Europe. The combination of the musical mixed sounds with the linguistic diversity of languages and accents in the film put an emphasis on the aural experience of sonic heterogeneity. The varied sound of languages, for example, suggests that Akın moves beyond Hamid

Naficy's theory of "accented cinema" by including accented languages and dialects for all protagonists, including western Europeans. This diversifies the languages of all characters, in any geographical setting. The chapter also includes brief discussions on the new sound of European noise in relation to the sound of music and voice.

Chapter 4, "Expanding the Scope of European Cinema: Akın's Cinematic Imagining of a Diverse Europe in Context," juxtaposes the findings from the previous chapters with the work of other European auteurs such as Emir Kusturica (the former Yugoslavia), Philippe Lioret, Mathieu Kassovitz, and Yamina Benguigui (France), Michael Haneke (Austria), Stephen Frears (UK), and Nuri Bilge Ceylan (Turkey). I chose these filmmakers because their work disseminates a similarly transnational vision of Europe. That is, so-called minority filmmakers and filmmakers without a particular discernible minority background both display a decidedly multiethnic Europe. As is typical for "global cities,"[125] in many such films, ethnic diversity becomes the underlying structure of a transnational Europe. In this chapter, I show how Akın's films recapitulate general tendencies within contemporary European cinema, by demonstrating how European cinema has adjusted to the changing demographic structures of the twenty-first century. At the same time, I am particularly interested in a comparison with New Turkish Cinema. Although often funded by European sources, Turkish cinema is seldom discussed as part of European cinema. It is, however, crucial for Akın's cinematic oeuvre. I include contemporary examples of New Turkish Cinema, which offer a particular perspective on diversity, especially regarding gender and ethnic inequalities.

The conclusion, "Intertextual Film—Transnational Film—Transnational Film History," discusses the creation of transnational film and film history through Akın's work. Looking back at the previous chapters, I argue that his cinema is a synthesis of the traditionally divided cinemas of Europe and Turkey. That is, first, Turkish cinema becomes a part of European cinema; and second, based on my findings, I suggest a move beyond a national and even European categorization of film and film history. Revisiting the examples from the films discussed in the first four chapters, I highlight the intertextualities in Akın's cinema. Juxtaposing in particular, but not exclusively, Turkish cinematic references and intertextualities (which includes classic Yeşilçam films from the 1950s through the 1970s, political Young Turkish Cinema form the 1970s and 1980s, and the artistically ambitious contemporary New Turkish Cinema) with German film historic references in Akın's films, I argue that Akın creates a transnational film history. Such a transnational film history changes our perception of traditionally existing national film archives and museums. Transnational film history not only allows the decoding of Akın's oeuvre thematically and stylistically, but it also requests a different mode of commemoration and recognition in film museums and archives, which are traditionally nationally organized.

Notes

1. See the same phrase also in Daniela Berghahn, *Gegen die Wand (Head-On)*, BFI Classics (London: BFI/Palgrave Macmillan, 2015), 18.

2. A decade later, *Aus dem nichts* (*In the Fade*, 2017), for which Akın won the Golden Globe for best foreign language film, was Germany's selection to compete for an Academy Award, and Diane Krüger, who played the protagonist in the film, was awarded the Best Actress prize in Cannes. With these awards and selections, Akın made a global reappearance, a reminder of his early start in the global film circuits more than a decade earlier.

3. Discussing the references to Turkish cultural traditions, Daniela Berghahn uses the term "aesthetics of hybridity" to describe Akın's *Head-On*. Berghahn, "Seeing Everything with Different Eyes," in *New Directions in German Cinema*, eds. Paul Cooke and Chris Homewood (London: I.B. Tauris, 2011), 254. An "aesthetic of heterogeneity," as I call it, refers to Akın's audiovisual style, composition, and general aesthetics in his cinema. See, for example, Berna Gueneli, "The Sound of Fatih Akın's Cinema: Polyphony and the Aesthetics of Heterogeneity in *The Edge of Heaven*," *German Studies Review* 37, no. 2 (2014): 339.

4. Exemplary films would be *Goodbye Lenin* (2003), *Der Untergang* (*Downfall*, 2004), and *Das Leben der anderen* (*The Lives of Others*, 2006).

5. For a reference to German cinema after New German Cinema, see Randall Halle, *German Film after Germany: Toward a Transnational Aesthetic* (Urbana: University of Illinois Press, 2008), 23–25; Eric Rentschler, "Postwall Prospects: An Introduction," in "Postwall Cinema," special issue, *New German Critique* 87 (2002); Eric Rentschler, "From New German Cinema to the Post-Wall Cinema of Consensus," in *Cinema and Nation*, eds. Mette Hjort and Scott MacKenzie (New York: Routledge, 2000).

6. Ian Christie, "Where is National Cinema Today (and Do We Still Need It?)" *Film History: An International Journal* 25, no. 1–2 (2013): 20, 28; Halle, *German Film after Germany*, 25, 26; Luisa Rivi, *European Cinema after 1989: Cultural Identity and Transnational Production* (New York: Palgrave Macmillan, 2007), 29.

7. Jill Forbes and Sarah Street, *European Cinema: An Introduction* (New York: Palgrave Macmillan, 2000), 8ff.; Ginette Vincendeau, "Issues in European Cinema," in *World Cinema: Critical Approaches*, eds. John Hill and Pamela Church Gibson (Oxford: Oxford University Press, 2000), 58; Sabine Hake, "German Cinema as European Cinema: Learning from Film History," *Film History: An International Journal* 25, no. 1 (2013): 113.

8. Halle, *German Film after Germany*, 8; for a discussion on globalization's effect on film, see Randall Halle, *The Europeanization of Cinema* (Urbana: University of Illinois Press, 2014); Anne Jäckel, *European Film Industries* (London: British Film Institute, 2003); and Mike Wayne, *The Politics of Contemporary European Cinema: Histories, Borders, Diasporas* (Bristol, UK: Intellect, 2002).

9. Katrin Sieg and Mary Wood discuss globalization's impact on European cinema, and Will Higbee and Song Hwee Lim introduce the term "critical transnationalism." See Katrin Sieg, *Choreographing the Global in European Cinema and Theater* (New York: Palgrave Macmillan, 2008), 39; Mary P. Wood, *Contemporary European Cinema* (London: Hodder Arnold, 2007), xi; and Will Higbee and Song Hwee Lim, "Concepts of Transnational

Cinema: Toward a Critical Transnationalism in Film Studies," *Transnational Cinemas* 1, no. 1 (2010): 2ff.

10. "Multiplex cinema" is the name Naficy coins to refer to the "emergence of a new mainstream cinema in the USA and Europe in our current moment of post-diasporic, post-internet, postmodern neoliberal globalization." These are films that are influenced by large numbers of contemporary "displaced and globalized populations" who are part of the film industry, as spectators and as producers. Ultimately, Naficy states that these multiplex films help "to rejuvenate mainstream cinema and giv[e] it a multiplex accent." Hamid Naficy, "From Accented Cinema to Multiplex Cinema," in *Convergence Media History*, eds. Sabine Hake and Janet Staiger (New York: Routledge, 2009), 3–4.

11. Leslie A. Adelson, *The Turkish Turn in Contemporary German Literature* (New York: Palgrave Macmillan, 2005), 12.

12. Adelson, *The Turkish Turn*, 15.

13. Adelson, *The Turkish Turn*, 14.

14. In the 2014 GSA seminar "Turkish German Studies: Past, Present, and Future," the coconveners Ela Gezen, David Gramling, and Berna Gueneli proposed and discussed the addition of the Turkish archive, to include Turkish texts and contexts, in the analysis and evaluation of Turkish German cultural productions. The resulting conference papers as well as the publications in the collected volume *Jahrbuch türkisch deutsche Studien, Jahrbuch 2015*, in addition to previous work by Karen Yeşilada, Kader Konuk, and others, have begun to reevaluate the Turkish archive for Turkish German studies. See, for example, Kader Konuk, *East West Mimesis: Auerbach in Turkey* (Palo Alto, CA: Stanford University Press, 2010); Karen Yeşilada, *Poesie der Dritten Sprache* (Tübingen, Germany: Stauffenburg, 2012); Mert Bahadır Reisoğlu, "From Poetry to Prose: Özdamar and the Ikinci Yeni Poetry Movement," in *Türkisch-deutsche Studien, Jahrbuch 2015* (Göttingen: V&R Unipress, 2015); Kristin Dickinson, *Translation and the Experience of Modernity: A History of Turkish German Connectivity* (PhD diss., University of California, Berkeley, 2015); Ela Gezen, "Converging Realisms: Aras Ören, Nazım Hikmet, and Bertolt Brecht," *Colloquia Germanica* 45, no. 3/4 (2012, publ. 2015); Berna Gueneli, "Remixing Film Histories: Fatih Akın and the Creation of a Transnational Film History," *Colloquia Germanica* 44, no. 4 (2011, publ. 2014); Randall Halle, "The Europeanization of Turkish German Cinema: Complex Connectivity and Imaginative Communities," in *Türkisch-deutsche Studien, Jahrbuch 2015* (Göttingen: V&R Unipress, 2015); as well as Lela Gibson's and Marc Baer's contributions to the GSA seminar in 2014: Baer, "Mistaken for Jews: Republican Turkish Accounts of Nazi Germany," paper presented at the annual meeting of the *German Studies Association*, Kansas City, Missouri, September 18–21, 2014; and Gibson, "The Ottoman Empire and Turkish-German Studies," paper presented at the annual meeting of the *German Studies Association*, Kansas City, Missouri, September, 18–21, 2014.

15. Adelson, *The Turkish Turn*, 12.

16. For these and other contributors who expand the inquiries within the field of Turkish German studies, see footnote 14 and also Ela Gezen and Berna Gueneli, "Introduction: Turkish German Studies: Past, Present, and Future" in *Turkish German Studies: Past, Present, and Future*, special volume, *Türkisch-deutsche Studien*, Jahrbuch 2015, eds. Yasemin Dayioğlu-Yücel, Michael Hofmann, Şeyda Ozil, guest eds. Ela Gezen and Berna Gueneli (Göttingen: V&R Unipress, 2015): 10.

17. Adelson, *The Turkish Turn*, 14.

18. Pegida is an acronym for *Patriotische Europäer gegen die Islamisierung des Abendlandes* (Patriotic Europeans against the Islamization of the West). The Pegida movement is a far-right anti-immigrant and anti-Islamic protest movement which began in Dresden, Germany, in 2014. The movement has quickly spread across Germany and Europe.

19. Daniela Berghahn's book on *Head-On* in the BFI Film Classics series appeared in the final stages of the preparation of this book. Berghahn's book offers an insightful reading of Akın's first internationally acclaimed feature film.

20. In an interview with the Goethe Institute in Greece, Akın discussed the filming of *The Cut*, and talked about his changing relationship to Turkey: "First there was disillusion, then frustration, and finally a certain distance. Now the time has come for separate paths, for a creative separation" [Zuerst kam Ernüchterung, dann Frustration, und schließlich ein gewisser Abstand. Jetzt kommt die Zeit der getrennten Wege, eine kreative Trennung.]. "Heute fühle ich mich als Grieche," Goethe Institut, May 2015, accessed September 24, 2015, https://www.goethe.de/de/uun/akt/20488257.html.

21. Rothberg discusses his theory of "multidirectional memory" in the context of Holocaust memory and the postcolonial world. In his path-breaking work, Rothberg questions the inflexible relativity between memory and an individual national history. He defines his concept as follows: "Against the framework that understands collective memory as *competitive* memory—as a zero-sum struggle over scarce resources—I suggest that we consider memory as *multidirectional*: as subject to ongoing negotiation, cross-referencing, and borrowing; as productive and not privative." He states that the "interaction of different historical memories [slavery, US racism, Holocaust] illustrates the productive, intercultural dynamic" of multidirectional memory. Rothberg's understanding is that such a conceptualization of memory "considers a series of interventions through which social actors bring multiple traumatic pasts into a heterogeneous and changing post–World War II present." Hence, he conceptualizes "collective memory in multicultural and transnational contexts." Rothberg states, "Fully cognizant of the differentials of access and power that mark the public space, I nevertheless provide a framework that draws attention to the inevitable dialogical exchange between memory traditions and keeps open the possibility of a more just future of memory. I identify the misrecognition of collective memory as zero-sum game—instead of an open-ended field of articulation and struggle—as one of the stumbling blocks for a more inclusive renarration of the history of memory and a harnessing of the legacies of violence in the interests of a more egalitarian future." Michael Rothberg, *Multidirectional Memory: Remembering the Holocaust in the Age of Decolonization* (Stanford, CA: Stanford University Press, 2009), 3, 4.

22. Gueneli, "Remixing Film Histories," 461.

23. Prior to the April 2017 referendum in Turkey (the referendum that decided whether Turkey should adopt a presidential system), Turkish ministers and politicians were campaigning for the referendum in Germany and other European countries due to the high number of dual citizens who can vote in Turkey. Several European cities did not allow the politicians to campaign for a variety of reasons, such as safety concerns. This led to an outcry among Erdoğan supporters. The Turkish president himself accused Dutch and German politicians of using Nazi methods, which resulted in consternation on the European end. See, for example, Samuel Osborne, "Recep Tayyip Erdogan Slams 'Fascist and Cruel' Europe and Says Turkey May Review Ties after Powers Referendum," *Independent*, March 21, 2017, accessed March 23, 2017, http://www.independent.co.uk/news/world/ europe/recep-tayyip-erdogan-europe-facist-cruel-turkey-president-powers-referendum-a7641171.html.

24. For a discussion of Turkey's interventions, see the Dresdner Symphony project website on Aghet. The same site also includes an open letter asking for a governmental recognition of the atrocities. This letter to the German chancellor and her government is signed by academics such as Fatma Müge Göçek, artists including Fatih Akın, and other figures from public life such as journalists and writers. "Dresdner Sinfoniker: Aghet Projektseite," accessed May 19, 2016, http://www.aghet.eu/aghet-aktu-intervention/; "Dresdner Sinfoniker: Offener Brief," May 10, 2016, http://www.aghet.eu/.

25. Gerard Delanty, "What Does It Mean to Be a 'European'?," *Innovation* 18, no. 1 (2005): 1. See also Catherine Fowler, introduction to *The European Cinema Reader* (London: Routledge, 2002), 1; and Halle, "The Europeanization of Turkish German Cinema," 18. See also Thomas Elsaesser, "Real Locations, Fantasy Space, Performative Place," in *European Film Theory*, ed. Temenuga Trifonova (New York: Routledge, 2009), 48; and Ray Hudson, "One Europe or Many? Reflections on Becoming European," *Transactions of the Institute of British Geographers* 25, no. 4 (2000): 409.

26. Akhil Gupta and James Ferguson, "Beyond 'Culture': Space, Identity, and the Politics of Difference," in *The Cultural Geography Reader*, eds. Timothy S. Oakes and Patricia L. Price (Hoboken, NJ: Routledge, 2008), 64, 65.

27. See for example, Fowler, introduction to *European Cinema Reader*, 2.

28. Thomas Elsaesser, for example, refers to the historical boundaries and the geographical reach of Europe from the Mediterranean to the Urals. Elsaesser further observes that Europe has always been "a continent settled and traversed by very disparate and mostly feuding ethnic entities." Thomas Elsaesser, "Real Locations," 48.

29. Thomas Elsaesser, "Real Locations," 48.

30. For a discussion on how within the last thirty years foreign labor and other immigrants to Europe turned from an ethnic group into a religious group, and for the growth of right-wing politics in western Europe, see the insightful case study of Danish immigration and related discourse in Ferruh Yilmaz, *How the Workers Became Muslims: Immigration, Culture, and Hegemonic Transformation in Europe* (Ann Arbor: University of Michigan, 2016). For a discussion of a variety of medial counter voices to German and European mainstream media images on Islam and Turkishness, see Berna Gueneli, "Reframing Islam: The Decoupling of Ethnicity from Religion in Turkish German Media," in "Faith, Fascination, and Fear in Twenty-First Century Culture," special issue, *Colloquia Germanica* 47, no. 1–2 (2014, publ. 2017).

31. For a discussion of the othering of eastern European cinemas, see also Dina Iordanova, *Cinema of the Other Europe: The Industry and Artistry of Central European Film* (London: Wallflower, 2003); Wayne, *Politics of Contemporary European Cinema*, 93ff.

32. Fatima El-Tayeb, "'The Birth of a European Public:' Migration, Postnationality, and Race in the Uniting of Europe," *American Quarterly* 60, no. 3 (2008): 659. In a different context, adding religion, El-Tayeb further points out that "the Muslim presence in Europe . . . is acknowledged in order to define a new, unified Europe characterized by a tolerant secularism—a tolerance, paradoxically, that is manifest not in the inclusion but the exclusion of the continent's largest religious minority." Fatima El-Tayeb, *European Others Queering Ethnicity in Postnational Europe* (Minneapolis: University of Minnesota Press, 2011), xxviii.

33. "Anne Will: Die Kanzlerin in der Flüchtlingskrise—Können wir es wirklich schaffen, Frau Merkel?," ARD Mediathek, aired on October 7, 2015, accessed October 8, 2015, http://www.ardmediathek.de/tv/Anne-Will/Die-Kanzlerin-in-der-Fl%C3%BCchtlingskrise-/Das-Erste/Video?documentId=30981456&bcastId=328454.

34. "Sarkozy Launches Presidential Bid with Anti-Turkey Stance," *EU Observer*, January 15, 2007, accessed February 1, 2016, http://euobserver.com/political/23251.

35. "Wir Europäer sind gemeinsam auf das Stärkste von der auf dem Boden judeo-christlicher Tradition entstandener Kultur geprägt; die Türken als weit überwiegend muslimische Nation gehören einem ganz anderen Kulturkreis an, der seine Heimat in Asien und Afrika hat, nicht aber in Europa." Translations into English are mine unless otherwise marked. Quoted in Leslie A. Adelson, "Opposing Oppositions: Turkish German Questions in Contemporary German Studies," *German Studies Review* 17, no. 2 (1994): 309.

36. "Wenn die Türkei ein Teil der Europäischen Gemeinschaft werden will, muss sie abstreifen, was noch an Asiatischem an ihr haftet." Quoted in Adelson, "Opposing Oppositions," 309.

37. Similarly, in the introduction to their anthology on literature and migration, the editors state that "kulturelle Grenzziehungen" ("cultural border drawings") are a result of the merging of discourses on migration, religion, and citizenship. Özkan Ezli, Dorothee Kimmich, and Annette Werberger, "Vorwort," in *Wider den Kulturenzwang. Migration, Kulturalisierung und Weltliteratur*, eds. Özkan Ezli, Dorothee Kimmich, and Annette Werberger (Bielefeld, Germany: Transcript, 2009), 12.

38. Yosefa Loshitzky, *Screening Strangers: Migration and Diaspora in Contemporary European Cinema* (Bloomington: Indiana University Press, 2010), 4.

39. Loshitzky, *Screening Strangers*, 2. See also William Brown, Dina Iordanova, and Leshu Torchin, *Moving People, Moving Images: Cinema And Trafficking in the New Europe* (St. Andrews, UK: St. Andrews Film Studies, 2010).

40. According to Katrin Sieg, cinema's "cultural and ideological importance" was recognized and subsidized early on with national funds. Today, in addition to regional and national film funds, the EU helps to finance many European film productions. Sieg and Anne Jäckel explain that since the late 1980s and early 1990s, pan-European funding programs have supplemented governmental subsidies. MEDIA and EURIMAGE are two examples of European programs that help produce, distribute, and exhibit films across national boundaries. Sieg, *Choreographing the Global*, 39–40; Jäckel, *European Film Industries*, 69–90; Wood, *Contemporary European Cinema*, 8–11.

41. "And the LUX Prize for European cinema goes to… 'Auf der anderen Seite' ('On the Edge of Heaven')," *European Parliament*, press release, October 24, 2007, accessed February 1, 2016, http://www.europarl.europa.eu/sides/getDoc.do?type=IM-PRESS&reference=20071023 IPR1210 9&language=EN

42. Rivi, *European Cinema after 1989*, 36, 41, 60–61.

43. Sieg, *Choreographing the Global*, 39–40; Jäckel, *European Film Industries*, 69–90; Wood, *Contemporary European Cinema*, 8–11.

44. "Douglas-Sirk-Preis für Fatih Akın," Filmfest Hamburg 2014, accessed July 31, 2014, http://www.filmfesthamburg.de/de/presse/2014/2014.07.25_SirkPreis.php.

45. For a discussion of Sirk's melodrama and its adaptation in the work of R. W. Fassbinder, whose own melodramas have been an inspiration and basis for the work of Pedro Almodóvar and others, see Brigitte Peukert, "Fassbinder Re-Framed," in *Fassbinder Now: Film and Video Art* (Frankfurt am Main, Germany: Deutsches Filminstitut Filmmuseum and Rainer Werner Fassbidner Foundation, 2013), 46.

46. Virginia Wright Wexman, introduction to *Film and Authorship*, ed. Virginia Wright Wexman (New Brunswick, NJ: Rutgers University Press, 2003), 3.

47. For a detailed historical description of the *Cahiers* group's background, see Wright Wexman's introduction, and for the actual texts see Andre Bazin's selected, collected writings in the English translation in *What Is Cinema*, compiled by Hugh Gray. Wright Wexman, introduction to *Film and Authorship*, 2–7; André Bazin, *What Is Cinema?*, trans. and ed. Hugh Grany (Berkeley: University of California Press, 1967).

48. Wright Wexman, introduction to *Film and Authorship*, 6.

49. Roland Barthes, "The Death of the Author," in *The Book History Reader*, eds. *David* Finkelstein and Alistair McCleery (London: Routledge, 2002); Michel Foucault, "What is an Author?" in *The Book History Reader*, eds. David Finkelstein and Alistair McCleery (London: Routledge, 2002).

50. Wright Wexman, introduction to *Film and Authorship*, 6.

51. Wright Wexman, introduction to *Film and Authorship*, 7.

52. Sheila Johnston, "The Author as Public Institution," in *The European Cinema Reader*, ed. Catherine Fowler (London: Routledge, 2002).

53. Johnston, "The Author as Public Institution," 122.

54. Johnston, "The Author as Public Institution," 124–125.

55. Johnston, "The Author as Public Institution," 127.

56. Ulrike Sieglohr, "New German Cinema," in *World Cinema: Critical Approaches*, eds. John Hill and Pamela Church Gibson (Oxford: Oxford University Press, 2000), 82.

57. Rosanna Maule, *Beyond Auteurism: New Directions in Authorial Film Practices in France, Italy and Spain Since the 1980s* (Bristol, UK: Intellect, 2008), 22.

58. See, for example, Janet Staiger, "Authorship Approaches," in *Authorship and Film*, eds. David A. Gerstner and Janet Staiger (New York: Routledge, 2002), 41.

59. For a more detailed discussion on the changing academic discourses on the auteur and a suggestion for a global auteur of the twenty-first century, see Seung-hoon Jeong and Jeremi Szeniawski, introduction to *Global Auteur*, eds. Jeong and Szeniawski (New York: Bloomsbury Academic, 2016).

60. Wood, *Contemporary European Cinema*, 41.

61. Dudley Andrew, "Fatih Akin's Moral Geometry," in *Global Auteur*, eds. Jeong and Szeniawski, (New York: Bloomsbury Academic, 2016).

62. For a discussion of Akın's media reception in Germany and Turkey, see Ayca Tunc Cox, "Hyphenated Identities: The Reception of Turkish German Cinema in the Turkish Daily Press," *Turkish German Cinema in the New Millennium: Sites, Sounds, and Screens*, eds. Sabine Hake and Barbara Mennel (Oxford: Berghahn, 2012); and Karolin Machtans, "The Perception and Marketing of Fatih Akın in the German Press," *Turkish German Cinema in the New Millennium: Sites, Sounds, and Screens*, eds. Sabine Hake and Barbara Mennel, (Oxford: Berghahn, 2012).

63. Many authors have referred to Akın and other Turkish German directors as auteurs, or as directors with particular film styles, but have not discussed how it applies to Akın's work particularly. Berghahn, "No Place like Home? Or Impossible Homecomings in the Films of Fatih Akin," *New Cinemas: Journal of Contemporary Film* 4, no. 3 (2006): 141; Berghahn, *Head-On* (*Gegen die Wand*), 33. Nezih Erdoğan, "Star Director as Symptom: Reflections on the Reception of Fatih Akin in the Turkish Media," *New Cinemas: Journal of Contemporary Film* 7, no. 1 (2009): 27; Deniz Göktürk, "Sound Bridges: Transnational Mobility as Ironic Drama," in *Shifting Landscapes: Film and Media in European Context*, eds. Christensen, Miyase and Nezih Erdoğan, (Newcastle, UK: Cambridge Scholars, 2008), 1-2; Deniz Göktürk, "Mobilität und Stillstand im Weltkino digital," in *Kultur als Ereignis: Fatih Akıns Film* Auf der anderen Seite *als transkulturelle Narration*, ed. Özkan Ezli (Bielefeld, Germany: Transcript, 2010), 35.; Barbara Mennel, "Bruce Lee in Kreuzberg and Scarface in Altona: Transnational Auteurism and Ghettocentrism in Thomas Arslan's *Brothers and Sisters* and Fatih Akin's *Short Sharp Shock*," *New German Critique* 87 (2002): 133.

64. I paraphrased and translated parts of the radio interview with film critic Andrej Plachow "Junges Russland: Fatih Akin—Ein Regisseur der Globalisierung," *Stimme Russlands*, April 24, 2009, accessed April 18, 2011, http://german.ruvr.ru/radio_broad cast/4001839/4001863 .html.

65. In footnote 72 of her chapter on *Head-On*, Çelik explains Akın's rejection to being connected to Fassbinder's filmmaking. Ipek A. Çelik, *In Permanent Crisis: Ethnicity in Contemporary European Media and Cinema* (Ann Arbor: University of Michigan, 2016), 167.

66. In an interview toward the end of the documentary *Fatih Akın—Diary of a Film Traveler*, Akın states that he is most pleased when his films are praised by his family, the general moviegoers, who are looking for entertainment, and by film critics writing for feuilletons or working at European art circuits. See Monique Akın, *Fatih Akın—Tagebuch eines Filmreisenden (Fatih Akin—Diary of a Film Traveler)*, 2007, extra features in *The Edge of Heaven* (Culver City, CA: Strand Releasing, 2008), DVD.

67. Göktürk mentions the "originality seal" ("Originalitätssiegel") that Akın's audio commentary and interviews provide for the audience of his films on DVDs. She states that these serve as an "auctorial gesture" ("auktoriale Geste"). Göktürk, "Mobilität und Stillstand im Weltkino digital," 17.

68. Such readings include, for example, Özkan Ezli, "Von der Identität zur Individuation: *Gegen die Wand*—eine Problematisierung kultureller Identitätszuschreibungen," in *Konfliktfeld Islam in Europa*, eds. Monika Wohlrab-Sahr and Levent Tezcan (Baden-Baden, Germany: Nomos, 2007); Jessica Gallagher, *Der neue deutsche Film ist türkisch: Issues of Space, Identity and Streotypes in Contemporary Turkish German Cinema* (PhD diss., University of Queensland, 2008); Matthias Knopp, "Identitäten zwischen den Kulturen: *Gegen die Wand*," in *Kontext Film: Beiträge zu Film und Literatur*, eds. Michael Braun and Werner Kamp (Berlin: Schmidt, 2006); Katherine Pratt Ewing, "Between Cinema and Social Work: Diasporic Turkish Women and the (Dis)Pleasures of Hybridity," *Cultural Anthropology* 21, no. 2 (2006); Diana Schäffler, *Deutscher Film mit türkischer Seele: Entwicklungen und Tendenzen der deutsch-türkischen Filme von den 70er Jahren bis zur Gegenwart* (Saarbrücken, Germany: VDM Verlag Dr. Müller, 2007).

69. Recent innovative readings include Claudia Breger, "Configuring Affect: Complex World Making in Fatih Akın's *Auf der anderen Seite* (*The Edge of Heaven*)," *Cinema Journal* 54, no. 1 (2014); Çelik, "In Permanent Crisis," 102–126; Gueneli, "The Sound of Fatih Akın's Cinema;" Göktürk, "Mobilität und Stillstand im Weltkino digital"; Roger Hillman and Vivien Silvey, "Remixing Hamburg: Transnationalism in Fatih Akın's Soul Kitchen," in *Turkish German Cinema in the New Millennium*; Barbara Mennel, "Überkreuzungen in globaler Zeit und globalem Raum in Fatih Akıns *Auf der anderen Seite*," in *Kultur als Ereignis*, ed. Özkan Ezli, (Bielefeld, Germany: Transcript, 2010).

70. See Berghahn, "Seeing Everything with Different Eyes;" Berghahn, *Head-On*; Özkan Ezli, "Von Lücken, Grenzen und Räumen: Übersetzungsverhältnisse in Alejandro Gonzáles Iñarritus Babel und Fatih Akıns *Auf der anderen Seite*," in *Kultur als Ereignis*, ed. Özkan Ezli (Bielefeld, Germany: Transcript, 2010); Gerd Gemünden, "Hollywood in Altona: Minority Cinema and the Transnational Imagination," in *German Pop Culture: How "American" is it?*, ed. Agnes C. Mueller (Ann Arbor: University of Michigan Press, 2004); Deniz Göktürk, "World Cinema Goes Digital: Looking at Europe from the Other Shore," in *Turkish German Cinema in the New Millennium*, eds. Sabine Hake and Barbara Mennel (Oxford: Berghahn, 2012); and Berna Gueneli, "Remixing Film Histories."

71. Isolina Ballesteros, *Immigration Cinema in the New Europe* (Bristol, UK: Intellect, 2015); Daniela Berghahn, *Far-Flung Families: The Diasporic Family in Contemporary European Cinema* (Edinburgh, UK: Edinburgh University Press, 2014).

72. Nilgün Bayraktar, *Mobility and Migration in Film and Moving Image Art: Cinema Beyond Europe* (New York: Routledge, 2016).

73. Çelik, *In Permanent Crisis*, 4ff., 27.

74. Çelik, *In Permanent Crisis*, 124.

75. Jeremy Barham and Holly Rogers, ed. *The Music and Sound of Experimental Film* (New York: Oxford University Press, 2017); Michel Chion, *Film: A Sound Art*, trans. Claudia Gorbman (New York: Columbia University Press, 2009); Mervyn Cooke, *A History of Film Music* (Cambridge: Cambridge University Press, 2008); Helen Hanson, *Hollywood Soundscapes: Film Sound Style, Craft & Production in the Classical Era* (London: Palgrave Macmillan, 2017); Kathryn Kalinak, *Sound: Dialogue, Music, and Effects* (New Brunswick, NJ: Rutgers University Press, 2015); David Neumeyer, *The Oxford Handbook of Film Music Studies* (New York: Oxford University Press, 2015); Gianluca Sergi, *The Dolby Era: Film Sound in Contemporary Hollywood* (Manchester, UK: Manchester UP, 2004); James Wierzbicki, *Film Music: A History* (New York: Routledge, 2009).

76. Göktürk, "World Cinema Goes Digital"; Hillman and Silvey, "Remixing Hamburg"; Kosta, "Transnational Space and Music"; Senta Siewert, "Soundtracks of Double Occupancy: Sampling Sounds and Cultures in Fatih Akin's *Head On*," in *Mind the Screen: Media Concepts According to Thomas Elsaesser*, eds. Jaap Kooijman, Patricia Pisters, and Wanda Strauven (Amsterdam: Amsterdam University Press, 2008): 199.

77. Venkat Mani, *Cosmopolitical Claims: Turkish German Literature from Nadolny to Pamuk* (Iowa City: University of Iowa Press, 2007), 8.

78. For a discussion of affect and Akın's cinema, see Breger, "Configuring Affect."

79. See, for example, Barbara Korte and Claudia Sternberg, *Bidding for the Mainstream? Black and Asian British Film since the 1990s* (Amsterdam: Rodopi, 2004); and Carrie Tarr, *Reframing Difference: Beur and Banlieue Filmmaking in France* (Manchester, UK: Manchester University Press/Palgrave Macmillan, 2005).

80. Loshitzy, *Screening Strangers*, 9.

81. Hamid Naficy, *An Accented Cinema: Exilic and Diasporic Filmmaking* (Princeton, N.J: Princeton University Press, 2001).

82. For a discussion of the hyphen and its use in literature, see Azade Seyhan, *Writing Outside the Nation* (Princeton, NJ: Princeton University Press, 2002), 15, 76.

83. For an example in literary studies, see Tom Cheesman, *Novels of Turkish German Settlement: Cosmopolite Fiction* (Rochester, NY: Camden House, 2007). For a film studies example, see Sabine Hake and Barbara Mennel, eds., *Turkish German Cinema in the New Millennium: Sites, Sounds, and Screens* (Oxford: Berghahn, 2012).

84. Sabine Hake and Barbara Mennel, introduction to *Turkish German Cinema in the New Millennium: Sites, Sounds, and Screens*, eds. Sabine Hake and Barbara Mennel (Oxford: Berghahn, 2012), 2.

85. Akın, often analyzed within the rubric of Turkish German cinema, has himself frequently emphasized that he is a German or European filmmaker who does not want to be classified solely under a niche reserved for diasporic or ethnic directors. For a brief discussion of this, see, for example, Gemünden, "Hollywood in Altona," 180 ff.; Machtans, "Perception and Marketing of Fatih Akın," 158ff.

86. Alexandra Ludewig, *Screening Nostalgia: 100 Years of German Heimat Film* (Bielefeld, Germany: Transcript, 2014), 400.

87. Discussing Tevfik Başer's films, Özkan Ezli states that the Turkish director depicts a fundamentally different "Turkish" culture for the observing "German" audience. Özkan Ezli, "Von der interkulturellen zur kulturellen Kompetenz. Fatih Akın's globalisiertes Kino," in *Wider den Kulturenzwang: Migration, Kulturalisierung und Weltliteratur*, eds. Özkan Ezli, Dorothee Kimmich, and Annette Werberger (Bielefeld, Germany: Transcript, 2009), 209.

88. Özkan Ezli, "Von der interkulturellen zur kulturellen Kompetenz," 208ff.; Deniz Göktürk, "Turkish Delight—German Fright: Migrant Identities in Transnational Cinema," *ESRC: Economic & Social Research Council—Transnational Communities Programme: Working Paper Series*, 2000, accessed January 15, 2008, http://transcomm.ox.ac.uk/working_papers.htm; Deniz Göktürk, "Migration und Kino—Subnationale Mitleidskultur oder Transnationale Rollenspiele?" in *Interkulturelle Literatur in Deutschland: ein Handbuch*, ed. Carmiene Chiellino (Stuttgart, Germany: Metzkler, 2000). For a similar periodization into three phases, see also Sabine Hake's and Barbara Mennel's introduction to their edited anthology *Turkish German Cinema in the New Millennium: Sights, Sounds, and Screens*, 5.

89. See also Daniela Berghahn, "Introduction: Turkish German Dialogue on Screen," *New Cinemas: Journal of Contemporary Film* 7, no. 1 (2009); and "Sowohl als auch: Das 'deutsch-türkische' Kino heute," filmportal.de, accessed March 1, 2014, https://www.filmportal.de/thema/sowohl-als-auch-das-deutsch-tuerkische-kino-heute.

90. "Studenten-Oscars 2015: Gold für İlker Çatak," *Sueddeutsche Zeitung*, September 18, 2015, accessed September 22, 2015, http://www.sueddeutsche.de/ kultur/nachwuchs-filmpreis-in-los-angeles-ilker-atak-gewinnt-goldenen-studenten-oscar-1.2653342.

91. Deniz Göktürk, "Beyond Paternalism: Turkish German Traffic in Cinema," in *The German Cinema Book*, eds. Tim Bergfelder, Erica Carter, and Deniz Göktürk (Suffolk, UK: BFI, 2002), 249.

92. Angelica Fenner, "Turkish Cinema in the New Europe: Visualizing Ethnic Conflict in Sinan Çetin's *Berlin in Berlin*," *Camera Obscura* 15, no. 2 (2000); Göktürk, "Beyond Paternalism"; Anna A. Kuhn, "Bourgeois Ideology as the (Mis) Reading of Günter Wallraff's Ganz Unten," in "Minorities in German Culture," special issue, *New German Critique* 46, (1989).

93. According to Randall Halle, in early depictions of ethnic minorities in German cinema, the narrative conflict is resolved by "radical excision"—that is, by "the death or departure" of the ethnic minority toward the end of the film. Halle, *German Film after Germany*, 141.

94. James Franklin, *New German Cinema: From Oberhausen to Hamburg* (Boston: Twayne, 1983), 22–23.

95. Rita Chin, *The Guest Worker Question in Postwar Germany* (Cambridge: Cambridge University Press, 2007), 30.

96. In this context, Göktürk has labeled most of the subsidy films from the 1960s–1980s as a "cinema of duty," borrowing the term from the British context. Deniz Göktürk, "Turkish Women on German Streets: Closure and Exposure in Transnational Cinema," in *Spaces in European Cinema*, ed. Myrto Konstantarakos (Exeter, UK: Intellect, 2000), 67.

97. Gökçe Yurdakul, *From Guest Workers into Muslims: The Transformation of Turkish Immigrant Associations in Germany* (Newcastle, UK: Cambridge Scholars, 2009), 31.

98. Naficy, *An Accented Cinema*, 191.

99. Göktürk, "Beyond Paternalism," 251; Rob Burns, "Images of Alterity: Second-Generation Turks in the Federal Republic," *The Modern Language Review* 94, no. 3 (July 1999): 748, 753.

100. For a long time, *Yasemin* has been referred to as a "milestone" in Turkish German understanding, while *Yasemin*, in fact, simply reaffirms "long-held stereotypes according to which German society is considered enlightened and civilized, while Turkish patriarchy is bound to archaic rituals and traditional beliefs." Göktürk, "Beyond Paternalism," 251.

101. See also, Göktürk, "Migration und Kino," 336.

102. Ludewig, *Screening Nostalgia*, 408.

103. David Horrocks and Eva Kolinsky, "Introduction: Migrants or Citizens? Turks in Germany between Exclusion and Acceptance," in *Turkish Culture in German Society Today*, eds. David Horrocks and Eva Kolinsky (Providence, RI: Berghahn Books, 1996), xx.

104. In *Berlin in Berlin*, as Fenner's analysis shows, the ethnic contemplation of difference is reversed. A German photographer turns into a foreigner, an exile in the apartment of a Turkish family in Berlin-Kreuzberg. Fenner, "Turkish Cinema in the New Europe," 114.

105. Halle, *German Film after Germany*, 146.

106. Rob Burns, "Turkish German Cinema: From Cultural Resistance to Transnational Cinema?," in *German Cinema: Since Unification*, ed. David Clarke (London: Continuum, 2006), 133.

107. Göktürk, "Turkish Women on German Streets," 72.

108. Gemünden, "Hollywood in Altona," 185; Göktürk, "Turkish Women on German Streets," 72; Mennel, "Bruce Lee in Kreuzberg," 135.

109. For a discussion of some of these films, see also Göktürk, "Beyond Paternalism," 251f, 253ff.

110. The term "Cinema of consensus" was coined by Eric Rentschler and refers to the cinema of the late 1980s and 1990s that has more commercial and less artistical aspirations. Thomas

Elsaesser referred to the same cinema as "cockily mainstream, brazenly commercial," a cinema that "wants no truck with the former quality label 'art cinema.'" David Clarke, ed., *German Cinema: Since Unification* (London: Continuum, 2006), 2–3; Rentschler, "From New German Cinema."

111. Göktürk criticized the spectatorship of Turkish German cinema, stating that many expect authenticity and "factual stories about outrages; [whereas] fantasies, fiction, or ironic distance are reserved for western mainstream or art cinema," and thereby inhibit a purely artistic production and reception of Turkish German cinema. Göktürk, "Beyond Paternalism," 250–251.

112. Berna Gueneli, "'*Wut*—Who Is Enraged? Violence in the 'Victim Society,'" *Türkisch-deutsche Studien, Jahrbuch 2013, Jugendbilder—Repräsentationen von Jugend in Medien und Politik*, eds. Yasemin Dayıoğlu-Yücel, Michael Hofmann, and Şeyda Ozil, (Göttingen: V&R Unipress, 2013).

113. "Europa—Gateway to the European Union," accessed January 15, 2011, http://europa.eu/index_en.htm.

114. Halle, *Europeanization of Cinema*, 9.

115. For the Schengener Übereinkommen, see the website of Auswärtiges Amt Deutschland, "Das Schengener Übereinkommen und Schengener Durchführungsübereinkommen," December 11, 2008, accessed January 30, 2009, http//www.auswaertiges-amt.de/en/WilkommeninD/EinreiseUndAufenthalt/Staatsangehoerig keitsrecht.html.

116. Ian Traynor and Patrick Kingsley, "EU Governments Push Through Divisive Deal to Share 120,000 Refugees," *The Guardian*, September 22, 2015. http://www.theguardian.com/world/2015/sep/22/eu-governments-divisive-quotas-deal-share-120000-refugees.

117. For a detailed discussion of the development of European cinema in the European Union, see Halle, *Europeanization of Cinema*.

118. Putting an emphasis on "transnational connections and on cosmopolitanism, on traveling back and forth, rather than on one-directional migration," Deniz Göktürk and Barbara Wolbert affirm that the current era warrants "thinking and feeling *beyond* the national." Deniz Göktürk and Barbara Wolbert, introduction to "Multicultural Germany: Art, Performance and Media," special issue, *New German Critique* 92 (Spring–Summer 2004): 3.

119. For books and anthologies examining diasporic and transnational cinema, see Daniela Berghahn and Claudia Sternberg, eds., *European Cinema in Motion: Migrant and Diasporic Film in Contemporary Europe* (Houndsmills, UK: Palgrave MacMillan, 2010); Berghahn, *Far-Flung Families*; and Halle, *German Film after Germany*.

120. Halle argues that globalization and transnationalism are intrinsically related. He states that transnationalism is a new word that addresses cultural dynamics and sociopolitical processes, whereas globalization belongs to the material economic processes. He further states that film "proves to be the most significant marker of simultaneous economic and cultural transformations, marker of globalization and transnationalism." Halle, *German Film after Germany*, 5–6.

121. Gueneli, "*Wut*—Who Is Enraged?," 96, 98.

122. Deniz Göktürk, "Strangers in Disguise: Role-Play beyond Identity Politics in Anarchic Film Comedy," in "Multicultural Germany, Art, Performance and Media," special issue, *New German Critique* 92 (2004), 103.

123. See for example, Hake and Mennel, *Turkish German Cinema*; Ela Gezen and Berna Gueneli, guest eds., "Transnational Hi/Stories: Turkish German Texts and Contexts," special issue, *Colloquia Germanica* 44, no. 4 (2011, publ. 2015); and Ela Gezen and Berna Gueneli, guest eds., *Turkish German Studies: Past, Present, and Future*, special volume, *Türkisch-deutsche*

Studien, Jahrbuch 2015, eds. Yasemin Dayioğlu-Yücel, Michael Hofmann, Şeyda Ozil (Göttingen: V&R Unipress, 2015).

124. Akın himself is quick to name influential directors such as Antonioni, Fassbinder, Polanski, Scorsese, and Yılmaz in his interviews accompanying the DVD releases of his films or even in the thank-you notes/credits of his films. Additionally, Göktürk and Ezli have pointed to global directors such as Iñárritu, Coppola, and Krzysztof Kieślowski in relation to Akın's global cinema. Ezli, "Von Lücken, Grenzen und Räumen," 71ff.; Göktürk, "Mobilität und Stillstand im Weltkino digital," 22, 35.

125. Nava discusses, for example, London as such a "global city." Mica Nava, *Visceral Cosmopolitanism: Gender, Culture and the Normalization of Difference* (Oxford: Berg, 2007), 13, 162.

CHAPTER 1

Mapping Europe

THE ROAD MOVIE GENRE AND TRANSNATIONAL EUROPEAN SPACE IN FILM

WHO AND WHAT defines Europe?[1] Various disciplines, organizations, and interest groups such as the EU, political parties, and academic disciplines have repeatedly constructed and defined Europe and things European. The building ban on minarets in Switzerland (2009), the outlawing of the *hijab* (veil) in French schools (2010), and the increasing numbers of refugees coming to Europe after the Arab Spring and the long war in Syria (post-2011) warrant once again a reevaluation of the changing sights and sounds of Europe. Cinema provides one way of imagining concepts of the continent, and Akın's films offer contemporary, popular examples for cinematic evaluations of Europe and Europeanness. Turkey's role in this new Europe is also important, especially considering Turkey's aspirations to become an EU member state.[2]

This chapter examines Akın's construction of an alternate filmic Europe. To this end, I discuss the intrinsically related specificities of European mobility, spaces, and sounds in his film *In July*. In particular, I highlight the role of the road movie genre for the construction of this filmic Europe in addition to foregrounding the politics of Akın's setting, casting, and soundtrack choices in *In July*, all of which impact the film's construction of Europe and Europeanness. The structure of this chapter is organized as such: Following an initial discussion of *In July*'s articulation of Europe, I provide a definition of the road movie genre, which helps Akın map his cinematic vision of Europe. The film uses this genre to destabilize a nation-centered map of Europe and its Others, and to create a porous and cosmopolitan Europe. I pay particular attention to the feature of mobility and the figure of the traveler from road movies. Cinematic mobility provides a mode of navigation through European spaces, and the film's figure of the traveler assists in mapping Europe for the viewer just as much as it portrays new, diverse European citizens as its navigators. Once the European navigators are clearly presented, I discuss the film's creation of European spaces in more detail. I analyze the depiction of borders, landscapes, and city spaces, which feature as stops in this European road movie. Finally, a discussion of the European sounds in *In July* complements, on the acoustic level, our understanding of the spatial construction of a filmic Europe.

The chapter thereby positions Akın and his cinema in a European context while attempting to decipher his audiovisual visions of Europe as expressed through elements of the road movie. Focusing on *In July*'s conception of Europe, this chapter thus lays the foundation for the next two chapters, which will offer a more detailed analysis of the aural composition in Akın's *Head-On* and *The Edge of Heaven* by discussing their transnational soundtracks.

In July's Europe

With *In July*, Akın sets the tone for his future films in his Turkish German entanglement period. The film showcases how Akın, with this very early feature film, has already begun to map Europe as a transnational space extending beyond existing EU borders. With the help of the road movie genre, the director subtly shifts geopolitical borders, depicts the arbitrariness of national borders, and creates a flexible, enlarged cinemascape of Europe.

Central features of Akın's filmic Europe are its multiethnicity and polyphony. This lighthearted road movie is different (in terms of genre, plot, and style) from Akın's later, critically acclaimed feature films such as *Head-On*, *The Edge of Heaven*, and *Soul Kitchen*. Yet *In July*'s visions of Europe are very similar to those later films. These films offer a coherent narrative of a connected and diverse cinematic Europe. Frequently such experiences of ethnic and linguistic diversity have been linked to experiences of cities that are under the influence of globalization.[3] Yet, in *In July*, such diversification is considered to be already in place throughout both the rural and urban settings of Europe. A combination of transnational sounds and visuals construct a fluid, almost borderless imagination of the European space, which explicitly includes pre-EU eastern Europe and Turkey.

European places figure prominently in *In July*, marking the film's setting immediately as European. The beginning of the film highlights eastern Europe with the title "somewhere in Bulgaria." The narrative begins with a young, dark-haired, mysterious-looking man, Isa (Mehmet Kurtuluş), getting out of his Mercedes, which has a Berlin license plate in pre-EU eastern Europe. This opening sequence introduces the audience to the main character, Daniel (Moritz Bleibtreu), who in travel-worn clothes tries to get a ride from Isa. After Daniel explains that he is on the way to find his love interest, Melek (Idil Üner), the story continues with Daniel's flashback narrative. The flashback explains why the teacher in training came from Hamburg to Bulgaria and is on his way to Istanbul. Starting in Hamburg and moving further southeast, Daniel travels through a Bavarian town, Vienna, and various eastern European locations. Eventually, the frame narrative continues with Daniel and Isa at the Bulgarian-Turkish border. From here, the last sequences portray Daniel on his way to a desired meeting spot in Ortaköy-Istanbul, where he hopes to see Melek. Instead, he encounters his former travel companion Juli (Christiane Paul), and both confirm their mutual love. The film ends with the continuation of their travel into the "shitty south."

Beginning "somewhere in Bulgaria" and ending on the way to the "shitty south," *In July* is both a European road movie and a politically conscious movie that makes deliberate choices to underscore the porousness of borders. The spatial continuity among the cityscapes and landscapes replaces previously established and commonly accepted geopolitical concepts of Europe, especially outside the Schengen zone (typically fortified through ritualized, politicized acts of border crossings). In Akın's film, this continuity is best symbolized by various characters traveling throughout post-1989 Europe. Akın connects iconic European cities such as Hamburg and Budapest with Istanbul. At the same time, rural landscapes in central and eastern Europe are linked to these cities in fluid continuity. Yet man-made borders interrupt and oppose the connections between these spaces. Thus, while thematizing the connectedness of European space, the film addresses the issue of borders explicitly by presenting them as complicated, metaphorical antagonists to the continuity of landscapes.

As the analysis of the road movie genre and the audiovisual dimensions of *In July* will demonstrate, Akın constructs cinematic imaginings of a diverse yet connected Europe. In this European space, multiethnicity and multilingualism are prominent in a variety of regions. Yet Akın's principal settings, like post–Cold War western and eastern Europe, as well as contemporary Turkey, are places that have often been seen as historically and politically distinct. Fatima El-Tayeb reminds us that a multiethnic and multireligious Europe has still not been accepted in contemporary conceptualizations of the continent.[4] In 2015, for example, when Europe began to experience a new "refugee crisis," widespread unfavorable opinions toward non-Christian, non–western European refugees and migrants in Europe epitomized the persistence of xenophobia across Europe. Such expressions reduce the idea of Europe to a one-dimensional, homogenous notion of the continent, which, in reality it has never been.

Akın's cinema imagines Europe as a changing entity with various dynamic interconnections. Hence, Akın presents European space not as a clear-cut, organized entity with centers and margins that can be firmly defined. Similarly, in the field of cultural geography, Doreen Massey conceptualizes space as a perpetually changing entity, which comes into being through multiple interconnections of people, places, and things material.[5] Akın's films reflect this interconnectedness of a formerly (sociopolitically) divided European North/South and East/West through his aesthetics of heterogeneity. That is, Akın's cinematic space regularly depicts interrelational, heterogeneous local sights and sounds across Europe. For example, he juxtaposes the sounds of global electronic dance music with decidedly localized Black Sea folk music from northeastern Turkey. He similarly intertwines Hamburg-based Brazilian-German reggae bands with the voices of Islamic prayers in his films. As a result, Akın's soundscapes reflect a vast and complex polyphony, which prior to his films was often excluded from conventional depictions of Europe. Languages such as English, Turkish, and Serbo-Croatian, as well as local idioms such as *Hamburgisch*, Bavarian, and Black Sea dialects, further enrich the new sonic heterogeneity of Europe. Ultimately, Akın's cinema portrays networks of European landscapes, city spaces, and sounds with links between local places in Turkey, eastern and western Europe, and South and North America. These transnational connections in Akın's cinematic Europe represent a sometimes polemic challenge to existing geopolitical, national European borders, which, as *In July* depicts, often enough impede transnational interactions beyond the Schengen zone in the lived European reality.

A central feature of this European space is its reliance on movement and mobility. Eventually, the travelers link local places and help create the filmic space of Europe. Similar to Doreen Massey's concept of space, Akın's cinematic visions of Europe are reflected in the interrelations of the people, places, and entities in his films. Massey proposes a progressive and "global sense of place." She suggests that a place comes into existence through the multiple connections it has to other places; it consists of networks of social relations, which are constantly in flux.[6] Through these networks, the specificities of places are perpetually reinvented. The connections in Akın's films are shown, for example, through landscapes that continue seamlessly across borders, parallel city spaces, and cosmopolitan travelers who cross each other's paths.

Such connections are also exemplified through Akın's soundtrack. A specific sound is not bound to a particular place and is capable of creating a link between geographically distant places. Within film sound studies, this detachment of sound recalls Michel Chion's elaborations on the "audiovisual scene." While the image refers to the frame and therefore has a "container," according to Chion, there is no "auditory container for sound."[7] "Film sound is what is contained or not contained in an image; there is no place of the sounds, no auditory scene already preexisting in the soundtrack—and therefore, properly speaking, there is no soundtrack."[8] This characteristic of cinematic sound makes it easy to demarcate flexibility and mobility. Chion further elaborates on his notion of the "acousmatic" to theorize sound.[9] Acousmatic sound, a sound, for example, that is recorded—or offscreen and nondiegetic sound in film—does not depict its place of enunciation. Such sound is therefore not bound to a specific body. It travels through space but carries with it the characteristics of the space from which it emerges. Looking at recorded sound, for example, it can clearly be dislocated in two ways—both by being detached from its space of enunciation (playback may happen at a different time, in another part of the globe) and within cinema, by being attached to or detached from specific bodies depicted in the film. That is, at all times, the viewer must be engaged in "mapping" the sound. In *In July*, sound maps Europe.

The following sections on the road movie genre and mobility, as well as on European spaces and sounds, provide more detailed insights about Akın's audio-visual conceptions of a connected Europe.

The Road Movie Genre

A widely popular genre, the road movie has been regarded as quintessentially American by some scholars,[10] while others have questioned the uncritical assumption of its "inherent Americanness" or highlighted the long traditions of road and travel movies in other geographies, such as in Europe.[11] In general, the road movie genre entails a variety of specific thematic, stylistic, and filmic components—and combinations thereof. Some of the prominent features of road movies include the depiction of a journey, the crossing of borders, the experience of mobility, the vastness and openness of the road, the use of a vehicle (typically a car), the staging of a traveling couple, and the cinematic techniques that create a particular feel and style, such as the traveling shot.[12]

While the topics can vary drastically, one of the recurring themes of the road movie is the act of border crossing—whether this implies a societal or cultural border crossing, or the physical crossing of a national border.[13] Describing the US context, David Laderman states, "The ability to cross borders via . . . highways becomes the central feature of the genre's *mise-en-scène*. To cross a state or country line is to leave the familiar behind, to venture into the new and unknown."[14] As Laderman further suggests, oftentimes the highway—or any other road symbolizing such a border crossing, for that matter—can thematically also involve a tension between "rebellion and conformity."[15]

Contemporary post-1989 European cinema has experienced a renewed interest in the road movie genre.[16] Ewa Mazierska and Laura Rascaroli describe this phenomenon as reflecting the new lifestyles of Europeans, characterized by a "lack of permanency," and the sociopolitical and economic changes seen in Europe. Mobility "has become the condition of large groups of citizens."[17] They further state that "experiences of displacement, diaspora, exile, migration, nomadism, homelessness, border-crossing and tourism are all relevant to contemporary Europe, as indeed they have been in earlier epochs."[18]

While Mazierska and Rascaroli analyze European road movies after 1989, they also discuss and restate the differences between the US and the European road movie. They agree that the main similarity between US and European road films is the motif of the journey, the fact that travel "commonly becomes an opportunity for explorations, discovery and transformation (of landscape, of situation and of identity)" in such films on either side of the Atlantic.[19] However, they are clear about differences, for example, regarding the depiction of space, transportation, and travelers. While US road movies favor open space and boundless highways that offer possibilities to "reinvent" oneself, the European movie depicts a more diverse space packed with a multitude of cultural and historical combinations. The authors further stress that European films differ from American ones in that they reflect a European reality, which is informed by "a mosaic of nations, cultures, languages and roads."[20] That is, European films highlight the traversing of national borders or landscapes. In terms of transportation, the authors suggest that the private car features prominently in US movies, while European films include a variety of transportation options, including walking, public transportation, and so forth. In terms of the travelers, they distinguish between the outcast, rebel US figure versus the rather "ordinary citizen . . . who is on the move, often for practical reasons (for work, immigration, commuting, or holiday-making" in European road films.[21] As my discussions will make clear in the following sections, Akın uses a mix of these different genre-specific forms of the road movie, making it difficult to clearly delineate between the influences of the US and European film genres.

Mobility and the Road Movie Genre: Creating the Cinematic Space of Europe

Mobility—a significant element in road movies—plays a key role in *In July*'s conception of space. I argue that through the different cinematic portrayals and experiences of mobility, the film visualizes the unfixed and unstable conditions in Europe. Mobility suggests dynamism and multidirectionality within Akın's cinematic Europe. The protagonists participate in this movement, too. In a different context, discussing human trafficking in cinema, William Brown rightly stresses that speed and fast movement in a globalized world (Europe) is restricted to the privileged and excludes trafficked people or people from the edges of a geopolitical Fortress Europe.[22] However, this is not so in Akın's cinema. While movement is generally a privilege of the legal citizens of Europe, legal and illegal subjects in *In July* traverse Europe and take part in the creation of a dynamic space. Mobility is symbolized by the film's heavy reliance on the genre conventions of the road movie, the various modes of transportation, the mobile narrative structure, and the movement of the characters.

The opening sequence of *In July* immediately situates the film within the road movie genre. The film begins with an emphasis on the setting by highlighting the geographic location. The establishing shot is of a sunlit country road with fields on either side. The image flickers to suggest intense heat to the viewer. Shortly after, the country road and landscape are introduced with the title "Thursday, July 7th, 12:10 p.m., somewhere in Bulgaria." The space is empty and depicts a vast landscape with fields and electric poles; no person is shown. A Mercedes is slowly driving toward the camera. While the car comes closer, the light dims, and the car pulls over and stops.

The opening shot pays particularly close attention to space and genre conventions through photography, camerawork, and setting. The establishing shot is focused on open space, which is shown in long shots that depict the landscape and the wideness of the field and road. This gives the illusion that the road and the fields continue beyond the camera frame, which suggests a continuity of open landscapes. At the same time, the setting is unknown and mysterious and implies adventure. This sequence is similar to scenes in classic US road movies, in which the road and the car take center stage. While the road symbolizes the "course of life" and "a lure of both freedom and destiny," it also provokes "anxiety" and "represents the unknown."[23] According to Laderman, the highway systems, as well as vast and open landscapes with "seductive horizons," are among the most important aspects of the genre; it is by moving through these open landscapes that the protagonists achieve a sense of freedom.[24] The opening shot of *In July* thus prepares the audience for a road movie adventure into "the unknown." However, instead of American highways, the audience is unmistakably introduced to traveling through eastern Europe with the title insert "somewhere in Bulgaria."

In July is generally categorized as a "romantic road movie," a "cross-Balkan road movie," or simply a "light-hearted road movie."[25] However, the *In July* scholarship does not thematize or discuss the function of the road movie genre closely. Rather, it is used to briefly contextualize the film as a journey, either as a "transnational journey" through eastern Europe or as a psychological journey toward oneself.[26] In terms of genre, Daniela Berghahn suggests that through generic templates of mainstream cinema, Akın can convey "ethnic identity themes in an accessible and popular format."[27] Berghahn thereby acknowledges the genre's function in bringing a complex theme (ethnicity) to a wider audience. There is, however, little or no discussion of the road movie genre as a possible form for thematic engagements within the post–Cold War context of eastern Europe.

Complicating the travel narrative of the film, I argue that the focus on movement and dynamism on various levels in *In July*, including the use of the road movie genre, functions as a metaphor for European mobility, especially in the Europe of post-1989. That is, I claim that the strategic use of generic material from road movies helps Akın to envision a continuous, dynamic European space.

While Akın's film is thusly a hybrid road movie, incorporating elements of European and US road movies as I discussed further above, Mazierska and Rascaroli's definition of the post-1989 European road movie in particular applies to *In July*.

An intense mobility characterizes contemporary, postmodern, post-1989 Europe and its filmic representation. Geopolitical, economic, and social shifts and changes such as the end of the Cold War, the expansion of the European Union, the Schengen regulations, economic and political uncertainties in the Balkans and elsewhere, as well as unrest, war, and economic inequalities in the global South and the Arab world, are among the factors that caused, and continue to cause, a new form of migration that informs the changes of the last decades in Europe. At the same time, while the post-Communist East/West boundary has slowly relaxed, the newly fortified boundary between North and South has become the latest European divide.[28] More recently, the increased migration movement caused by the Arab Spring and the Syrian war epitomizes the newly reestablished Southeast/Northwest divide. New eastern/central European EU member states, such as Hungary and the Czech Republic—now themselves enjoying a Schengen freedom of movement—have become the new enforcers of borders and try to limit the movement of migrants who enter under enormous hardships into Fortress Europe, and who often try to continue to move throughout Europe into more central and northwestern locations.

Certainly, Akın's films—*In July* in particular—take part in depicting Europe's increased mobility. Yet, additionally, they could also be seen as a challenge to the conceptions of such old and new divides and dividing lines mentioned above, promoting free movement across borders. Illegal Turkish travelers such as Ayten in *The Edge of Heaven* as well as urban businesswomen such as Selma in *Head-On* travel from Turkey to Germany as other characters in the films travel from Germany to Turkey. Akın introduces a multidirectional travel narrative in his films, which includes a diverse palette of travels. His depiction of Turkish travelers furthermore lacks the earlier, one-dimensional filmic depiction of economic or political migrants from Turkey to Germany. That is, Akın's characters travel, legally and illegally, predominantly back and forth in these directions: northwest to southeast.

The newly mobile post–Cold War Europe has impacted European films, particularly those with an immigration theme. While earlier depictions of immigration focused on showing a move from a so-called old home to a new home, films in the new millennium such as Michael Haneke's *Code Unknown* (*Code Inconnu*, 2000) and Pawel Pawlikowski's *Last Resort* (2000) "show that home no longer exists in the sense of a permanent hub."[29] Most certainly, Akın's *In July* is not an immigration film per se; it has a vacation travel narrative. Yet European immigration mobility still features in the film, particularly in the scenes depicting Budapest. In Budapest, former Yugoslavian traveler Luna and the ethnically ambiguous bartender are either working in or traversing through eastern Europe. Also, their knowledge of German hints at possible connections to Germany. Luna, in particular, traveling in a truck marked with "Ex" on the Yugoslavian license plate, becomes a metaphor for recent Balkan history, which has mobilized many people, either forcing them to move from a war-torn country, or permitting them to move freely after the fall of Communism.

In sum, *In July* is a Turkish German example of a post-1989 European road movie that is inspired by US road movies. The European aspects of the road movie are exposed by following the film's narrative of navigating and traversing through nation-states, regions, and cities of northern and eastern Europe. In that sense, *In July* has the qualities that Mazierska and Rascaroli state for European films, namely, "the ability to mirror and interpret phenomena such as shifting European borders; the formation of new personal, regional and transnational identities; the transformation of communities; and, more generally, the character of movement in postmodernity."[30] However, in many ways the film also enthusiastically cites US road movies. *In July* displays vast and open landscapes, a road that symbolizes "the unknown," "adventure," and "freedom"—all of which are quintessentially American elements of the road movie.[31]

Through the adaptation of the road movie genre, Akın is ultimately able to project a cinematic vision of a mobile, traversable, and connected Europe (even if predominantly for European travelers). The different modes of transportation provide for a depiction of different levels of speed while navigating Europe. By traveling on the ground (as opposed to flying), the "map" of Europe becomes more visible, and the European space becomes physically experienced by the travelers. This allows for a more immediate and tactile experience of a connected European space. For instance, although Hamburg is mainly experienced through walking, other cities such as Budapest are seen through high-speed car chases. At the same time, many rural and agrarian areas are predominantly experienced through walking, traveling on a boat, or riding in a car or truck in a much slower motion. The various modes of transportation lead to a diversified perception and cinematic experience of the European landscapes and city spaces.

The Figure of the Traveler: Navigating Europe

As is typical for road movies, the figure of the traveler is another important component of Akın's *In July*. Travelers are set into motion and through their movements assist in drawing a map of Europe. Their journey constructs a cinematic Europe that is traversable and navigable. Emotional involvement leads to a dynamic, physical movement of the characters, who chase each other across Europe. It is through their movement that Akın visualizes European mobility. While the film depicts a variety of travelers, the main characters are four young, urban

Europeans. Their movement is not financially or politically motivated but rather emotionally motivated. For the most part, they freely move between nation-states for personal reasons. Isa and Melek individually travel from Germany to Turkey for a family burial with plans to meet each other in Istanbul. Daniel's travel to Istanbul is motivated by his desire to meet his newly discovered love interest, Melek. Finally, Juli joins Daniel on his way to Istanbul and eventually gains his love and affection.

The figure of the traveler, as well as the casting choices for these figures, help fashion the new inhabitants and travelers of Europe. That is, moving from Berlin to Hamburg and from Hamburg, through eastern Europe, to Istanbul and beyond, these travelers themselves become the new representatives of young, diverse Europeans on screen. This is achieved by, first, reversing cultural stereotypes, thereby allowing European diversity to take center stage; and, second, by focusing on their multidirectional mobility, thereby subtly emphasizing a mobile and decentralized Europe.

Already the opening sequence in Bulgaria suggests a play on cultural stereotypes and viewer expectations. After the establishing shot of *In July*, the first sequence continues with a man in black shades and snakeskin boots (Isa) getting out of his car. He looks at the solar eclipse, which caused the darkening of the sky. After the eclipse, when the sunlight is fully established again, the action continues. Isa is portrayed as peculiar: he has a scar on his head and a gold tooth in his mouth. He moves suspiciously toward the trunk of his car, looking around to see if anybody is watching him. He opens the trunk to reveal a dead body. While he sprays air freshener on it, a second man, Daniel, approaches him. Afraid that Daniel might have detected the body, Isa starts to fight him. The last part of the sequence begins with fast-cut back-and-forth fight scenes between Daniel and Isa. Later it is revealed that Daniel needs a ride to Turkey. Isa is initially not interested in a travel companion and wants to leave him behind. After accidentally hitting Daniel with his car while trying to get away, Isa feels guilty and eventually takes him along, and both men continue their journey together. The sequence ends with Daniel explaining to Isa that he is following his love interest (Melek) to Istanbul.

The casting, acting, and costume choices in the film aid in further undermining persisting cultural stereotypes by disseminating a notion of European ambiguity—suggesting, for example, an initial play on cultural stereotypes. Akın uses popular contemporary actors in Germany, such as Moritz Bleibtreu and Christiane Paul, as well as less popular actors at the time, such as Mehmet Kurtuluş and Idil Üner. Bleibtreu additionally has a recognition factor among global audiences through his part in Tom Tykwer's internationally successful film *Lola rennt* (*Run Lola Run*, 1998).[32] Generally, Akın's use of Bleibtreu and Paul has been credited with making *In July* a commercially successful film.[33] While this is a valid assumption, these and other casting choices should be addressed further. The casting of Bleibtreu, Paul, Kurtuluş, and Üner plays a significant role in the diffusion of Akın's new visions of Europe and Europeanness—as does the casting of Serbian-born Branka Katić, Hungarian-born Gábor Salinger, and Turkish-born Birol Ünel in supporting roles.

The male protagonists Isa and Daniel share certain features (fig. 1.1). The physical aspects of German actor Bleibtreu, who plays Daniel, a German, are similar to those of Turkish German actor Kurtuluş, who plays Isa, a Turkish German character. Both actors are of similar height and weight and have dark hair and dark eyes, so that ambiguity about their ethnic background is implied. Also, Bleibtreu's role as "Abdul the Arab" in Thomas Jahn's 1997 film *Knockin' on Heaven's Door* certainly stresses the ambiguity of his physical features, showing him as a versatile actor who can convincingly play an Arab German character as well as a German one.[34] Kurtuluş's prior acting career was dominated by minor roles playing Turkish German characters in TV productions, until he became critically acclaimed for his part in Akın's 1998 feature *Kurz und Schmerzlos* (*Short Sharp Shock*). In this film he played a lead role as a Turkish German gangster, for which he received a Bronze Leopard at the International Film Festival of Locarno and an Adolf Grimme award. This prior role might shape initial perceptions about the character he plays in *In July*.

In the opening sequence, Isa and Daniel are portrayed as dissimilar. Initially, Isa's acting seems highly stylized through his gangster image (supported by costume and attire). In scenes depicting his curiosity about the solar eclipse and his eventual interest in and concern for Daniel, his acting becomes less stylized. That is, the portrayal of Isa's character seems artificial when he is acting out a certain stereotype of a Turkish German gangster. Dressed in a pair of jeans, snakeskin boots, tight black shirt, and black shades, Isa fits a stereotypical depiction of a Turkish German (petty) criminal.[35] Other elements that ground an initial ethnicized depiction are props and design. Isa drives an old Mercedes (a stereotypical car of Turkish guest workers), which has a blue eye hanging on the front mirror (the *Nazar boncuk*: Turkish talisman against the evil eye).[36] The audio is a popular song by Turkish pop star Sezen Aksu, "Değer mi?" (Is it worth it?) on tape. Thus, the car and its decor are full of clichéd props of a Turkish German character. Isa's gangster persona is enforced in combination with the dead body in his car, his use of a butterfly knife, his propensity toward fire, and his initial aggressive behavior toward Daniel. Daniel's costume and his desperate need of transportation, on the other hand, fit the stereotypical depiction of an illegal immigrant. Dark-haired and unshaven, Daniel wears a dirty white shirt and pants. He seems to be confused but determined to get help for the continuation of his travel.

The initial play on these cultural stereotypes suggests that contemporary young navigators of Europe cannot be easily categorized. The costume and

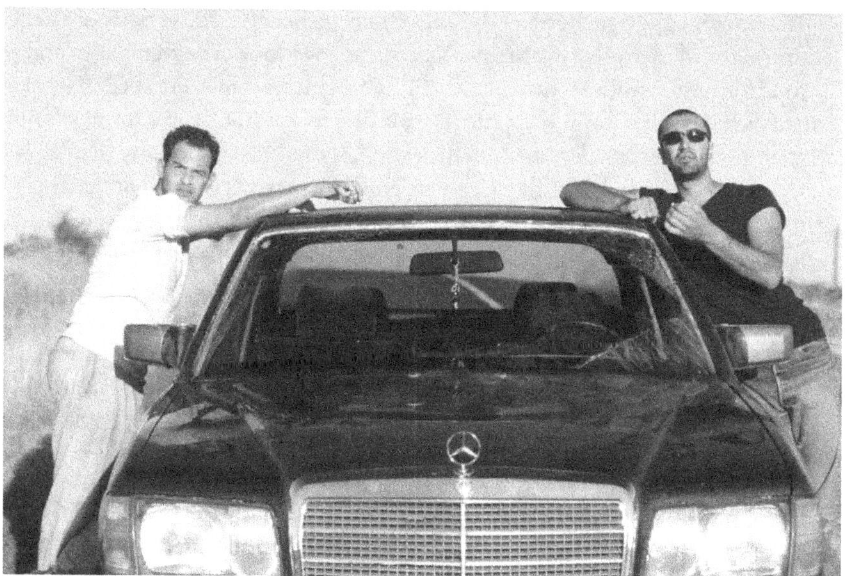

Figure 1.1. Daniel (Moritz Bleibtreu) and Isa (Mehmet Kurtuluş) meet on the road "somewhere in Bulgaria." © Wüste Film, Photo: Gordon Timpen. With kind permission of Wüste Film.

behavior of both characters use and break stereotypes about both German and Turkish German characters—stereotypes that are more directly developed in later parts of the film. In this sequence, the audience is invited to ask why Daniel, a schoolteacher, looks "wie 'n Penner" (like a bum) or like a stereotypical illegal immigrant in the middle of Bulgaria, [37] as well as why the gangster-style Turkish German has a body in his car yet is ultimately nice and willing to help Daniel.

Similar to Daniel and Isa, Juli (Paul) and Melek (Üner), who appear in later sequences, are cast as attractive, ethnically ambiguous European characters. Paul and Üner share physical as well as lifestyle similarities in their film roles. They represent free-spirited, independent, open-minded characters. Deniz Göktürk describes Üner's prior role in Akın's *Short Sharp Shock* as "independent and strong-minded," which echoes her role in *In July*.[38] Economically mobile, Melek, for example, does not strike the audience as a victimized Turkish daughter or wife; nor does she seem to be restricted in her movements, traveling from Berlin to Hamburg, across Hamburg-Altona, to Istanbul, and to Edirne.

All principal characters represent contemporary European travelers who are citizens of a traversable Europe. They are portrayed as open-minded, diverse, tolerant, and cosmopolitan, representing model EU citizens; at the same time, they are also portrayed as illegal border crossers (Daniel travels without a passport) and facilitators of illegal border crossings (Isa transports the dead body of an illegal immigrant), representing the problematic restrictions of movement in and to Europe for non-European travelers.[39] All four principal travelers speak German fluently and have an unproblematic relationship to one another in terms of their ethnicities. (Underprivileged ethnicities and nationalities, especially their limitations of movement within the EU, are briefly referenced at the end of the film.)[40] Daniel falls in love with Melek. Upon asking the meaning of her name, Daniel is not taken aback by Melek's Turkish background and follows her to Istanbul. Juli does not differentiate among nationalities. Bavaria, for that matter, is more foreign to her than Budapest, for example.

Akın's road movie manages to map a dynamic European space, particularly through these travelers. Through their legal and illegal movements, walking and driving through various metropolitan and rural areas—even if these spaces are occasionally interrupted by national borders, as discussed in the next section—they ultimately visualize the inherent connectedness of Akın's cinematic Europe, well beyond the limits of Fortress Europe.

European Spaces: Borders, Landscapes, and City Spaces

Borders

Crossing borders of different kinds is a key feature of road movies.[41] Multiple borders are crossed in *In July* (fig 1.2). The following sequence is an example of the arbitrariness and constructedness of national borders. In the film, neither Hungary nor Romania is an EU member state. Neither state belongs to the borderless Schengen zone. Therefore, this sequence operates as a portrayal of a pre-EU eastern/central European state aspiring to become a member, with open borders, of the European Union. At the same time, this scene unintentionally foreshadows the future attempts of Hungary—which has been an EU member state since 2004—to stop refugee migration from the political southeast into central Europe via the rebuilding of a razor-wire fence and reinstated border patrols in 2015.

Akın's pre-EU Hungarian-Romanian border sequence depicts Daniel in the midst of his trans-European travel. He arrives with a stolen car at the stylized, though primitive, border. The setting is an open, sunny space, seemingly in a Mediterranean climate, dominated in the center by a building that is divided in half—one half being the Hungarian border office building and the other the Romanian. The border is marked by a simple pole, the uniforms of the two officers, their automatic guns, and the large national flags. Daniel explains to the Romanian officer (Akın) that his documents were stolen. The officer calmly eats sunflower seeds and plays a game of *tavla* (backgammon) with his Hungarian counterpart at the symmetrical center of the border, which coincides with the center of the frame. He does not allow Daniel to enter Romania: "No passport,

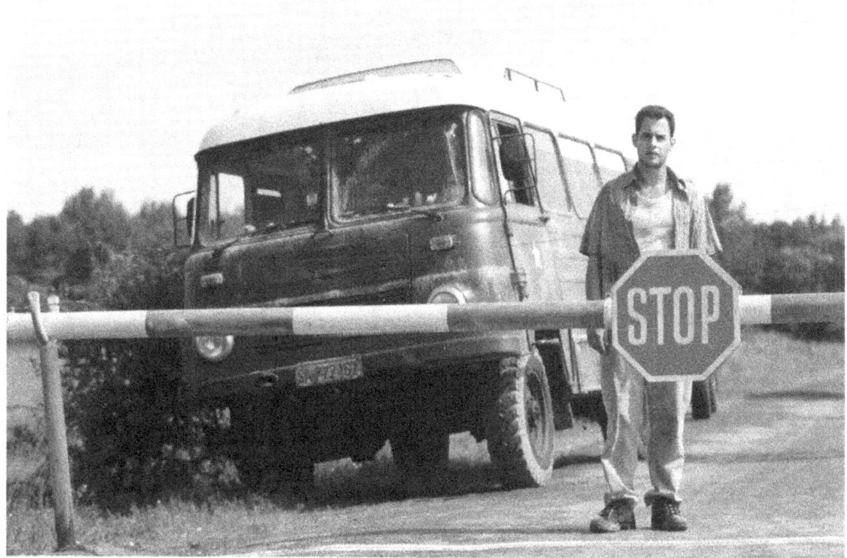

Figure 1.2. Daniel (Moritz Bleibtreu) stares at the other side of the border. © Wüste Film, Photo: Gordon Timpen. With kind permission of Wüste Film.

no Romania!" Disheartened, Daniel stares into the endless road and fields, which continue seamlessly on the other side of the border. He then sees Juli on the Romanian side. For Daniel to cross the border, they agree to perform a ritual of marriage (figure 1.3). The Romanian officer witnesses the wedding ritual and allows Daniel to enter Romania, but not without asking for his vehicle as a "wedding present." The neutralization of the border through this fake wedding unmasks the border as arbitrary and manmade.

This sequence particularly relies on the opposition of stylized versus non-stylized formal details to make suggestions about borders. While the landscape is open and continuous, the stylized border breaks the center of the frame. It symbolizes an artificial divide of the otherwise seamlessly continuous rural space. The setting (border props) emerges as almost stage-like. The overall design of the border is exaggeratedly symmetrical, which, in addition to the comedic acting of Akın, further questions the highly conventionalized ritual of border crossings. Through the staged wedding at the equally staged border, the film reminds the audience of the constructedness of national borders. The unofficially wed groom crosses a previously impermeable border without his passport. The barriers that seem to momentarily inhibit movement are exposed as artificial, physically constructed, and, ultimately, obsolete. As randomly as they seem to have been established, they are abolished.

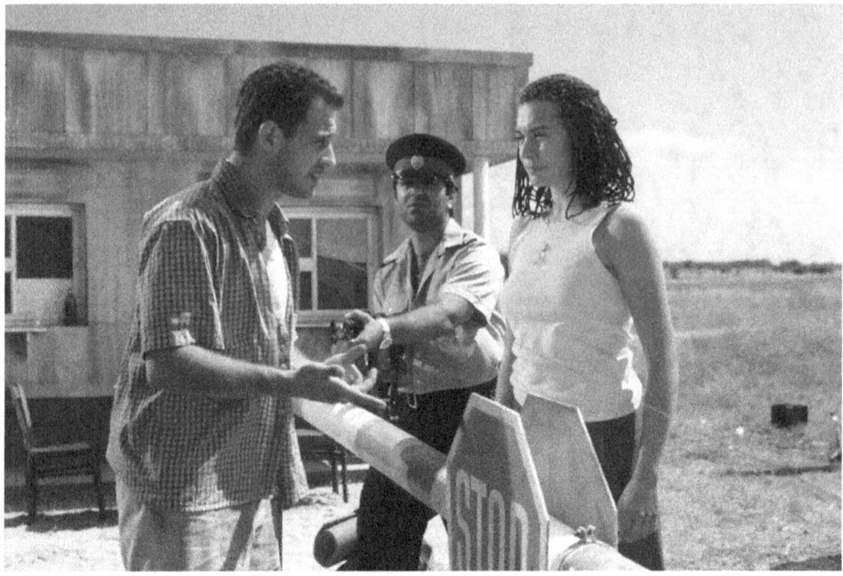

Figure 1.3. Juli (Christiane Paul) and Daniel (Moritz Bleibtreu) discuss getting married at the border crossing. The border official (Fatih Akın) witnesses it. © Wüste Film, Photo: Gordon Timpen. With kind permission of Wüste Film.

Acting, in conjunction with costume and setting, supports the implied message of the film, which is to challenge such fortified European borders. The comic treatment of the border crossing diminishes the meaning of such barriers. The nonstylized acting of the two travelers (Daniel and Juli) is juxtaposed with the exaggerated performance of the border officials. The opposition between the officials and the travelers is further supported by costume. Daniel wears dirty, travel-worn pants and a shirt; Juli is dressed in a casual travel outfit; and the border officers wear national uniforms. The travelers' clothing reflects practical garb, while the more elaborate uniforms of the officials represent the symbolic extension of the border, a transition from the material (border pole) to the symbolic (national emblems). Since the romantic road movie genre conventionally invites the viewers to favor the travelers of the film, the unarmed, un-uniformed travelers are the favored characters in the narrative, as opposed to the uniformed guards of the national border.[42]

Through this favoritism, the film brings into view the perspective on border crossing without political obstacles. In everyday life, artificially constructed borders, be they regional, national, or continental, are naturalized through conventions and rituals. Akın's border crossing scenes remind the viewers of this artificiality. Göktürk additionally reads these unconventional border crossings, especially the appearance of Akın himself, as "ironic moments" in the film.[43] This irony is further reflected in the camera angles in the scene.

Audiences are lured into empathizing with Daniel through photographic details, which are at times contradictory to viewer expectations. For example, a low- and high-angle shot/reverse shot scene between the Romanian officer and Daniel reverses the role of the person in political power (the border official's perspective is shown at low angle, looking up at Daniel) versus the petitioner (Daniel), the person without political power (perspective shown from high angle, looking down at the Romanian border officer). Thus, the camera angle is contrary to the expected perspective of the person with or without political power. By looking down at the Romanian officer through the high-angle perspective, Daniel's position is elevated by the film's formal language, while the Romanian border official's authority is denied in filmic terms. This scene could also be read in terms of economic power. Although Daniel is penniless at this stage of the film, he is a representative of a capitalist, western European country. Daniel's German perspective could symbolize the hegemonic position, from which he is looking down at the economically less powerful nation-state Romania in eastern Europe, represented by the border official. Yet, the border official, on whom Daniel literally looks down, is also the director of the film, and thus has directorial authority over the film. It is, ultimately, also the border official who denies/allows Daniel to cross the border and thereby regains his authority in the filmic narrative. In contrast, Daniel and Juli are depicted with shot/counter shot at eye level, suggesting equality between the two travelers at all times. In presenting perspectives that might run counter to viewer expectations and established modes of representing national borders, Akın encourages the audience once more to revise possibly existing preconceptions about national borders. The comedic road movie genre facilitates the depiction of unconventional border crossing, disregarding (eastern European) national regulations.

Representing a post-1989 and pre-EU eastern European region (Romania became an official EU member state in 2007), the Hungarian-Romanian border sequence introduces the film's audience to these "unchartered," new parts of Europe that were less accessible to a western European audience before 1989. Turkish guest workers and other travelers, however, driving from West Germany to Turkey often traversed eastern European countries such as Bulgaria or the former Yugoslavia during the Cold War. In *In July*, these images represent new regional areas in eastern Europe, which incorporate images of today's post-Communist Europe. The eastern European landscape in the film thus becomes integrated into the life-changing experiences of a north European traveler.

By the time Daniel arrives at the Hungarian-Romanian border, the protagonist has experienced nightlife, drugs, and carnal desires, as well as adventurous trips in Hungary and across the Balkans. He is connecting to the people and places in eastern Europe and is becoming more comfortable in these regions as he learns to navigate and communicate through various eastern European settings. Eastern Europe, as represented through settings, characters, and the soundtrack, becomes a part of Daniel's travel narrative. His quest through eastern Europe becomes his alternative to classic western European *Bildungsreisen* (educational journeys represented in literature most prominently by Johann Wolfgang von Goethe). Early in the film, Daniel and Juli discuss the route for their travel. While Daniel suggests going south via Italy and then taking a ferry to Greece, Juli prefers to go through eastern Europe, an idea that initially seems undesirable and foreign to Daniel.

Daniel's suggested route through Italy is, on the one hand, one that many Turkish guest workers took during the post-Communist Balkan wars, when driving through eastern Europe was not advisable; but, on the other hand, it is also a route reminiscent of the *Bildungsreise*. For Goethe, for example, Italy (and Greece) represented the origins of Western civilization, and therefore visiting Italy was a necessity for young men in order to become educated citizens. Ultimately, having Turkey—via eastern Europe—as the goal ironically mirrors Goethe's *Bildungsreise*, adding a twenty-first-century twist to the educational trip. The path for educational growth for the German teacher becomes a route through central and eastern Europe and ends, at least in this story, in Istanbul. Daniel's *Bildungsreise* leads him to the country of origin for the largest immigrant community in Germany. Ultimately, his travel moves from the geographical northwest to the southeast of Europe, thereby connecting and creating a new, accessible route to Turkey via eastern European countries.

Landscapes

Nationality, while still a valid category for state officials and some scholars, is a fading academic concept in early twenty-first-century Europe; it has increasingly been replaced by a focus on regionality in cultural productions; in the daily life, workings, and administration of the EU; and in academia.[44] *In July* also shows a growing interest in a regional conceptualization of Europe. This is visualized in the film with an emphasis on regional continuities of European rural and urban spaces. While the countryside settings connect various rural spaces throughout Europe, as in the border sequence, the vivid and cosmopolitan city settings seem to connect European urban spaces, as I will analyze further below.

The relevance of the countryside in the film is twofold. As discussed above, by continuing across borders, rural settings show a unity and connectedness of regions. At the same time, the European landscape functions as a *locus amoenus*. In literature, a locus amoenus is a place outside the city, away from people, buildings, and technology. Michael Squires describes the "lovely place" as "a natural site, both shaded and beautiful, whose basic ingredients are trees, a meadow, and a spring or brook."[45] Juli and Daniel are depicted in such contemporary,

European *loci amoeni*: the Danube river and the heath and the forests in Romania. The film combines these settings of "river," "heath," and "forest," turning the landscapes of central and eastern Europe into a large locus amoenus. At the same time, this locus amoenus is located close to rundown gas stops, rusty ships, or narrow, unpaved roads. By being edgier and rougher, these settings are an ironic reversal of classic European ideas about what constitutes a locus amoenus.

The Danube River, originating in the German Black Forest and passing through central and eastern European capitals, empties into the Black Sea and as such, connects, most naturally, the regions and nation-states in central and eastern Europe. Floating on the river as stowaways on a small eastern European cargo ship, Juli and Daniel smoke cannabis, sing a classic American love song ("Blue Moon Revisited [Song for Elvis]," performed by the Cowboy Junkies), and compose the poetic love vows to be used on Melek. While the couple travels on the ship, the background depicts, first, city lights, which resemble shining stars, and later, forest silhouettes in the dark. This locus amoenus does not exclude the rusty vehicle of transportation that Daniel and Juli boarded illegally.

A similar bonding moment between the two is set in the Romanian heath. Sitting on grass, picking flowers, Juli and Daniel contemplate how to proceed with their travel. The heath continues beyond the camera frame to suggest an open, infinite landscape. A counter shot reveals their closeness to a run-down gas station. Instead of resulting in a moment of disillusionment, the scenery is incorporated into this alternate locus amoenus, which allows for these sights of decay. Deciding to steal a car in Bonny and Clyde fashion, Juli and Daniel become petty criminal lovers in eastern Europe. Ultimately, these romanticized landscapes function as edgy loci amoeni, which include the stereotypically harsher realities of eastern Europe (rusty boats, decrepit gas stations, and criminal activities). Eastern Europe provides a seemingly uninterrupted locus amoenus. At the same time, the landscapes also provide an opposition to the city spaces, which present another layer of the film's connected European space.

City Spaces

The three major European cities in *In July* are Hamburg, Budapest, and Istanbul. Although these cities are marked by their differences due to their individual histories, geographies, and economies, they are revealed as connected. Ethnically diverse characters, musical mixtures, and local landmarks predominantly mark Akın's cityscapes. They offer an audiovisual experience of classic European cities, which become the backdrop for the film's love story. By specifically emphasizing entertainment venues and marketplaces in Hamburg and Budapest, the film grounds the similarities that connect these west/central European cities.

The nightlife sequence set in Hamburg begins with a close-up of the lead singer of the real-life, local band Niños con Bombas, beginning the Spanish song

"Velocidad" (Speed) with a loud scream straight into the camera. The camera zooms out, showing the band's open-air stage, and then cuts to Daniel. Accompanied by the rhythmic, upbeat song, the camera adopts Daniel's perspective and slowly moves into the vibrant entertainment venue. People dancing, drinking, and talking are positioned on either side of the frame. Daniel moves timidly through the young partygoers. Meanwhile the band, which is now shown with a case of the local Astra beer underneath its upright bass, has introduced their next song. The singer says "Ramona" is a "love song" that goes beyond borders. Shortly thereafter, Daniel meets Melek outside the bar.

The Hamburg nightlife sequence in the opening shot establishes the major components of the European city: ethnic diversity, cultural multiplicity, and dynamic interrelations of the people and places that ultimately create the local city space of Hamburg.[46] The nocturnal city becomes a site of musical entertainment. The vibrant music becomes a part of the city and the young metropolitan audience. This Hamburg-based band features members from Chile, Brazil, and Germany, but at the same time represents the very local music scene of Hamburg. The lyrics are in Spanish, true to the band's habit of presenting musically and lyrically mixed forms. The band often also incorporates English and French to their songs, which are influenced by ska, jazz, punk, and cabaret. That is, through the opening scene, the film introduces major components of the European city as envisioned by Akın.

These components of the city are reiterated during Daniel's trek across Hamburg-Altona. Hamburg allows for sonic mixes in the soundtrack to create a polyphonic city space, which offers varied sensual, aural, and visual experiences. Daniel and Melek walk through iconic places in Altona. These are all marked as ethnically diverse and represent today's European "global city,"[47] in which multiethnicity becomes an important component. They visit a Turkish restaurant, which has an oriental décor, depicting the Bosporus Bridge in Istanbul. The diegetic sound of Turkish classical music, featuring the instruments saz and ud, which are central to Turkish musical traditions, accompanies the couple's conversation. Later, they take a walk to the "Elbstrand," the Elbe river beachfront between Blankenese and Altona. Here, the couple receives a bottle of Astra from a man with a presumably eastern European accent, and Melek sings a song in Turkish.

Through these interrelations, the city becomes a cosmopolitan venue. Cosmopolitanism in *In July* emerges, among other things, with the experience of ethnic diversity. Thereby, the film connects to a larger discourse. The discourse on cosmopolitanism has rapidly emerged in the social sciences and in the humanities within the last decade. Cosmopolitanism is intrinsically linked to globalization. It is reflected in a "willingness to engage with the other" and to have a global awareness in general.[48] Mica Nava identifies cosmopolitanism as a mainstream phenomenon in today's global cities. It signifies openness to the world.[49] This kind of global openness is prominently depicted in the film's local places, which are the product of local/global networks. However, it should be stressed that Akın's cinematic cosmopolitanism is not blind to violence, deportation of migrants, manslaughter, or terrorism. While Akın's cosmopolitanism connotes openness to the world, it also exhibits aspects of the sometimes harsh realities of the characters' lives, such as the difficulties of legal bureaucratic or illegal border crossings. These are exemplified in more depth in *Head-On* and *The Edge of Heaven*.

The night scene in Budapest is similarly cosmopolitan. The scene, set in an underground dance club, is infused with dance music, drugs, and petty criminality. The sequence begins with Daniel and Luna (Daniel's interim travel companion played by Branka Katić) navigating through twisted paths into a glossy Hungarian club. The ethnically ambiguous Luna and the bartender (Birol Ünel) provide Daniel's dinner. Shortly after, a close-up of Luna's hand shows her pouring narcotics into Daniel's drink. The sequence continues, depicting the scenery in slow motion, suggesting Daniel's narcotized perception of the place. Daniel joins the people on the dance floor to the tunes of "Suicide Swing" performed by J*Let featuring Nero Gato. It is unclear whether this eclectic song is diegetic or nondiegetic, reflecting Daniel's narcotized condition. The sequence ends with Daniel being thrown out of Luna's truck, after she has seduced him and stolen his ring.

Like the open-air club in Hamburg, the underground Hungarian club offers a pulsating entertainment venue. Lured by Luna's sexuality, Budapest at night becomes a place for Daniel's sensual encounter. Some of the characters seem edgier, wearing flamboyant outfits and hairstyles. Luna, from the former Yugoslavia, the bartender, and a street vendor in Hungary (in a later scene) represent segments of the mixed population in the Balkans. The casting of Serbian-, Hungarian-, and Turkish-born actors is a way of visualizing the diversity of central/eastern Europe in Budapest. The languages spoken include Serbo-Croatian, Hungarian, German, and English, suggesting a cosmopolitan environment.

While the cities are depicted as entertainment venues at night, during the day they offer a glimpse of unique architectural sights. The marketplace, symbolic of meeting places for different demographic populations since the early modern period,[50] figures prominently in both cities. Hamburg's borough of Ottensen, which has been transformed and gentrified from a working-class neighborhood in the 1950s to a neighborhood with a mixed population including artists, young urban professionals with and without families, students, and multiethnic citizens, appears on screen first. The colorful flea market scene is set in Ottensen. The market's location is a plaza at an intersection that juxtaposes historic buildings and contemporary bars and restaurants. It is here that Juli, a street vendor, encourages Daniel to buy a ring with a Mayan sun symbol and hands him a Spanish flyer to join an event. After the lively market interlude, the scene continues with Daniel's walk through Hamburg-Ottensen.

The scene introduces the viewers to the architecture of nineteenth-century apartment buildings in Ottensen. Daniel lives in such a house. On the stairs, Daniel meets his Afro-German neighbor Kodjo (Ernest Herrmann). Kodjo is dressed in a Jamaican sports jersey, has hair spotted with dye, smokes a bong, and talks in a fake Jamaican-English accent about his travel to Jamaica. Asking Daniel to house sit, however, he quickly switches to his native Hamburg dialect, showing his playful code switching and role playing. The interior of the building, colored in orange and blue paint, relativizes the illusion of the nineteenth-century atmosphere created through the restored facade of the buildings. It allows for a contemporary portrayal of the place. The house, which is reminiscent of historic Ottensen through its architecture, is portrayed as a place for contemporary, ethnically diverse, and energetic Hamburg citizens such as Kodjo, and less vibrant personalities such as Daniel.

In Budapest, the market scene is similarly colorful. Daniel witnesses how Luna sells his ring to a Hungarian street vendor. After Daniel forcefully retrieves his ring, the action extends from the market scene into the city. A car race scene through the historic old town of Budapest leads the audience through Hungary's eighteenth- and nineteenth-century architecture. This sequence includes a long shot of the famous Lánchíd (Chain Bridge) crossing the Danube River. The bridge is a nineteenth-century building that links the city's two historic parts, Buda/west and Pest/east.

Ultimately, both cities depict the market as a starting point for architecturally unique sights. The scenes in Hamburg are short and only represent the beginning of the travel narrative, yet Akın manages to portray an ethnically, musically, and architecturally diverse and vibrant city, which also coincides with its northern characteristics (e.g., at the Elbstrand). The same is true for Budapest, which is a central European stop in the midst of Daniel's travel. These cities become both representatives of classical European cities with old towns, marketplaces, historic buildings, and a river along their cityscapes, and places for cultural, linguistic, and musical heterogeneity, in which locality is emphasized.

Massey's discussions about space and place relate to *In July*'s filmic projection of European local city spaces. In arguing for a progressive and global idea of locality/place, Massey states that instead "of thinking of places as areas with boundaries around, they can be imagined as articulated moments in networks of social relations and understandings, but where a large proportion of those relations, experiences and understandings are constructed on a far larger scale than what we happen to define for that moment as the place itself, whether that be a street, or a region or even a continent."[51] The idea of a place does not need to be reactionary and require boundaries. Massey stresses that "what gives a place its specificity is not some long internalized history but the fact that it is constructed out of a particular constellation of social relations, meeting and weaving together at a particular locus."[52]

In *In July*, European cities are portrayed as distinctly vibrant places that are connected through their vivid cosmopolitanism. Although many of the characteristics described above could be seen as part of any metropolitan cityscape, these are nonetheless constructed as distinctly European through the specific composition of languages, the infrastructure, and the architecture. These cities are explicitly marked as Hamburg and Budapest, as a part of a larger European history, culture, and lifestyle, but also as places in flux with blurring boundaries, which do not exclude interactions and exchanges with places beyond a geopolitical Europe. These cinematic cities are momentary constructs as suggested by Massey. Budapest thus refrains from being an eastern "margin" to the "central" position of Hamburg in Europe and becomes an equally desirable and cosmopolitan European urban space.

Furthermore, the cities are constructed as a space for love. Metropolitan settings like Paris and Berlin have prominently denoted sexuality and carnal desires in literary and filmic works.[53] Akın decentralizes these traditional spaces of desire by choosing Hamburg, Budapest, and Istanbul to equally represent such sites for love and desire.[54] The final sequence in the film portrays daytime scenes in Istanbul that highlight this further.

Daniel arrives at a bus terminal in Harem, on the Asian side of Istanbul. He walks through the crowded city, along the Bosporus, passing the *kız kulesi* ("maiden tower") in historic Üsküdar. The scene then cuts to the European side of Istanbul. Daniel walks through the plaza in the historic district Ortaköy. This was already a cosmopolitan neighborhood during the Ottoman Empire with diverse religious and ethnic communities living together. Here, Daniel meets Juli and declares his love. Encircled by the waters of the Bosporus, the first Bosporus bridge, the Ottoman Neo-Baroque-style Ortaköy mosque, and the people standing around them at the plaza, Daniel and Juli kiss. The camera, showing close-ups of the kissing couple, grounds the circular construction of the frame by moving around Daniel and Juli, mimicking the "[Fassbinder-]Ballhaus" circle depicting Martha and Helmut Salomon in Fassbinder's *Martha* (1973)—a much different, stylized depiction of an equally complicated relationship.[55] Ultimately, Istanbul, like Hamburg and Budapest—contoured with diversity and multiethnicity, historical landmarks, and contemporary musical mixtures in the nondiegetic sound—becomes the setting for expressions of love.

European Sounds

Like the landscapes and city spaces, the soundscapes in *In July* construct a diverse and decentralized Europe. The interwoven connections of the protagonists and settings are achieved through the mise-en-scène and through language and music in the soundtrack. Turkish pop music, Spanish-language songs from Hamburg, Canadian pop songs on the Danube, and German psychedelic music in Hungary expose the aural diversity of the film. Furthermore, Turkish, English, eastern European languages, and the different accents of the protagonists emphasize linguistic diversity. The film provides an acoustic potpourri of languages and music, and thereby normalizes linguistic variations and sonic mixture.

As typical for Akın's later films, the music in *In July* is polyphonic in the metaphorical sense: it is varied and represents different textures and origins. The opening sequence in Bulgaria, for example, ends with the diegetic music of acclaimed Turkish musician Sezen Aksu. Here, Aksu's tape in the car is a hint at the multidirectionality of migration.[56] Before moving southeast with Isa, the tape traveled from Turkey to Germany (a reference to cultural transfers between the two nations). Aksu's song has become a part of a new European sound. In the 1970s and 1980s, Turkish green grocers in German cities had started to import Turkish cultural goods such as newspapers (starting in the 1960s) and music tapes and videocassettes. Today, many foreign media are readily available in private and public spheres in Germany (and elsewhere in Europe). The presence of Turkish media commodities in Germany is often viewed critically. As Andreas Goldberg states, Turkish music, video, or TV broadcasts have often been read as a "retreat from society," as an act of self-isolation from German society. Calling the Turkish media consumption in Germany a "medial ghettoization," Goldberg further states that the function of the media recalled fears about immigrant integration.[57] There were "anxieties, that the strong dedication to (Turkish) mother tongue media would gradually lead to a social exclusion of the foreign population from German communication structures."[58] In *In July*, these "anxieties" are replaced by an inclusiveness of the media. Turkish music does not feature as an exotic commodity, nor as an alien element that alludes to foreignness. The Turkish pop song becomes one alternative, which exists simultaneously along with other (pop) songs.

Aksu's song becomes a part of the European soundtrack of the film next to music by the New York-based, multiethnic band Brooklyn Funk Essentials, which is an acid-jazz, funk, and hip hop collective that features a diversity of artists.[59] They feature songs with Turkish folk music rhythms, instruments, and artists such as Laço Tayfa. Aurally, this results in a musical heteroglossia, a dialogic creation of music, which blends styles, traditions, and instruments. Generally, in Akın's films, music as diverse as US funk bands, Turkish pop, classic *Yeşilçam* film music, folklore, or modern dub versions of eastern European songs—I will return to the specificities of the musical soundtrack in more detail in chapter three—become commonplace in the creation of the European soundscapes.

Ultimately, regions starting in Hamburg and passing through central and eastern Europe and Turkey are linked through a diverse European soundscape.

These connections help lift binaries, such as centers and margins. In Akın's films, Europe's polyphony is further enriched through languages. The languages—like the music and travelers—are not bound to a specific region. For example, to begin *In July* in Bulgaria with two German-speaking characters suggests a blurring of language borders: the editing disconnects language and country/place. Similarly, the sequence in Budapest, where Slavic languages, English, and German are spoken, normalizes linguistic diversity in the European soundtrack, disconnecting language from a particular geopolitical space. This invites an interpretation of culture and place as suggested by anthropologists Aghil Gupta and James Ferguson. They discuss the assumption of many disciplines that certain cultures live in fixed geographical locations. This seems particularly inadequate in today's globalized world with its moving cultures and peoples. They claim that "the distinctiveness of societies, nations, and cultures is predicated on a seemingly unproblematic division of space, on the fact that they occupy 'naturally' discontinuous spaces." For Gupta and Ferguson, the display of "people, tribes and cultures" on maps depicting an "inherently fragmented space" is inadequate. Cultures and people "cease to be plausibly identifiable as spots on a map." Certain fields still present people and places as "solid, commonsensical [*sic*], and agreed on," when they are in fact "contested, uncertain and in flux." They argue that mainly national elites and states construct and maintain reified and naturalized national representations. Gupta and Ferguson suggest moving "beyond naturalized conceptions of spatialized 'cultures' to explore instead the production of difference within common, shared, and connected space."[60]

The soundtrack of *In July* manages to display the diversity of European sounds and creates a multisonic Europe, the various implications of which I will analyze in the upcoming chapters. The diverse characters in geographically different settings speak numerous languages. The speakers travel with their languages and create acoustic connections between the spaces. The protagonists' dialects and accents are heard in scenes from Hamburg to Istanbul. All characters speak with specific accents. German characters, for example, speak foreign languages with German accents. This creates an aesthetically orchestrated sonic diversity.

This polyphonic sound is in dialogue with the visualization of landscapes and city spaces. It reiterates on an acoustic level the film's visions of a diverse and multiethnic Europe creating a new aural experience of the continent, refraining from setting boundaries or conceptualizing centers and margins. As Chion states, through sound "value" is "added" to the image, which he defines as the

> expressive and informative value with which a sound enriches a given image so as to create the definitive impression, in the immediate or remembered experience one has of it, that this information or expression 'naturally' comes from what is seen, and is already contained in the image itself. Added value

> is what gives the (eminently incorrect) impression that sound is unnecessary, that sound merely duplicates a meaning which in reality it brings out, either all on its own or by discrepancies between it and the image.[61]

I interpret sound as "bringing out" European diversity on an acoustic level. Moreover, looking directly at the filmic voices, Akın's linguistic diversity adds more languages to the European soundtrack—a technique established, for example, by Wim Wenders's 1994 film *Lisbon Story*. However, Mazierska and Rascaroli point out that Wenders excluded certain languages (e.g., Turkish, Irish, Serbo-Croatian) from his opening of *Lisbon Story* and used languages associated with the core of Europe, such as German, French, Spanish, Portuguese, and English.[62] Akın adds previously marginalized languages to the acoustics of post-1989 Europe.

Decentralizing Europe?

With the assistance of the road movie genre, *In July* imagines Europe as a cosmopolitan, decentralized space that is promoted as open and traversable. It includes previously "othered" European spaces such as eastern Europe and Turkey. Europeanness in this imagined, cinematic Europe becomes an attitude, a mobile, cosmopolitan lifestyle, echoing Delanty: "To be European is . . . to recognize that one lives in a world that does not belong to a specific people."[63] An example for cosmopolitanism in progress is Daniel's quest. A seemingly bourgeois, uptight, and naive teacher turns into an open-minded cosmopolitan. His educational journey (*Bildungsreise*) does not take place along the traditional route of German classicism (to/through Italy), but along an unconventional route through a still largely unknown post-1989 eastern Europe. This journey suggests a desire for new explorations. Turkey as a destination might be as educational as Italy was imagined to be for Goethe. By negotiating with the people and places on his travel, Daniel becomes a more balanced person, whose *Bildung* (education) consists of the acquisition of a cosmopolitan identity, a value the EU likes to endorse.

The EU has recognized and accordingly utilized cinema as a tool for projections of European values and lifestyles. Sieg reminds us that it is by funding cultural programs that the European institution "has sought to foster positive popular identification with European identity and values. The EU's cultural policy has stimulated the visual, narrative and theatrical imagining of European community as cosmopolitan, tolerant, and diverse."[64] Daniel's metamorphosis turns him into a—to use Sieg's words—"cosmopolitan, tolerant, and diverse" European subject traversing eastern Europe. Daniel's and his companion's desires and movements are represented as nonstylized (acting and costume) and understandable (empathy) as opposed to the stylized depiction of borders. The film thus appeals to a wider European audience that envisions a cosmopolitan, traversable Europe. Generally speaking, this could be a vision of Europe that might be compatible with the cultural agenda of the EU. However, Akın's Europe includes spaces beyond the margins of geopolitical EU borders (e.g., Turkey) and subtly refers to the limitations of movement to and from such places. These limitations might remind viewers of the refugee movements across the EU borders, traversing Fortress Europe through hardships to reach central and western Europe, imagining a better life beyond those guarded borders.

At the same time, Akın's film seems to project both a vision of a cosmopolitan subjectivity, which allows for multiple affiliations, and—through a variety of transnational connections—a diverse and decentralized Europe. Akın might be part of a larger trend in which contemporary directors envision a decentralized Europe, which I elaborate on in more detail in chapter 4. Yet Akın's visions that normalize heterogeneity and polyphony and promote a "mobile sense of place" have not been accepted in all of European realities. Current rules and regulations that limit religious symbolism in public spaces as well as the xenophobic treatment of refugees and migrants by right-wing and ultraconservative Europeans stand opposed to the aestheticized diversity in Akın's films. That Akın is a spokesperson for an open-minded Europe has been exemplified through his response to the 2009 Swiss ban of minaret buildings. Akın states that as the child of Muslim parents, for whom minarets represent an "architectural completeness" of religious buildings—and not a politicized Islam—he was personally offended by the xenophobic referendum. He canceled his appearance at the *Soul Kitchen* premiere in Switzerland.

It remains a matter of interpretation how much artistic productions such as films represent or comment on geopolitical, social, or historical changes. The boundaries between Akın the director/public figure and his work are often blurred, as he frequently, and deliberately, connects the two by commenting on current sociopolitical events, as in the examples above. In addition, his award-winning films often feature a distinctly European cast, setting, and soundtrack, and reference European issues as well, all of which would seem to invite an interpretation of his work within a European framework. Here, Akın's films in fact comment on sociopolitical situations in Germany/Europe by displaying a particular cinematic imagining of a new Europe, a Europe that aspires to be cosmopolitan, open-minded, and connected, while challenging the existing geopolitical or xenophobic impediments

Notes

1. Parts of this chapter previously appeared in "Fatih Akın's Filmic Vision's of a New Europe: Spatial and Aural Constructions of Europe in *Im Juli/In July* (2000)," *East, West, and Centre: Reframing Post-1989 European Cinema*, eds. Michael Gott and Todd Herzog (Edinburgh, UK: Edinburgh University Press, 2015), 79–93.

2. Turkey has officially been under consideration for EU candidacy since 1997, and the initial negotiations towards Turkey's potential membership began in 2005.

3. Barbara Mennel states, for example, that "ethnoscapes," a term coined by Arjun Appadurai to refer to the many people whose movement marks the shifting spaces in the global world, "are often recreated in the cinematic representation of global cities inhabited by people moving transnationally into, out of, and through them." For a more detailed discussion on cities and globalization in film as well as Appadurai's concept of ethnoscapes in this context, see Barbara Mennel, "The Global City and Cities in Globalization," in *Cities and Cinema* (New York: Routledge, 2008), 195–209, 202.

4. Fatima El-Tayeb, "'The Birth of a European Public': Migration, Postnationality, and Race in the Uniting of Europe," *American Quarterly* 60, no. 3 (2008): 652–653.

5. Doreen Massey, *For Space* (London: Sage, 2005), 9, 13.

6. Doreen Massey, "A Global Sense of Place," in *The Cultural Georgraphy Reader*, eds. Tomothy Oakes and Patricia L. Price (Hoboken: Routledge, 2008), 262–263.

7. Michel Chion, *Audiovision: Sound on Screen* (New York: Columbia University Press, 1994), 67–68.

8. Chion, *Audiovision*, 68.

9. For an extended reading and discussion of the audiovisual scene and the acousmatic, see Chion, *Audiovision*, 71–94.

10. David Laderman, *Driving Visions: Exploring the Road Movie* (Austin: University of Texas Press, 2002), 2. And Steven Cohan and Ina Rae Hark state, for example, "The road movie is . . . like the musical and the Western, a Hollywood genre that catches peculiar American dreams, tensions, and anxieties, even when imported by the motion picture industries of other nations." Steven Cohan and Ina Rae Hark, eds., *The Road Movie Book* (London: Routledge, 1997), 2.

11. Devin Orgeron, *Road Movies: From Muybridge and Méliès to Lynch and Kiarostami* (Houndmills, UK: Palgrave Macmillan, 2008), 6; Ewa Mazierska and Laura Rascaroli, *Crossing New Europe: Postmodern Travel and the European Road Movie* (London: Wallflower, 2006), 4.

12. For a detailed definition and discussion of US road movies, see Laderman, *Driving Visions*; Katie Mills, *The Road Movie Story and the Rebel: Moving through Film, Fiction, and Television* (Carbondale, IL: Southern Illinois University Press, 2006); and Cohan and Hark, *The Road Movie Book*. For a detailed discussion including road movies beyond the American context, see, for example, Orgeron, *Road Movies*; and Mazierska and Rascaroli, *Crossing New Europe*.

13. Laderman, *Driving Visions*, 2, 14.

14. Laderman, *Driving Visions*, 14.

15. Laderman, *Driving Visions*, 20.

16. See, for example, Michael Gott, *French-Language Road Cinema: Borders, Diasporas, Migration and "New Europe"* (Edinburgh: Edinburgh University Press, 2016); and Mazierska and Rascaroli, *Crossing New Europe*.

16. Mazierska and Rascaroli, *Crossing New Europe*, 1.

17. Mazierska and Rascaroli, *Crossing New Europe*, 1.

18. Mazierska and Rascaroli, *Crossing New Europe*, 1.

19. Mazierska and Rascaroli, *Crossing New Europe*, 4.

20. Mazierska and Rascaroli, *Crossing New Europe*, 5.

21. Mazierska and Rascaroli, *Crossing New Europe*, 5.

22. William Brown, "Negotiating the Invisible," in *Moving People, Moving Images: Cinema and Trafficking in the New Europe*, eds. William Brown, Dina Iordanova, Leshu Torchin (St. Andrews, UK: St. Andrews Film Studies, 2010), 39–40.

23. Laderman, *Driving Visions*, 2.

24. Laderman, *Driving Visions*, 14, 15.

25. Rob Burns, "Turkish-German Cinema: From Cultural Resistance to Transnational Cinema?" in *German Cinema: Since Unification*, ed. David Clarke (London: Continuum, 2006), 146; Deniz Göktürk, "Sound Bridges: Transnational Mobility as Ironic Drama" in *Shifting Landscapes: Film and Media in European Context*, eds. Miyase Christensen and Nezih Erdoğan (Newcastle, UK Cambridge Scholars, 2008), 153; Daniela Berghahn, "No Place like Home? Or Impossible Homecomings in the Films of Fatih Akin," *New Cinemas: Journal of Contemporary Film* 4, no. 3 (2006): 144.

26. Rob Burns, "Toward a Cinema of Cultural Hybridity: Turkish-German Filmmakers and the Representation of Alterity," *Debatte* 15, no. 1 (2007): 3–24, 13; Rob Burns, "On the Streets and on the Road: Identity in Transit in Turkish-German Travelogues on Screen," *New Cinemas: Journal of Contemporary Film* 7, no. 1 (2009): 22.

27. Berghahn, "No Place like Home?" 141.

28. Mazierska and Rascaroli, *Crossing New Europe*, 141.

29. Mazierska and Rascaroli, *Crossing New Europe*, 142.

30. Mazierska and Rascaroli, *Crossing New Europe*, 2.

31. Steven Cohan and Ina Rae Hark are convinced that the road movie is "like the musical or the Western, a Hollywood genre that catches peculiarly American dreams, tensions, and anxieties, even when imported by the motion picture industries of other nations"; *The Road Movie Book*, 2. David Laderman also follows Cohan and Hark in classifying the road movie as inherently American; *Driving Visions*, 2, 13.

32. *Lola rennt*, directed by Tom Tyker, 1998 (Culver City, CA: Sony Pictures Home Entertainment, 1999), DVD.

33. Berghahn, "No Place like Home?" 144.

34. *Knockin' on Heaven's Door*, directed by Thomas Jahn, 1997 (Planegg, Germany: Koch Media GmbH, 2003), DVD.

35. His costume seems to be a relic of the 1990s *Kanak* movement and the rap and hip-hop culture of that time. Starting with Feridun Zaimoğlu's *Kanak Sprack* and *Abschaum* in the literary world, gangster images and *Kanak*-style aesthetics also emerged in filmic works. Lars Becker's *Kanak Attack* and Akın's *Kurz und schmerzos* are only two prominent examples. For a discussion of similar texts of the 1990s, see Maria Stehle, *Ghetto Voices in Contemporary German Culture: Textscapes, Filmscapes, and Soundscapes* (Rochester, NY: Camden House, 2012).

36. There are several Turkish films about Turkish guest workers returning to Turkey with a Mercedes. See, for example, *Mercedes mon amour (The Yellow Mercedes)*, directed by Tunç Okan (1993; Berlin: Salzgeber & Co. Medien GmbH, 1997), VHS.

37. There is a long tradition in German literature and culture of depicting German teachers as uptight and overly proper. In film, these figures are often used to depict the transgression of boundaries. See *Die Feuerzangenbowle*, directed by Helmut Weiss (1944; Berlin: Studiocanal, 2009), DVD; and *Der Blaue Engel*, directed by Josef von Sternberg (1930; New York: Kino Lorber Films, 2001), DVD.

38. Deniz Göktürk, "Turkish Women on German Streets: Closure and Exposure in Transnational Cinema," in *Spaces in European Cinema*, ed. Myrto Konstantarakos (Exeter, UK: Intellect, 2000), 72.

39. For further discussions of human trafficking in the new Europe (and its cinema), see William Brown, Dina Iordanova, and Leshu Torchin, *Moving People, Moving Images: Cinema and Trafficking in the New Europe* (St. Andrews, UK: St. Andrews Film Studies, 2010).

40. Isa expresses criticism of limited and restricted visit and travel permits issued by the German government to Turks who want to visit their relatives in Germany. This episode addresses the exclusion of certain countries from European privileges such as the freedom of movement.

41. Laderman, *Driving Visions*, 14.

42. This overcoming of the border might also be related to the film's romance narrative, which often uses the trope of overcoming obstacles. In the film the obstacles would be the border and the border officials.

43. "In this absurdist enactment of border control, the director's cameo appearance and mockery of his own role introduces a moment of authorial self-irony, implying a tongue-in-cheek complicity with an initiated audience. Such ironic moments have become a trademark of Hamburg-based Turkish-German director Fatih Akın's film style." Göktürk, "Sound Bridges," 153–154.

44. Ray Hudson, "One Europe or Many? Reflections on Becoming European," *Transactions of the Institute of British Geographers* 25, no. 4, New Series (2000): 409. For a discussion of regionality and nationality in film, see also Mike Wayne, *The Politics of Contemporary European Cinema: Histories, Borders, and Diasporas* (Bristol, UK: Intellect, 2002); and Randall Halle, *Europeanization of Cinema: Interzones and Imaginative Communities* (Urbana: University of Illinois Press, 2014).

45. Michael Squires, "Adam Bede and the Locus Amoenus," *Studies in English Literature, 1500–1900* 13, no. 4 (1973).

46. For a discussion of urban diversity in Akın's cinema, see Berna Gueneli, "The Sound of Fatih Akın's Cinema: Polyphony and the Aesthetics of Heterogeneity in *The Edge of Heaven*," *German Studies Review* 37, no. 2 (2014); and Roger Hillman and Vivien Silvey, "Remixing Hamburg: Transnationalism in Fatih Akın's *Soul Kitchen*," in *Turkish German Cinema in the New Millennium: Sites, Sounds, and Screens*, eds. Sabine Hake and Barbara Mennel (Oxford: Berghahn, 2012.

47. For discussions of multiethnicity and migrant populations in European "global cities," see Elizabeth Meehan, "Rethinking the Path to European Citizenship," in *Migration and Cultural Inclusion in the European City*, eds. J.V. William Neill and Uve-Hanns Schwedler (New York: Palgrave Macmillan, 2007).

48. Mika Savage, Gaynor Bagnall, and Brian Longhurst, *Globalization & Belonging* (London: Sage, 2005), 181.

49. Mica Nava, *Visceral Cosmopolitanism: Gender, Culture and the Normalization of Difference* (Oxford: Berg, 2007), 3–4.

50. Michaela Fenske, *Marktkultur in der Frühen Neuzeit. Wirtschaft, Macht und Unterhaltung auf einem Städtischen Jahr- und Viehmarkt* (Cologne, Germany: Böhlau, 2006).

51. Massey, "A Global Sense of Place," 262.

52. Massey, "A Global Sense of Place," 261–262.

53. For a discussion of Paris and Berlin in this context, see, for example, Katharina Gerstenberger, *Writing the New Berlin: The German Capital in Post-Wall Literature* (Rochester, NY: Camden House, 2008), 24–26; and Barbara Mennel, "The City of Love: Paris," in *Cities and Cinema* (New York: Routledge, 2008), 61, 62.

54. Hamburg as a sailor city has long connoted sexuality/prostitution, but here it becomes a romanticized space for love.

55. Ralph Michael Fischer references this 360-degree camera movement of Fassbinder's cameraman Michael Ballhaus in *Martha* (1973), which depicts the first encounter between Martha and Helmut Salomon as a key scene. The circular tracking shot has been also adapted by Runa Islam's artwork in museum space. Ralph Michael Fischer, "A Film-Historical Whirl of Love and Multimedia Criticism of Illusions in Museum Space—Runa Islam's *Martha* Adaptation *Tuin*," in *Fassbinder Now: Film and Video Art* (Frankfurt am Main, Germany: Deutsches Filminstitut Filmmuseum and Rainer Werner Fassbinder Foundation, 2013), 212, 214.

56. Discussing travelers in *Head-On*, Göktürk also refers to the multidirectionality of migration. Göktürk, "Sound Bridges," 155, 168.

57. Andreas Goldberg, "Medien der Migrant/Innen," in *Interkulturelle Literatur in Deutschland: ein Handbuch*, eds. Carmine Chiellino and Andreas Goldberg (Stuttgart, Germany: Metzler, 2000).

58. Goldberg, "Medien der Migrant/Innen," 434.

59. "Brooklyn Funk Essentials," Last.fm, accessed August 9, 2010, http://www.last.fm/music/Brooklyn+Funk+Essentials.

60. Akhil Gupta and James Ferguson, "Beyond 'Culture': Space, Identity, and the Politics of Difference," in *The Cultural Geography Reader*, eds. Timothy S. Oakes and Patricia L. Price (Hoboken, NJ: Routledge, 2008), 61–66.

61. Chion, *Audiovison*, 5.

62. Mazierska and Rascaroli, *Crossing New Europe*, 204.

63. Gerard Delanty, "What Does It Mean to Be a 'European'?" *Innovation* 18, no. 1 (2005): 19.

64. Katrin Sieg, *Choreographing the Global in Europe Cinema and Theater* (New York: Palgrave Macmillan, 2008), 2, 62.

CHAPTER 2

The Sound of Polyphony

MULTILINGUALISM, MULTIETHNICITY, AND LINGUISTIC EMPOWERMENT IN *HEAD-ON*

At international film festivals and on film circuits, whether in Sarajevo, Venice, Berlin, Antalya, or San Sebastián, Akın responds to interview questions in one of his main languages of communication: Turkish, German, and English. As a trilingual producer, director, writer, and actor, Akın also effortlessly emphasizes multilingualism in his work. He thereby naturalizes trilingualism, which becomes a quotidian characteristic of mainly urban, but also rural, Europe in his films. Considering the EU's goal of trilingual proficiency among its citizenry,[1] Akın and his films inevitably turn into important promoters of multilingualism, within and beyond the borders of the European Union.[2] As stated by the EU website, "Multilingualism is central to the EU's cultural diversity."[3] By adding Turkish as one of the linguistic competences of his filmic characters to the canon of European languages, Akın complements the diversity of the EU's twenty-four official languages with that of its most long-standing candidate country. With the numbers of non-European refugees escaping to central and northern Europe reaching a peak in 2015 (more than a million)—these numbers can be compared to post–World War II mass migration of displaced people—Akın's cinematic normalization of a diversity of sounds, including those of non-EU languages, becomes ever more relevant. Immigration has played a major role in many European countries for a long time, especially considering their colonial history and postwar labor recruitments, and it continues to impact and shape their city- and soundscapes. By growing up bilingual and learning one to three languages in state schools, most minority children in Germany become by default the polyglots that the EU seeks to make of all its citizenry through education. Yet, in Akın's films, we also see the complexities of multilingualism: a language is not a simple add-on skill that exists in a vacuum but is fraught with a complex set of power dynamics, identifications, and affiliations.

Through his portrayal of a multilingual Europe, Akın stages a polyglot flexibility within Germany and Europe and its people. This chapter is occupied in particular with the cinematic portrayal of Turkish German characters as examples of multilingual Europeans.[4] How do these figures evolve through their language use (their dialogues, monologues, and choices of music)? To what extent does Akın use, play on, or reject images that are based on stereotypes or earlier representations of Turkish Germans in cinema? Close readings of selected scenes from *Head-On* will reveal Akın's depiction of a diverse set of Turkish German characters emblematic of a complex European heterogeneity and polyphony. Ultimately, I argue that through the speech of his characters, Akın complicates national and ethnic categories, loosens notions of belonging, and readjusts one-dimensional gender expectations of Turkish German characters, while at the same time inevitably promoting and demystifying multilingualism among Europeans.

Head-On is a love story between two second-generation Turkish Germans who live in Hamburg. The protagonists, Sibel (Sibel Kekilli) and Cahit (Birol Ünel), meet in the waiting room of a psychiatric practice, where they both had to sign in after their respective suicide attempts. There, Sibel asks Cahit to marry her so that she can escape her conservative father, Yunus Güner (Demir Gökgöl), and brother, Yılmaz (Cem Akın). Cahit agrees to help her. Once away from the paternal household, Sibel tries to live out her repressed sexual desires. Although this is initially a marriage of convenience, Cahit eventually falls in love with her. When Sibel also becomes aware of her own growing affections for him, the situation escalates: Cahit accidentally kills an ex-lover of hers and is imprisoned. Abandoned by her father and brother because of adultery and scandal, Sibel moves to Turkey. She plans to stay with her welcoming cousin Selma (Meltem Cumbul) in Istanbul while waiting for Cahit. After his release from prison, however, Cahit finds Sibel settled down with a new boyfriend and daughter in Istanbul. The film ends with Sibel deciding to stay with her new family and Cahit taking a bus to Mersin, his birthplace in southern Turkey.

This film can be approached from a variety of angles. Most scholarship has extensively analyzed it from the perspective of identity, minority culture, multiculturalism, transnationalism, and gender, pinpointing Akın's innovation in terms of Turkish German representation.[5] Others have examined it from aesthetic, film-theoretical, or genre-specific angles.[6] I focus on the lesser-analyzed yet highly relevant linguistic dimension of the film because it demonstrates another level of diversity among his characters. While there have been initial discussions of language use in Akın's cinema,[7] there is hardly any scholarship that provides an in-depth study of Akın's cinematic multilingualism, the sound of such linguistic variety, and its implications for an ever more diverse Europe. This chapter scrutinizes the spoken and sung word in film in combination with other cinematic elements such as casting, mise-en-scène, and costume. The sonic element of code-switching and multilingualism adds a different, affective level to the linguistic diversity that Azade Seyhan, Leslie Adelson, and Yasemin Yıldız, among others, have examined in multilingual literary practices.[8] Prominent subjects of such studies within Turkish German studies include Feridun Zaimoğlu's and Emine Sevgi Özdamar's work, which is linguistically mixed and aestheticized; but also outside of Turkish German literature there are important literary texts with elements of code-switching, such as the work of Yoko Tawada in the Asian-German and Ilija Trojanow in the Bulgarian-German contexts, to name two prominent examples. Adding to these literary studies, I provide an extended critical reading of Akın's filmic use of languages. In my analysis, his linguistic soundtrack becomes an example of a newly developed, and continuously developing, diverse, multilingual demography in European cinema. While this multilingualism does not automatically imply a smooth and peaceful diversity—after all, in *Head-On* the audience follows the emotional ups and downs of two suicidal protagonists—it unquestionably normalizes a diversity of sounds. That is, multilingualism, while being promoted in the film, also stays decoupled from images of either a utopian happy-go-lucky Europe or a depressing xenophobic Europe.

More concretely, the polyphonic language in *Head-On*'s soundtrack grounds two major issues: First, the language use, especially the code-switching episodes, addresses notions of belonging. Belonging becomes more flexible and allows multilocal affiliations. That is, the act of code-switching diversifies categories such as "German," "Turkish," and "European." Thereby, the second-generation Turkish German characters in the film can simultaneously be an integral part of a diverse Germany/Europe, *and* they can identify with a variety of other places, people, music, and lifestyles. This is a novel concept of European belonging that goes against traditional notions of mononational and ethnic belonging.

Second, multilingualism in the film functions as empowerment of the characters, which is particularly intriguing in the case of two women figures: Sibel and Selma. The polyglot women in the film, for example, help erase or at least challenge clichés and misconceptions about Turkish and Turkish German conceptions of femininity. They thereby question and complicate class-based, national, and ethnic categorizations and stigmatizations. Additionally, as multilingual, multidirectional travelers, these women figures are able to navigate in a mobile and connected European space reaching from Hamburg to Istanbul, and beyond. For this section, I focus on Sibel's and Selma's language use. While Sibel is portrayed as an emotional figure, who unconventionally acts upon her urge to break free from her imposed role as an obedient daughter, Selma is associated with a rational, urban femininity in a neoliberal capitalist world—an image of femininity seldom depicted in earlier Turkish German cinema. The depiction and sounding of these women criticize and ultimately undo existing gender stereotypes about Turkish and Turkish German figures.

Switching Codes, Switching Places: Code-Switching as a Marker of Belonging

Code-switching in language use is the act of switching between one language or dialect and another. This is a phenomenon that frequently appears with bi- and multilingual speakers. Its strategic use in commerce, its affective use in literature and the creative arts, its analysis in the social sciences, and its linguistic particularities have been well documented.[9] Additionally, code-switching can relate to more global questions of power, politics, and performance, as Mary Louise Pratt has shown: Beginning with a reference to Jane Hill's 1980 research on language use in the Malinche Volcano region in Mexico, Pratt reminds us that power dynamics can be a part of bi- and multilingual language use. She concludes Hill's specific research example by saying that

> the two languages [the indigenous Nahuatl and the official language, Spanish], and the ideologically loaded symbolic relations between them, are fully in play, at all times. In these entanglements of Spanish and Nahuatl, and in the symbolic divisions of labor between them, we see the afterlife of Spanish as an imperial language in Mexico. But we are also seeing the afterlife of Nahuatl as an imperial language, first as a lingua franca of the Aztec empire and then in the modern era as a sustained practice of resistance to Spanish imperial and Mexican national hegemonies.[10]

That is, the contemporary language use of these speakers exemplifies the embedded political implications and power dynamics between the two languages that have been established over centuries. Pratt's essay ultimately acknowledges the *long durée* of multilingualism and its political implications, throughout the global history of mankind and its linguistic interactions.

Power relationships between different languages can also influence linguistic choices made in films. The prestige of and the fantasy about a language and its sound might play a role in the selection of sonic elements in German and European film. The sonic perception of French as musical and of Italian as staccato-like might stereotypically involve fantasies about romantic and passionate love affairs, or recall fantasies of vacationing on the Mediterranean coast (after all, for many Germans, Spain, Italy, and France are beloved vacation spots).[11] These places and their national languages have figured prominently in German road movies and vacation films since the postwar years, ranging from art house cinema with road movies such as Wim Wenders' *Lisbon Story* (1994) that navigate from western-central to southwestern Europe; to mainstream "cinema of consensus" travel films like Peter Timm's *Go Tabi Go* (1991) that depict an ironic travel narrative from eastern Germany to Italy in the wake of the German reunification; to satirical comedies such as Hanns Christian Müller's *Man spricht deutsch* (*We Speak German*, 1988) that portrays petty bourgeois budget travelers in Italy; or to current entertainment cinema by Dorris Dörrie, whose *Alles Inklusive* (*The Whole Shebang*, 2014) depicts the titular all-inclusive budget travel to Spain. Yet non-EU languages—often largely absent from school curricula in the EU—might, due to ignorance and limited exposure, be less likely to call up associations with romance, pleasure, and significance. On the contrary, those languages might even evoke fears of and anxieties about the unintelligible and unfamiliar (linguistic) sounds.

Akın incorporates non-EU languages into his films by adding Turkish (and Kurdish) to the soundtrack, a language most often associated with guest workers, asylum seekers, and their offspring. In *Head-On*, Turkish is used in a variety of contexts. The sound of Turkish does not function as a single placeholder for preconceived ideas about an essentialized group of people. Thus, Akın's use of Turkish in the dialogue complicates one-dimensional experiences of languages. First and foremost, through his diverse and multilingual cast and figures, Akın portrays a normalization of multiethnicity and multilingualism in Germany and Europe. Second, by including speakers of Turkish, those who speak other languages in addition to Turkish, he also portrays an opening of the concept of (linguistic) belonging to include multiple regions. Akın's use of code-switching episodes (between Turkish and German and Turkish and English) helps to subversively make statements about such experiences of belonging. A discussion of two representative scenes—Cahit's taxi ride in Istanbul and a conversation between Cahit and his brother-in-law, Yılmaz, in Hamburg—illustrates this well.

Code-Switching One: A Taxi Ride in Istanbul

The taxi ride scene depicts Cahit, who has just arrived in Istanbul, and Nejat, the taxi driver who chauffeurs him from the airport to a hotel. The scene begins with a long shot depicting wide and open sights of Istanbul framed by the taxi windows. The outside view of Istanbul is sunlit and warm. The sights are accompanied with the diegetic sound of Turkish folk music that the car radio provides; this type of music is often associated with Anatolia[12] as well as with nostalgic, emotional experiences of *gurbet* (roughly: being abroad, in exile).[13] The dialogue between Cahit and Nejat begins with classic shot/reverse shot granting both characters equal importance in the narrative. Throughout the conversation, the slightly disoriented Cahit curiously looks through the rear window at the sights of Istanbul, which include the historic Galata Kulesi (Galata Tower) on the north shore of the Golden Horn and the Galata Köprüsü (Galata Bridge).

NEJAT: Yolculuk nereden? (Turkish: Where are you coming from?)

CAHIT: Hamburg.

NEJAT Hamburg? Du bist aus Hamburg, oder was? (Hamburg? You are from Hamburg, or what?)

CAHIT: Jo. (Yeah.)

NEJAT: Ey alter, ich bin aus München, Mann. (Dude, I am from Munich, man.)

CAHIT: O'Gott, bist'n Bayer, oder was? (Gee, are you a Bavarian, or what?)

NEJAT: Ja, in meinem letzten Leben war ich ein Bayer. Aber jetzt bin ich halt hier. Die ham' mich abgeschoben . . . die Schweine . . . rausgeschmissen. (Yes, in my last life I was a Bavarian. But now, I am just here. They've deported me . . . those pigs . . . [they've] thrown me out.)

In this scene, Nejat initially speaks in Turkish to his customer, and Cahit's replies are rudimentary, due to his limited knowledge of Turkish. However, when Nejat discovers Cahit's origin, he immediately switches to German. Born and raised in Germany, Nejat was deported to Turkey for drug trafficking (as we find out later in the dialogue). He speaks with a Bavarian accent, foregrounding his origins from Munich. Briefly interrupting his touristic gaze at Istanbul, Cahit looks at Nejat with surprise: "Gee, are you a Bavarian, or what?" Cahit identifies Nejat as Bavarian, not as a "Turk," "German," or "Turkish German," and, thereby, ironically alludes to stereotypical, regional north/south animosities between Hamburg, his hometown, and Munich, Nejat's hometown.[14] The local identity and affiliation of the two interlocutors is highlighted and established through dialect. At the same time, as soon as the mutual "German" background is established, the two speak German with each other without hesitation. Such language use, including the amalgamation of both languages, is linguistically known as code-switching and appears among most bilingual speakers. This prominent episode of code-switching in Istanbul between a Turkish German visiting Turkey (Cahit) and another Turkish German deported to Turkey (Nejat) illustrates two things: First, their preferred language of communication is German in any geographical location, including Turkey, and, second, their language use offers political criticism. The use of a German dialect by a deported Turkish German who has been denied German citizenship and homeland pungently foregrounds the legal and geographical incongruity between these Turkish German characters' personal lived experiences and preferences, on the one side, and the legal and governmental regulations, on the other.

Nejat's language is marked by a Bavarian accent, but at the same time he speaks fluent Turkish, listens to Turkish Arabesque music, and is able to navigate through Istanbul, which is further symbolized through his work as a taxi driver in Istanbul. Akın's humorous depiction of two Turkish German men speaking to each other in their regional German dialects in Turkey invites the reading of these characters as Bavarian, northern German, as well as Turkish. *Speaking* their local identities, their language use is an intuitive verbalization of their belonging. Thereby, Nejat's and Cahit's characters challenge traditional notions of Germanness. According to this scene, their belonging is multiple and ambiguous. That is, the scene clearly suggests that multiple affiliations are possible in today's globalized world, in which people might travel, migrate, study, and work in multiple places, either by choice or by forced migration. As this example shows, language plays a pivotal role in Akın's *Head-On*, as it does in his other films. Through their intuitive language use, the protagonists mark their belonging to specific regions; in fact, they might assert multiple affiliations.

Head-On's filmic figures are depicted as parts of a new, diverse society within the Turkish German community that cannot be easily categorized as "foreign" or "Turkish," and certainly not as "in-between" identities. In the new millennium, a generation of young adults with a migratory background is increasingly and visibly productive in Germany. Like Nejat's and Cahit's, their visual and sonic presence challenges traditional notions of Germanness, which had been linked to a German bloodline (*ius sanguine*) until the changes in the German citizenship laws in 2000 and 2005.[15] The visibility and audibility of various ethnicities and discussions about and with them in German media, in the workforce, and in other domains of public and intellectual life—whether benevolent, affirmative, or xenophobic in tone—have impacted cultural productions. Akın's films, and this scene in particular, also contribute from a cinematic point of view to the continuous conversations about diversity, citizenship, and belonging within German and European society.

Code-Switching Two: An Auto-Repair Shop in Hamburg

In the next scene, the notion of belonging is even further complicated through the use of dialect. In Hamburg, two Turkish German figures with divergent ideological backgrounds are conversing in a northern German dialect (a variety of *Hamburgisch*). Via their language use, both demonstrate aurally their connection to the port city of Hamburg. Their narratives are part of Germany, and, by extension, of Europe, as paradoxical, controversial, and complicated as they might be.

This is the final dialogue between Yılmaz (Sibel's brother) and Cahit in Hamburg. After his release from prison, Cahit visits Yılmaz in his auto-repair shop to inquire about Sibel's address in Turkey. The scene begins with a long shot of Cahit, who is framed by the shop's door. The direct sound is of mechanical repairs in a body shop, creating a metallic, harsh sonic environment. Cahit's background is sunlit, while the foreground is indoors and therefore darker. The reverse shot is a long shot of Yılmaz indoors in his work environment. Yılmaz is surprised to see Cahit. A jump cut leads to their conversation, which takes place in the shop's office. A medium shot/reverse shot depicts Cahit, sitting in front of a sunlit window, and Yılmaz, sitting in front of a world map, which hangs on his office wall. Both men are drinking Turkish tea. Here, Cahit begins his inquiry about Sibel.

YILMAZ: Enişte? (Brother-in-law? Form of address in Turkish)

CAHIT: Wo ist deine Schwester? (Where is your sister?)

YILMAZ: Ich habe keine Schwester mehr. (I don't have a sister anymore.)

CAHIT: Ihr habt doch die gleiche Mutter. (But you have the same mother.) Wie geht es denn deiner Mutter? (So, how is your mother doing?)

YILMAZ: Wir mussten unsere Ehre retten. Verstehst du das? (We had to save our honor. Do you understand that?)

CAHIT: Und? Habt ihr sie gerettet, eure Ehre? (So? Did you save your honor?)

The content of the conversation and the language choice initially play against each other. After the Turkish form of address, Yılmaz switches to German. Yılmaz's language is authoritarian and formulaic. A medium close-up reveals his stern and serious facial expression when he uses clichéd phrases about honor in German to answer Cahit's questions: "I don't have a sister anymore," and "We had to save our honor." These utterances remain especially peculiar considering the world map behind Yılmaz, which ironically suggests openness to the world, and, by extension, open-mindedness. Even though the content of his language is rather controversial and focused on stereotypical, patriarchal Turkish-Islamic values, his language of choice remains regional German, which, again, suggests a regional connection to Hamburg. Initially, the content of his language seems to go against the dialect he uses to disseminate his thoughts. (This surely does not mean that an expression of such ideas in Turkish would authenticate such statements any more). However, by expressing clichéd assumptions about Islamic fundamentalism through a regional German dialect, the expressions become necessarily, and more obviously, a part of Hamburg, notwithstanding its content. Thereby, the content and dialect of his language create an uneasy tension. The "otherness" of the content of his speech becomes familiar through the dialect—a dialect that ironically calls for multiple, even conflicting, stereotypical associations, such as the Hamburg bourgeoisie of the Hanse City, the Hamburg harbor and its sailors, and the Reeperbahn—the entertainment and red-light district of Hamburg.

This dialogue has two functions within the narrative of the film. First, although the camera gives equal relevance to both figures, Yılmaz's clichéd answers are revealed as stereotypical and empty. This is best shown when he is depicted as speechless following Cahit's final, ironic remark: "So? Did you save your honor?" The scene ends with a medium shot of a defeated Yılmaz, who is looking down, not able to answer Cahit's last question. Perhaps this is a process of reflection? Second, both Cahit and Yılmaz are portrayed as belonging to Germany and thus to Europe. Their diverse belief systems and lifestyles are both part of a regional German setting: Hamburg-Altona. Their language marks them aurally as northern Germans, while the camera places them on an equal plane through similar shot/reverse shot pattern. Although the content of their dialogue alludes to discourses of honor killings in Muslim families living in Europe (as overgeneralized in German media),[16] and thus marks Yılmaz initially as an "other," eventually the scene depicts both Turkish German characters as Europeans with two different personalities and with two different stances on "honor" and adultery. Both exist simultaneously in the new Europe and are a part of its complicated diversity. Such depictions counter far-right European voices. Although depictions such as Yılmaz's might initially confirm clichéd ideas about aggressive Muslim masculinities,[17] his possible change of heart and the depiction of nonpracticing Muslims such as Cahit in this context no longer fit such clichés easily. Politically far-right European opinions often negate a plurality among European citizens, and especially among European minorities. Akın's portrayals thus indirectly challenge xenophobic voices that oppose a Europe embodying diversity of and within ethnicities, languages, religions, and lifestyles.

Yılmaz's and Cahit's multilingualism is juxtaposed with the sound of various languages in the speech of the other characters and in the several music events in *Head-On*. The multilingualism in the film suggests a decentralized experience of belonging, where multiple linguistic and geographical affiliations become possible. One place, such as Hamburg, for example, might invite extensions to other places, such as Istanbul. Venues and events in Hamburg that are as multiethnic and multilingual as the characters offer such heterogeneous settings;[18] examples are *Taxim*, a Turkish dance club (which is also the actual name of a vibrant entertainment and commercial district in Istanbul); techno clubs with global, commercial electronic dance music; or cultural centers such as Die Fabrik (The Factory, an existing music venue in Hamburg) that feature international bands, including Romani musicians. Hamburg in *Head-On* offers a diverse soundscape, similar to soundscapes in *In July* and *The Edge of Heaven*. There is a tendency in Akın's films to interweave musical, linguistic, and ethnic diversity. Such diversity of characters, sounds, and settings—as expressed, among other things, through code-switching and multilingualism in the soundtrack—has become a trademark of Akın's cinema.

Multilingualism as Empowerment: Polyglot Turkish and Turkish German Femininities

Language use in *Head-On* complicates gendered, national, and ethnic categories. Akın's use of polyglot characters in his films undercuts simplified and essentialized classifications of multiethnic figures. This is true for protagonists of any gender. However, it is particularly striking for the female figures in *Head-On*. Linguistic mastery among guest workers was often assumed as masculine, and the depiction of a Turkish and a Turkish German woman as switching codes, as linguistically flexible and capable, as owning linguistic competence, might in itself be seen as subversive.[19] Akın's inclusion of a female multilingual Turkish character in his film thereby challenges stereotypical representations of Turkish women in German and European film. Focusing mainly on the figures of Sibel and Selma, and analyzing their language use in comparison with earlier depictions of Turkish and Turkish German figures, I suggest that their multilingualism functions as empowerment.

Sibel's Language Use

In general, second-generation Turkish Germans in *Head-On* all use German as their language of choice. They speak a variety of the Hamburg and Bavarian dialects. They additionally use English and Turkish to varying degrees. Sibel's character is a second-generation Turkish German woman, born to Turkish parents in Hamburg. Her character resists categorization based on gender and ethnicity in any essentialist fashion. This disruption of essentialism is conveyed, among other things, through Sibel's language use. She speaks German and Turkish fluently and in various registers. She speaks a fairly accent-free idiolect of German. Her register and tone change according to addressees and situations. In contact with unknown Germans (flirting with men, working in the hair salon) Sibel uses a fairly polite and standardized German, whereas in situations in which she is not comfortable (being followed by her ex-lover Nico), she switches to an aggressive tone and language in a low register. Sibel's language use varies most noticeably in conversations with Cahit. Depending on the context, her language and tone sound persuasive, aggressive, or sensual. She employs both vulgar and standard German, and high and low registers, showing her proficiency within the language.

While the competent use of German is not necessarily rare for characters in Turkish German cinema, its combination with the proficient use of Turkish is striking and calls for attention. Sibel's language, and generally, the language of other second-generation characters in the film, changes to Turkish and is automatically characterized by a higher register when in interactions with first-generation Turkish Germans. The first generation in the film, represented by

Sibel's parents, Yunus and Birsen Güner, use Turkish exclusively as their language of communication. Both Mr. and Mrs. Güner speak standard Turkish, with occasional colloquialisms.

The negligible use of Turkish when speaking to her parents and her humble posture when in their presence (especially her father's), highlight Sibel's verbal and physical performance of the obedient and passive daughter role. While talking and listening to her father, whether at home or in the hospital, Sibel adopts a humble, shy, and silent language. She reduces her language to a minimum of words: "Evet, baba" (Yes, father). While speaking she looks at the ground and has her head bowed. Toward her mother she shows more confidence and speaks more freely and warmly. Nevertheless, the communication with her mother also stays at a minimum. Her silence as well as her brief and shy Turkish utterances toward her parents, especially toward her father, are visually framed through the mise-en-scène in the "proposal sequence" in the Turkish German home of her parents. The petty-bourgeois Turkish household with rustic furniture, a popular Turkish show on TV, and an enclosed, small space in the kitchen and in the living room, seem to be suffocating and silencing Sibel. The mise-en-scène thus accentuates her role as a silenced daughter. Sibel is depicted with medium-long and long shots in the confining sphere of the patriarchal household serving tea, answering her parents' questions, washing dishes in the kitchen framed (and imprisoned) by the kitchen door. In the same sequence, Cahit and his friend are similarly framed visually by the suffocating patriarchal context, offering an intriguing parallelism of spatial confinement (fig. 2.1).

However, Akın refrains from limiting the sound of Turkish to only represent the aurally repressive environment of Sibel's patriarchal family household. Other instances in the film suggest an emotional and quotidian context for the use of Turkish, both positive and negative. When communicating with Cahit, already early in the film, Sibel uses certain Turkish phrases and colloquial expressions to address him even though Cahit's Turkish is extremely rudimentary. Cutting Cahit's hair in their newly decorated, now colorful and sunlit living room, for example, she tells him playfully: "Çükünü keserim!" (I'm gonna cut your penis off!). Traditionally, this expression is used in a low register to threaten misbehaving children. Sibel uses it humorously in a familiar, slightly sensual setting with Cahit. The diegetic sound of a Turkish rap song accompanies the rest of their conversation in German. Sibel's Turkish expression is followed by Cahit's first sensual encounter with her, in which the camera angle shows a close-up of Cahit's face leaning on Sibel's breast while he is having his haircut.

The sound of Turkish accompanies highly emotional situations. One such scene is the prison scene between Cahit and Sibel. Here, the only other sound is Sibel's sobbing. A shot/reverse close-up shows Sibel's and Cahit's faces, when Sibel utters the only phrase in the scene to him: "Bekleğeceğim seni!" (I will wait

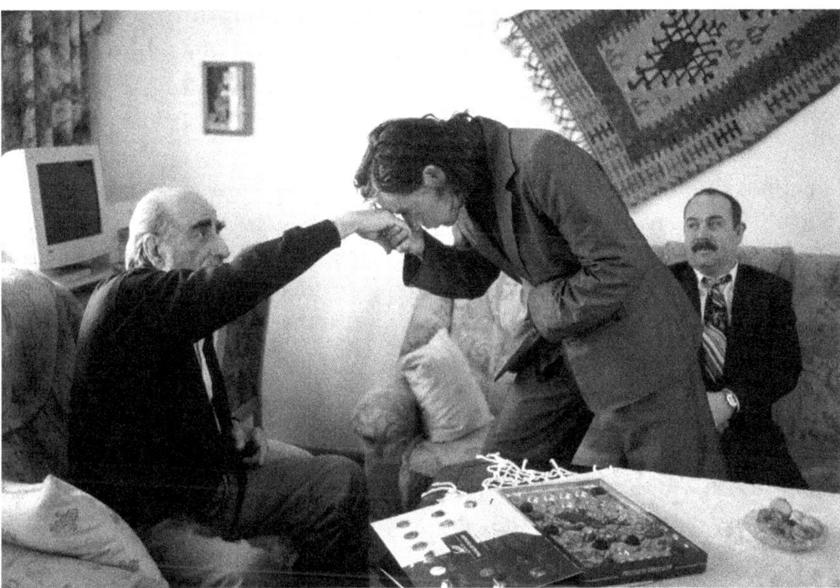

Figure 2.1. Cahit (Birol Ünel) is encircled by Sibel's father (Demir Gökgöl), brother (not pictured here), and mother (Aysel Iscan, not pictured here), his friend Şeref (Güven Kıraç), and the Turkish Kilim carpet on the wall in the confined living room space. © Wüste Film, Photo: Kerstin Stelter. With kind permission of Wüste Film.

for you). In an emotional letter she writes to Cahit from Istanbul, in a later scene, Sibel closes the German text with a Turkish formula. A voice-over narration of this letter to Cahit is heard with scenes depicting Sibel in Istanbul: in front of the employee entry of the Marmara hotel; in a coffee shop, where she drinks Efes Pilsen beer and writes a letter; and walking through vibrant Istanbul streets. Sibel closes the melancholic voice-over narration in Turkish with "Hadi öptüm, Sibel" (Kisses, Sibel), as she enters a dark underground bar, which has esoteric music in the background. Here again, Turkish underlines the emotional episodes in the film. Her longing for Cahit is expressed in her voice-over, and the scene ends with Sibel's stern request, in Turkish, for drugs to alleviate her pain.

Another emotionally and psychologically laden scene depicts Sibel's second suicide attempt in the film's narrative. She does not speak Turkish but plays a Turkish-language Ağır Roman CD before she cuts her veins.[20] The song "Ağla Sevdam" ("Cry, my beloved") immediately follows the nondiegetic English song by Wendy Rene, "After Laughter (Comes Tears)." Rene's song is still audible as a sound bridge as Sibel opens the CD player. A miniseries of close-ups follows (putting the CD into the player, pushing the play button, turning up the volume), and functions as an introduction to a suicide ritual in preparation for the cutting of the veins. While the camera then shows close-ups of Sibel crying, slapping herself, wrapping up her wound, and, later, her wound being stitched up by a doctor, the only sound is the diegetic, and later nondiegetic, song "Ağla Sevdam." The Turkish song, which accompanies Sibel's suicidal action, is very much imbued with deep emotions of sorrow. The soundtrack expresses Sibel's emotions through a variety of Turkish linguistic and musical sounds. Asuman Suner talks about *Kara Sevda* (dark passion) in relation to the general theme of the film.[21] The theme of *Kara Sevda* is closely associated with painful love, suffering, and sometimes with suicidal actions or thoughts of the lover(s). Suner highlights the affinity for such love themes in Turkish cultural traditions (music, novels, cinema, and so on.).[22]

The variety of Sibel's own Turkish register is further emphasized through conversations with Turkish friends in Hamburg, with Selma, and with her daughter, Pamuk (born in Istanbul). While Sibel generally uses a fairly standardized Turkish with a slight accent that many Turkish Germans born and/or raised in Germany have, she also uses vulgar words and an aggressive tone when she gets attacked at night in Istanbul. In Turkey she mostly prefers to speak Turkish, yet when she meets Cahit in Istanbul, her communication switches automatically to German. Her effortless code-switching shows her flexibility and expertise in both languages.

Sibel uses a variety of registers and styles within Turkish and German. The versatility with which Sibel performs in the languages manifests her linguistic competence in *both* languages. Most of Akın's figures speak a variety of German and Turkish and illustrate their linguistic flexibility. They speak variations within different languages, and in these languages they express and perform a range of ideas, opinions, and lifestyles. In combination with the code-switching episodes discussed above, these examples of Sibel's language use help to give insight into, but also complicate, the representation of various Turkish German characters in films, freeing them from earlier one-dimensional cinematic depictions.

Language Use in Previous Turkish German Cinema

Akın's cinematic characters' linguistic particularities are especially noticeable when juxtaposed with earlier representations of language use in Turkish German films. Films from the 1960s and 1970s about Turkish Germans often depict mute and victimized subjects with hardly any knowledge of German, as in Helma Sanders-Brahms's *Shirin's Wedding* or Tevfik Başer's *40 Square Meters of Germany*. Here the subjects are often marked as eternal "others," who cannot communicate with their neighbors or are (linguistically and economically) in a less advantageous, if not inferior, position than their German counterparts. This linguistic depiction goes hand in hand with what Göktürk referred to as the "cinema of duty," the state-funded films that make benevolent efforts to depict the pitiful experiences of guest workers and their families.[23]

In the films from the 1980s, Turkish was often exclusively replaced with German. Hark Bohm's 1988 film *Yasemin* illustrates this phenomenon well. In contrast to the first generation in the film, who have hardly any or no knowledge of German, the second generation prefers to speak German only. Turkish does not figure very prominently. They speak at the most an accented and ungrammatical Turkish. This language behavior in the film suggests a complete assimilation of the second generation into German society through language use. Simultaneously, this generation's ignorance of Turkish suggests a break with ethnic ties to Turkey and the Turkish language, which seems to mirror a political stance of assimilation in the FRG of the 1980s.[24]

Whereas in *Yasemin*, the young generation speaks like their German counterparts,[25] in later films (predominantly in the 1990s), the German spoken by Turkish German youth is often portrayed as different, for example, through the so-called sociolect *Kanak Sprak*, or Kietzdeutsch. Some groups of the second and later generations of migrants speak this sociolect, or variations thereof. Linguistically, it is a variety of German, marked by a specific lexicon, syntax, and accent, influenced by Turkish and other languages. Therefore, a depiction of Turkish Germans as speaking exclusively a variety of *Kanak Sprak* linguistically marks these speakers as "others"[26] for a mainstream audience. Akın goes beyond a *Kanak Sprak* depiction of Turkish Germans, which became popular in film and music of the 1990s. Interestingly, even in Akın's 1998 gangster film *Kurz und Schmerzlos* (*Short Sharp Shock*), which is located in the milieus of minority petty criminality, the protagonists speak a local variety of the Hamburg dialect, or other idiolects, and not necessarily a so-called *Kietzdeutsch* or *Kanak Sprak*.

A palette of Akın's trademark linguistic soundtrack is also played out in his autobiographical documentary *We Forgot to Return Home*, decentralizing belonging and regional affiliation. Here he offers his audience a potpourri of accents, dialects, and languages. Akın depicts, for example, his mother and father, who speak a variety of the so-called *Gastarbeiterdeutsch* (guest worker German), which is commonly associated with the first generation of guest workers in Germany and is often marked by an accent and some ungrammatical expressions. His parents speak differently from each other, each with their own idiolect of German. At the same time, Akın interviews his brother, Cem Akın, and several of his Hamburg-based friends, who all speak a variety of *Hamburgisch* and are locally tied to Hamburg-Altona, despite different national affiliations. In Akın's filmic representation of Turkey, we encounter a variety of Turkish dialects as well as variations of English and German. Through the differing languages of his interviewees and through the portrayal of various locations and settings, ranging from Hamburg-Altona, to neighborhoods in Istanbul, and to the Black Sea region, which are all connected through the narrative of the documentary, Akın constructs the diverse soundscape of a decentralized Europe on screen. At the end of the film, for example, the audience is invited to ask why Akın's cousin—a businesswoman in Istanbul, born and raised in Hamburg, fluent in German—is not also a part of Hamburg-Altona, which she longs for, but which she is no longer allowed to visit spontaneously due to governmental regulations and travel restrictions in Germany.

Ultimately, Akın portrays a much more complicated relationship between language, belonging, ethnicity, and gender in his films. In *Head-On*, there is no need to choose between a German or Turkish affiliation. The portrayal of ethnic and regional belonging stands opposed to German citizenship laws, which generally require Turkish applicants to choose between their citizenships to avoid dual citizenship.[27] The film proposes that the second-generation Turkish German characters manifest themselves through their language use. No legally and governmentally imposed regulations can change those personal feelings of belonging, as the taxi driver scene in Istanbul suggests.[28] *Head-On* depicts the simultaneous expression of different lifestyles, languages, and opinions, which can be paradoxical at times, but which do not need to be mutually exclusive. For example, Sibel is proficient in Turkish and German, using both languages in various registers. Like her languages, her lifestyle choices are not fixed. She cooks traditional Turkish food, dances to techno music, but also listens to Ağır Roman and Turkish pop music; she has multiple sexual partners, is married to Cahit, and finally has a different, extramarital steady partner and a daughter. All these actions and performances are part of her complicated young-adult personality in the film's narrative and thus eliminate a one-dimensional reading of her character.

The Cousin from Istanbul: Selma's Language Use

Akın further complicates the depiction of Turkish German characters by introducing a Turkish figure from Istanbul into the narrative of the film. With her, Akın undermines existing stereotypes about Turkish femininities on screen. In addition to undoing Turkish German gender stereotypes and modernizing Turkish femininities, the urban, Turkish businesswoman also symbolizes geographical extensions from Hamburg to Istanbul/Turkey. Played by popular Turkish actress Meltem Cumbul, Selma personifies a "Europeanized," or even globalized, Turkish femininity. This is marked by her lifestyle, fashion, work, and, ultimately, language use. I use one typical scene that illustrates the figure of Selma as one of the first—if not the first—secular, professional, urban woman figures in Turkish German cinema.

In order to inquire about Sibel, Cahit visits Selma in a luxury hotel, the Marmara, in cosmopolitan Taxim Square, where Selma has a management position.

The scene begins with a long shot of the entrance of the Marmara. The camera then tilts up to the top of the high-rise building, showing a worm's-eye perspective of the hotel. This perspective suggests economic growth and prosperity. The voice-over of Selma talking to her employees (in Turkish) is heard at all times during these shots of the Marmara. The scene then cuts to the interior of the hotel restaurant on one of the top floors. The setting is an empty, sunlit, sterile-looking restaurant. The camera adopts Cahit's perspective and moves toward Selma. Selma, dressed in a professional black suit, is surrounded by men, who are following her orders in a business meeting. Once Cahit is introduced, the meeting is postponed, and she orders red wine for herself and water for Cahit. They start and end their conversation in Turkish. After the formalities of greeting and hospitality are established, Cahit begins to inquire about Sibel, and the conversation becomes more serious. In between, the camera pans to the windows, showing a panoramic view of the Bosporus, a postcard image of Istanbul, which is framed by the windows. A close-up of Cahit's face as he drinks water follows. Unable to express his emotions entirely in Turkish, Cahit switches to English. This interlude situates English as the Hollywood language of love, as the global language of music, and ultimately also as the language of commerce.[29] The code-switching eventually shows Selma's command of English, which is stronger than Cahit's. Throughout the scene, Cahit and Selma are shown in close-ups or in medium close-ups, revealing their concerns and thoughtfulness in their facial expressions during their conversation.

The depiction of Selma's language use and the portrayal of Turkish femininity in this episode is opposed to stereotypical presuppositions about Turkish femininities as mute, passive, or victimized characters, as shown in earlier Turkish German productions. In the films from the 1970s to 1990s that depict Turkish femininities, the audience is often confronted with rural or folkloric images of silenced Turkish women. The image of Selma in *Head-On* provides a rare, talkative, urban, and secular view of Turkish femininity in German film. Selma's Turkish is educated; she uses a high register and speaks an Istanbul dialect. Her English proves to be fluent, as it is adequate for an ambitious businesswoman. Selma can communicate in the lingua franca of commerce. Her character therefore shifts the perspective of Turkish femininity from that of mute subjects with limited communications skills to a multilingual subject in an urban business setting. Intriguing is also the location of the Marmara hotel at Taxim Square, which is a real site, and which would become the site for antigovernment rallies during the actual Gezi protests of 2013 and 2014 in Istanbul, and which has been a place for (secular) protests in the past decades.

In the scene that is set at a site representing secular Turkey, Selma too becomes secularized. By ordering wine, Selma is portrayed as a secular figure (fig. 2.2). She decouples a stereotypical, naturalized link between "Turkishness"

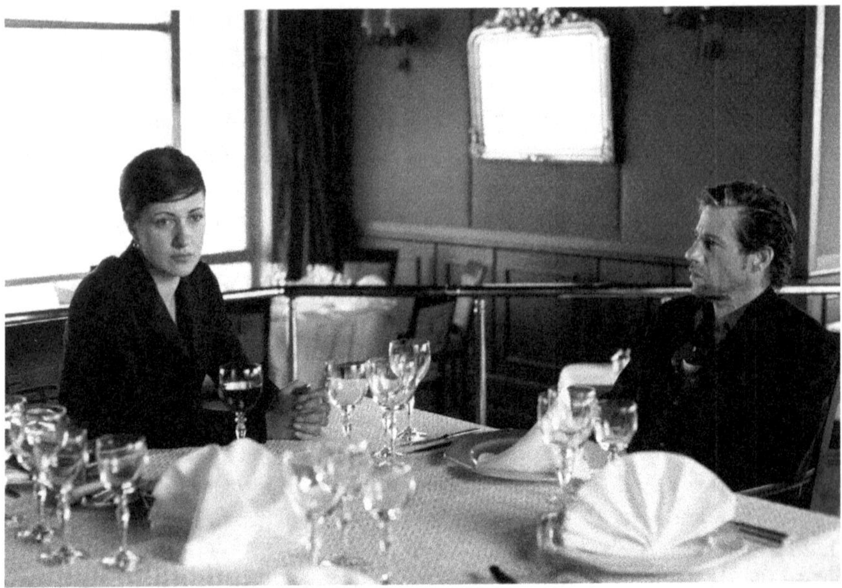

Figure 2.2. Selma (Meltem Cumbul) drinks wine talking with Cahit (Birol Ünel) at a luxury hotel, The Marmara. © Wüste Film, Photo: Kerstin Stelter. With kind permission of Wüste Film.

and Islam.[30] Such decoupling of ethnicity from religion has been increasingly displayed in recent Turkish German media productions, as I have argued elsewhere.[31] However, by having a woman perform such decoupling, the scene gains more importance. First, by ordering an alcoholic beverage, Selma, as a Turkish woman, is secularized and freed from clichéd depictions of Turkish femininity. The camera enforces this decoupling process by showing a medium close-up of Selma as she takes a sip before continuing her conversation with Cahit. Second, Selma tells Cahit (still the legal husband of Sibel) that she will not help him to find Sibel (who now has a lover and a child). In doing so, Selma further challenges stereotypes about Turkish femininity. She approves of a secular, adulterous partnership and an extramarital child as a lifestyle. This lifestyle goes against traditional notions of Islamic family constellations, which typically prescribe a religious matrimony and conception of a child within the marriage and prohibit extramarital sexual activity.

Although the type of Turkish femininity presented by Selma's character is new in Turkish German cinema, it is noteworthy that the director replaces one stereotype with another. Akın constructs a stereotype of an urban, global businesswoman; thus, the victimized, mute, folkloric Turkish woman of so many earlier films turns into a single, frustrated, divorced, workaholic woman of a global, capitalist society. The last shot of Selma is a long shot showing her sitting alone at the long table, drinking wine. This image of a lonely, partially callous, overworked person from the global business world might be familiar to western European audiences. Through the figure of Selma (an Istanbulite), Istanbul becomes connected to Europe. It becomes easy to equate Selma, through her audiovisual portrayal, with other lonesome professionals in global London, Paris, or Berlin. Thus, Istanbul might be recognized as a place that is similar to any European urban business setting.

Multilingual Travel

This urbanism as expressed through Selma's character is similar to narratives and images of travel in *Head-On*. The film creates new images of the traveling, urban Turkish German/Turkish woman. This becomes evident looking at the multilingual travels of Sibel and Selma, who can easily move southeast (or northwest) to begin a new life, to attend a wedding, or to pursue their love interests. While Selma can effortlessly travel back and forth between Turkey and Germany for pleasure, Sibel (as well as Cahit) is shown as a restless character in transit. Sibel travels to Turkey and is able to communicate, although this might result at times in miscommunications, frustrations, and violent encounters. Certainly, modes of transportation and accessibility of travel have changed in the last decades. Nevertheless, their travel calls for comparisons with prior images of Turkish migration.

The filmic depiction of second-generation Turkish Germans traveling to Turkey is different from early media depictions (fiction and nonfiction) of Turkish work migrants, who were shown moving in the reverse direction, arriving in Germany in crowded trains, speaking hardly any German, and staying in overcrowded hostels.[32] The new generation is no longer a part of the same immigration culture with which their parents' generation is still associated. Even if Sibel's initial work as a silent chambermaid in a Turkish hotel ironically recalls images of work migration to Germany (reminiscent of unskilled Turkish migrants working in low-paid jobs), this occupation remains merely an allusion to the first generation of work migrants, since in another episode we see Sibel consuming alcohol and abusing drugs, in stark contrast with most of the earlier depictions of Turkish migrant women in film. Sibel goes to Turkey to escape her unforgiving father and brother, and Cahit follows her to Istanbul to reunite with his love interest. It is an emotionally driven movement instead of an economically driven one. Most importantly, the characters, once they arrive in Turkey, can communicate and negotiate with their surroundings. They are not bound to a specific place, but can, in fact, decide to move in any direction. These travelers are marked by a flexible mobility, which they are in control of, for the most part, and which was absent from the depiction of their parents' migration. Talking about the protagonists in motion in Akın's and Angelina Maccarone's films, Alexandra Ludewig states that they "provide a non-glamourized and unsanitized glance into the realities of (to use Bhabha's terms) 'people of the pagus-colonials, postcolonials, migrants, minorities, wandering peoples.'"[33] Most importantly in *Head-On*, the characters of Sibel and Cahit naturalize a flexible mobility in an unembellished and sober style, neither soliciting pity, nor eliciting envy from the audience because of their travel. Akın's portrayal of a flexible, mobile Europe avoids depicting an idealized, unproblematic multicultural world. He does this by showcasing the main Turkish German travelers of this cinematic Europe as his version of complicated "abject heroes"—to use Elsaesser's term.[34]

Demystifying the privilege of multidirectional travel, the characters in *Head-On* possess flexibility in their mobility that allows them to move in either direction across the Bosporus. Selma partakes in complicating images of Turkish travel. To attend Sibel's wedding, she travels from Istanbul to Hamburg by plane and stays in a hotel while in Germany. All these localities—airport, planes, and hotels—are shown with brief long shots indicating their relevance. This travel episode depicts Selma in non-work-related travel from the southeast to the northwest of Europe in the twenty-first century, freeing the privileged image of flexible travel from a mainly Western, capitalist society. Selma epitomizes flexible and self-confident movement, opposing two stereotypical depictions of Turkish travel and migration. On the one hand, looking back to the 1970s, Selma's movement contrasts with earlier depictions of Turkish guest workers' migration, which was often shown as a one-way migration, traveling from the southern old home to the new destination in the European Northwest, which promised economic progress.[35] On the other hand, looking toward the new millennium, Selma's travel is also opposed to depictions of mass migration; it thereby opposes fearful imaginings of Turks who will rush into Germany, into the "Christian Club" of the European Union to stay for good, once Turkey is accepted into the EU. Selma's travel exemplifies the possibility of a transitory traveling Turkish woman figure, a movement that was for a long time reserved for European—especially western European—vocational and holiday travelers in films.

Through Akın's travelers, Istanbul, and thus Turkey, becomes connected to Germany/Europe. It is not portrayed as remote and distinct from European regions, as prior films like Bohm's *Yasemin* or Yilmaz Arslan's 1998 film *Yara* might have suggested. In these previous films, Turkey was referred to as a threatening place. With Akın's film, Istanbul can be experienced like any European cosmopolitan city. This is further alluded to with settings shown in Istanbul. These mirror events and occurrences in Hamburg. The film juxtaposes a vibrant nightlife, diverse work and business environments, and harsh milieus of violence and drug abuse in both cities. Both cities prove to be metropolises that are connected through the multilingual characters and through the dynamism that the dense cityscapes and the people therein provide.

However, Akın's depiction of the rather effortless travel between Germany and Turkey for the linguistically versed Turkish German or Turkish protagonists in *Head-On*, becomes complicated when considering the real-life events in North African regions and the Middle and Near East, leading to mass migration of refugees after 2011, and especially after 2015. Traveling under extreme difficulties and often ending in fatal tragedies, most refugees from these regions try to escape their war-torn homes through either the Mediterranean or eastern Europe, via non-EU countries such as Serbia and Turkey. These travelers, their fates, and their media depiction in overcrowded trains and train stations, in buses, and in boats are surely far from being featured in Akın's depiction of flexible European travel in *Head-On* (although the theme of illegal and less conventional border crossing comes up with a friend of Cahit's, Şeref (played by Turkish actor Güven Kıraç), and is more directly depicted in *In July, The Edge of Heaven,* and *The Cut).*

Nevertheless, perhaps Akın's depiction of multilingual travel can be relevant, especially in times when a plurality of public and political opinions about migrants and refugees—ranging from xenophobic neo-Nazi slogans to benevolent calls for philanthropic help—are disseminated via the media, at street demonstrations, and at public venues such as local pubs and coffee shops. As discussed above, flexible mobilities within the narrative of *Head-On* exist. Akın's protagonists have reached a status as accepted European travelers in film, overcoming their previous exclusion from this role. Perhaps through their depiction as multilingual navigators of Europe, via eastern Europe, into and back from Turkey, the film could speak to the travel and migration of others. Considering the global migratory movements in the new millennium, in combination with the travel restrictions and impediments for non-European migrants, which, in the case of Europe, brings out "Europe's [b]est and [w]orst,"[36] it is even more intriguing to see filmic depictions of a passage through eastern Europe, Turkey, and the Mediterranean for European and non-European citizens, foreshadowing larger migratory movements.

An Inclusive, Polyphonic, and Traversable Europe for Polyglot Travelers

As stated in the beginning of this chapter, Akın's polyglot characters become a version of the multilingual Europeans that the EU envisions, investing much in educational and promotional strategies for reaching its goal. Through *Head-On*, Akın creates—effortlessly, so it seems—a polyphonic, traversable Europe, with empowered Turkish German femininities. The Turkish German characters

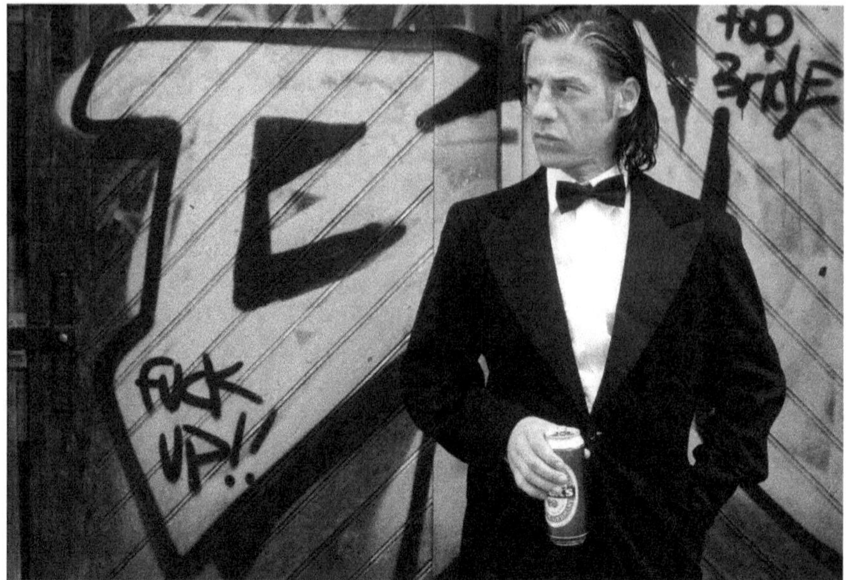

Figure 2.3. Cahit leaves his apartment, holding a Becks beer can, to go to his own wedding. © Wüste Film, Photo: Kerstin Stelter. With kind permission of Wüste Film.

in the film—no matter whether they represent a specific minority, ethnicity, class, political ideology, or psychological state—identify with various languages, places, musical traditions, tastes, and lifestyles, and thereby refrain from being categorized in any preconceived image about a particular group of people. They are complicated fictional characters with complex and paradoxical wishes and fantasies. Akın manages to portray a linguistic and cultural diversity that is inherent in each of his figures. He depicts a diversified vision of previously essentialized categories. By revisiting glimpses of clichéd images and utterances (such as Sibel as oppressed daughter and as low-paid unskilled worker, or Yılmaz as the male protector of family honor) that are familiar from earlier Turkish German films and media discourses on ethnic minorities, and then reversing them with unexpected turns and twists, Akın invites the audience to rethink their possible preconceptions. This is particularly effective with the depiction of Selma as a secular, urban Turkish businesswoman, or Cahit as a self-loathing, unkempt disorganized man (fig 2.3) as opposed to a patriarchal, aggressive figure such as Yılmaz. Akın's characters voice different ideological stances among the Turkish and Turkish German filmic communities, all of which become a part of Europe's complex diversity. Akın achieves this, among other things, through language. By recording a diversified sound of Turkish, German, and English (as spoken, for example, by Sibel, Mr. and Mrs. Güner, Selma, Cahit, and Şeref) in the film, Akın makes linguistic and ethnic diversity a part of Europe's sights and sounds. Through Akın's cinematic multilingualism, the film ultimately propagates, on a sonic level, an acceptance of these differences on a daily basis within the spheres of Europe, which, in his imagining, also includes Istanbul.

Notes

1. The EU's website states that the "EU's guiding principle is that every person should be able to speak two foreign languages in addition to their mother tongue." There are also research teams that have worked on projects to enhance multilingualism. Linguistics Professor emeritus Henning Wode and his team at the University of Kiel, for example, have started the Kiel project, which has advocated and researched the early immersion of schoolchildren in order to become trilingual. For more details on the EU's policy on trilingualism, please see European Commission: Multilingualism, "EU Languages and Language Policy," updated November 24, 2010, accessed February 9, 2011, http://ec.europa.eu/education/languages/languages-of-europe/index_en.htm.

2. On its official website, the EU encourages its citizenry to study and learn other European languages to promote mobility and flexibility within Europe. The site further highlights the current multilingualism in many EU member states due to migration and immigration. It has become ever more important to be multilingual, according to the EU officials. European Union, "EUROPA-Languages-Language Learning," February 4, 2008, accessed April 1, 2010, http://europa.eu/languages/en/chapter/14. For the imperatives for language learning in the EU, see http://ec.europa.eu/languages/policy/ learning-languages/index_en.htm; and http://ec.europa.eu/languages/index_en.htm.

3. For the languages used in the EU and the statement on multilingualism, see European Union, "EU administration," updated August 25, 2015, accessed September 10, 2015, http://europa.eu/about-eu/facts-figures/administration/index_en.htm.

4. For a discussion of the technical and sociolingusitic aspects of polylingualism in Mediterranean countries and their cinematic portrayal of bi- and multilingualism in the context of immigration, see Verena Berger and Miya Komori, eds., *Polyglot Cinema: Migration and Transcultural Narration in France, Italy, Portugal and Spain* (Münster, Germany: LIT, 2010).

5. Daniela Berghahn, "Seeing Everything with Different Eyes: The Diasporic Optic of Fatih Akin's *Head-On* (2004)," in *New Directions in German Cinema*, eds. Paul Cooke and Chris Homewood (London: B. Tauris, 2011); Mine Eren, "Cosmopolitan Filmmaking: Fatih Akin's *In July* and *Head-On*," in *Turkish German Cinema in the New Millennium: Sights, Sounds, and Screens*, eds. Sabine Hake and Barbara Mennel (Oxford: Berghahn, 2012); Mine Eren, "The Antiheroine in Fatih Akin's *Head On*," in *Muslim Women, Transnational Feminism and the Ethics of Pedagogy: Contested Imaginaries in Post-9/11 Cultural Practice*, eds. Lisa K. Taylor and Jasmin Zine (New York: Routledge, 2014); Özkan Ezli, "Von der Indentität zur Individuation: Gegen die Wand—eine Problematisierung kultureller Identitätszuschreibungen," in *Konfliktfeld Islam in Europa*, ed. Monika Wohlrab-Sahr and Levent Tezcan (Baden-Baden, Germany: Nomos, 2007), 295; Petra Fachinger, "A New Kind of Creative Energy: Yadé Kara's *Selam Berlin* and Fatih Akin's *Kurz und schmerzlos* and *Gegen die Wand*," *German Life and Letters* 60, no. 2 (2007); Matthias Knopp, "Identitäten zwischen den Kulturen: *Gegen die Wand*," in *Kontext Film: Beiträge zu Film und Literatur*, eds. Michael Braun and Werner

Kamp (Berlin: Schmidt, 2006); Jessica Gallagher, "Der neue deutsche Film ist türkisch: Issues of Space, Identity and Stereotypes in Contemporary Turkish German Cinema" (PhD diss., University of Queensland, 2008); and Polona Petek, "Enabling collisions: Re-Thinking Multiculturalism through Fatih Akin's *Gegen die Wand/Head On*," *Studies in European Cinema* 4, no. 3 (2007).

6. Senta Siewert discusses Akın's unique soundtrack strategies in the film; Alexandra Ludewig points to *Head-On*'s function in the redefinition of the Heimatfilm genre; Roger Hillmann and Göktürk highlight its transnationalism; Daniela Berghahn and Ipek A. Çelik discuss the genre of melodrama, to name a few. Senta Siewert, "Soundtracks of Double Occupancy: Sampling Sounds and Cultures in Fatih Akin's *Head On*," in *Mind the Screen: Media Concepts According to Thomas Elsaesser*, eds. Jaap Koojiman, Patricia Pisters, and Wanda Strauven (Amsterdam: Amsterdam University Press, 2008); Alexandra Ludewig, *Screening Nostalgia: 100 Years of German Heimat Film* (Bielefeld, Germany: Transcript, 2008); Deniz Göktürk, "Mobilität und Stillstand im Weltkino digital," in *Kultur als Ereignis. Fatih Akıns Film* Auf der anderen Seite *als transkulturelle Narration*, ed. Özkan Ezli (Bielefeld, Germany: Transcript, 2010); Daniela Bergman, *Gage die Wand* (*Head-On*), BFI Classics (London: BFI, 2015); Ipek A. Çelik, *In Permanent Crisis: Ethnicity in Contemporary European Media and Cinema* (Ann Arbor: University of Michigan Press, 2015), 102–126, 161–168.

7. Deniz Göktürk, Barbara Mennel, and David Gramling, among others, discuss aspects of language use in Akın's work. Göktürk and Mennel address the languages spoken in *The Edge of Heaven* within their work on globalization in Akın's films, and David Gramling gives a brief overview of the multilingualism in Akın's oeuvre, discussing the gradual changes from rather comical relief (in *In July*) to a "more precise conceptualization of polyglot film [in *The Edge of Heaven*]." Göktürk, "Mobilität und Stillstand im Weltkino digital"; David Gramling, "On the Other Side of Monolingualism: Fatih Akın's Linguistic Turn," *The German Quarterly* 83, no. 3 (2010): 359; Barbara Mennel, "Überkreuzungen in globaler Zeit und globalem Raum in Fatih Akın's *Auf der anderen Seite*," in *Kultur als Ereignis*, ed. Özkan Ezli (Bielefeld, Germany: Transcript, 2010). See also Jochen Neubauer, *Türkische Deutsche, Kanakster und Deutschländer: Identität und Fremdwahrnehmung in Film und Literatur: Fatih Akin, Thomas Arslan, Emine Sevgi Özdamar, Zafer Şenocak und Feridun Zaimoğlu* (Würzburg, Germany: Königshausen & Neumann, 2011), 252.

8. For scholarly discussions on such multilingual texts, see Leslie Adelson, *The Turkish Turn in Contemporary German Literature* (New York: Palgrave Macmillan, 2005); Azade Seyhan, *Writing Outside the Nation* (Princeton, NJ: Princeton University Press, 2000); Yasemin Yildiz, *Beyond the Mother Tonque: The Postmonolingual Condition* (New York: Fordham University Press, 2012). For further discussions see, Tom Cheesman, "Talking 'Kanak': Zaimoğlu contra Leitkultur," "Multicultural Germany: Art, Performance and Media," special issue, *New German Critique* (2004); Soheila Ghaussy, "Das Vaterland verlassen: Nomadic Language and 'Feminine Writing' in Emine Sevgi Özdamar's *Das Leben ist eine Karawanserei*," *The German Quarterly* 72, no. 1 (1999); Azade Seyhan, "Lost in Translation: Re-Membering the Mother Tongue in Emine Sevgi Özdamar's *Das Leben ist eine Karawanserei*," "Culture Studies," special issue, *The German Quarterly* 69, no. 4 (1996); Maria Stehle, *Ghetto Voices in Contemporary German Culture: Textscapes, Filmcsapes, Soundscapes* (Rochester: Camden House, 2012); Monika Totten and Yoko Tawada, "Writing in Two Languages: A Conversation with Yoko Tawada," *Harvard Review* no. 17 (1999); Yoko Tawada and Rachel McNichol, "From Mother Tongue to Linguistic Mother," *Manoa* 18, no 1 (2006); Yasemin Yildiz, "Political Trauma and Literal Translation: Emine Sevgi Özdamar's 'Mutterzunge,'" *Gegenwartsliteratur* 7 (2008); Yasemin Yildiz, "Kritisch 'Kanak': Gesellschaftskritik, Sprache und Kultur bei Feridun Zaimoglu," in *Wider den Kulturenzwang: Migration, Kulturalisierung, Weltliteratur,*

eds. Özkan Ezli, Dorothee Kimmich, and Anette Werberger (Bielefeld, Germany: Transcript, 2009).

9. Jannis Androutsopoulos, "Networked Multilingualism: Some Language Practices on Facebook and Their Implications," *International Journal of Bilingualism* 19, no. 2 (2015): 185–206; Penelope Gardner-Chloros and Daniel Weston, "Code-Switching and Multilingualism in Literature," *Language and Literature* 24, no.3 (2015):; David Luna and Laura A. Peracchio, "Moderators of Language Effects in Advertising in Bilinguals: A Psycholinguistic Approach," *Journal of Consumer Research* 28, no. 2 (2001); David Luna and Laura A. Peracchio, "Sociolingusitic Effects on Code-Switching Ads Targeting Bilingual Consumers," *Journal of Advertising* 34, no.2 (2005); Lourdes Torres, "In the Contact Zone: Code-Switching Strategies by Latino/a Writers," "In the Contact Zone: Language, Race, Class, and Nation," special issue, *Melus* 32, no. 1 (2007).

10. Mary Louise Pratt, "Language and the Afterlife of Empire," *PMLA* 130, no.2 (2015), 350.

11. For a short discussion of the sound of languages see, for example, Bernd Brenner, "Der Klang der deutschen Sprache—'Wie eine Schreibmaschine, die Alufolie frisst,'" Deutschlandfunk. Deutschlandfunk.de, December 26, 2014, accessed September 18, 2015, http://www.deutschlandfunk.de/der-klang-der-deutschen-sprache-wie-eine-schreibmaschine.1184.de.html?dram:article_id=307163; Daniel Szewczyk, "Warum Deutsch hart klingt—und Arabisch forsch," Welt Online, August 18, 2013, accessed September 18, 2015, http://www.welt.de/wissenschaft/article119098264/Warum-Deutsch-hart-klingt-und-Arabisch-forsch.html; and "Tourismus—Beliebteste Urlaubsziele der Deutschen 2015," Statista, accessed September 18, 2015, http://de.statista.com/statistik/daten/studie/170822/umfrage/tourismus—beliebteste-urlaubsziele-der-letzten-12-monate/.

12. Anatolia generally refers to the Asian and eastern parts of Turkey.

13. I translate *gurbet* into German as "die Ferne, die Heimweh/Nostalgie erzeugt." Gurbet means an exile or foreign place; this might be experienced, for example, through migration from southeastern, rural Anatolia to the western cities of Turkey, or through work or other migration to foreign destinations. An example for such a migration is the guest worker.program. This migration often resulted in nostalgia for the familiar, rural, or urban homelands, including family and friends or lovers, but also, more generally, in a longing for places, music, and customs left behind. Many migrants who traveled from the eastern parts of Turkey to Istanbul have brought along this kind of Arabesque music. The same is true for many migrants, who went to Germany or other European countries. Arabesque was initially often associated with workers and peasants of Anatolia. Through the exponentially growing number of listeners, which was the result of cassette exports to Germany, musicians traveling to Germany for concerts, and also new radio stations dedicated to these kinds of music, it has become a popular form of music in Turkey as well as among several groups of Turkish Germans in Germany and elsewhere in Europe. Often the themes of Arabesque are about unfulfilled love. The popular concept and theme of *kara sevda*—which translates into "dark love" ("painful, unfulfilled love")—is often used in these songs. Following Martin Stokes, Daniela Berghahn explains that while Turkish "arabesque music was originally the music of labor migrants who moved from the southeast of Turkey to the big cities, it soon developed into a more encompassing social and cultural phenomenon and manifested itself in other forms of cultural production, notably cinema." Daniela Berghahn, "No Place like Home? Or Impossible Homecomings in the Films of Fatih Akin," 154. For further discussions of Turkish melodrama, Arabesque, and *Head-On*, see, Berghahn, *Gegen die Wand (Head-On)*, 70–75.

14. The playful north/south animosity is also directly shown in Akın's *In July*. There, Bavaria is depicted as unfamiliar and strange to the northern German travelers.

15. For a long time, German citizenship was based on bloodline alone, *ius sanguine* (instead of *ius solis*). Until 2000, in order to be German by birth, a child born in the Federal Republic

of Germany had to have at least one German parent. Also after the renewal of citizenship and immigration laws (in 2000 and 2005), in order for a Turkish citizen to become German, the applicant has to fulfill certain prerequisites, including the disposal of the Turkish citizenship/nationality. Only for children born in Germany after 2000 have the conditions slightly changed with the new citizenship laws. Now a child born to foreign (Turkish) parents in Germany can claim German citizenship if the parents have been in Germany for eight years or more in good standing. It is possible for these children to have two citizenships until they are eighteen years old, by when they have to choose which one they will keep. There are exceptions to these laws, especially if the applicants are from other EU countries. For more details see the web page of the Auswärtiges Amt in Germany: "Law on Nationality," Auswärtiges Amt, September 16, 2005, accessed January 8, 2010, http://www.auswaertiges-amt.de/diplo/en/WillkommeninD/Einreise UndAufenthalt/Staatsangehoerigkeitsrecht.html.

16. For examples of honor killing coverage in German media, see "Gülsüm wurde nach Abtreibung erschlagen," *Die Welt*, April 2, 2009, accessed December 14, 2009, http://www.welt.de/vermischtes/article3491080/Guelsuem-wurde-nach-Abtreibung-erschlagen.html; Yassin Musharbash, "Man lebte in Kreuzberg, aber wohl nicht in Deutschland," *Spiegel Online*, April 13, 2009, accessed December 14, 2009, http://www.spiegel.de/panorama/justiz/0,1518,411283,00.html; Sebastian Fischer, "Ich bin sehr froh, dass ich die Tat begangen habe," *Spiegel Online*, October 10, 2007, accessed December 14, 2009, http://www.spiegel.de/panorama/justiz/0,1518,510671,00.html; Constanze von Bullion, "In den Fängen einer türkischen Familie," sueddeutsche. de, February 25, 2005, accessed December 14, 2009, http://www.sueddeutsche.de/ politik/118/358943/text/; and Ferda Ataman, "Studie zu Ehrenmorden: Was den Mord zum Ehrenmord macht," *Zeit Online*, December 7, 2009, accessed December 14, 2009, http://www.zeit.de/gesellschaft/generationen/2009-12/ehrenmord-studie.

17. For an enlightening discussion of the perception of aggressive Muslim masculinities in the French context, see Fatima El Tayeb, "'The Birth of a European Public:' Migration, Postnationality, and Race in the Uniting of Europe," *American Quarterly* 60, no. 3 (2008).

18. In her published magister (MA) thesis on Akın's films, Margaret Mackuth discusses the demography of Hamburg-Altona. Hamburg itself has a "foreigner" component of 14.9 percent, the district of Hamburg-Altona has a slightly higher immigration population with 15.7 percent, and, finally, the Ottensen district within Hamburg-Altona even has an immigrant population of 16.8 percent. That is, we can assume that this neighborhood in Hamburg-Altona has grown to become a center for multiethnic and multilingual diversity. Akın, who himself grew up in these districts, carefully chooses his neighborhood to be mediated for most of his feature films as a new diverse demography in German film. For the numeric details about Hamburg's populations, please see Margaret Mackuth, *Es geht um Freiheit. Interkulturelle Motive in den Spielfilmen Fatih Akins* (Saarbrücken: VDM Verlag Dr. Müller, 2007), 22.

19. It is a common tendency and stereotype, especially regarding the first wave of migrants, to place guest workers and their families in an Islamic patriarchy, and hence to assume linguistic voice and public presence for men, more so than for women.

20. For further discussion on Arabesque aesthetics and the use of an Arabesque CD in *Head-On*, see Eren, "Cosmopolitan Filmmaking," 183–184.

21. Asuman Suner, "Dark Passion," *Sight & Sound* 15, no. 3 (March 2005).

22. Suner, "Dark Passion."

23. Deniz Göktürk, "Turkish Delight—German Fright. Unsettling Oppositions in Transnational Cinema," *EIPCP: European Institute for Progressive Cultural Policies*, October 2000, accessed January 15, 2008, http://eipcp.net/transversal/0101/goektuerk/en.

24. In *Yasemin*, the break with "Turkishness" is further epitomized through the protagonist's flight from her patriarchal family with the help of a German teenager at the end of the

film. The modern prince (he has a white motorcycle) helps the princess with Oriental trades to become completely German by escaping her threatening Turkish surrounding. This "Turkish surrounding" is portrayed as an all-male mob trying to kidnap Yasemin and send her to Turkey.

25. In *Yasemin*, young Turkish German teenagers are framed as being completely assimilated into their German surrounding. Yasemin's high school teacher, for example, talks about Yasemin as one of her best students in class. Also, Yasemin's younger sister does not speak Turkish at all and answers her parents in standard German.

26. Generally *Kanak Sprak* refers to a sociolect that developed among speakers of the second- and third-generation ethnic minorities. This sociolect has been named *Kanak Sprak* after the popularization of Zaimoğlu's 1995 book by the same name. Especially in the 1990s, there seemed to be an aestheticization of German urban "ghetto culture." These were elevated also into the realms of literature and cinema (e.g., Lars Becker's 2000 film *Kanak Attack*, Zaimoglu's 1995 book *Kanak Sprack* or 1997 book *Abschaum*), but were also visible and audible in the music and hip-hop culture of the late 1980s and 1990s. The depiction of Turkish German youth as part of street gangs or the aestheticization of these in the arts often led to a misconception of a whole generation as marked by a certain sociolect that, consequently, marked them as "others." For a discussion of *Kanak Sprak*, see Schulte von Drach, Markus C. "Jugendsprache: Yalla, Lan! Bin ich Kino?," *Sueddeutsche Zeitung*, May 19, 2010, accessed August 2, 2017, https://www.sueddeutsche.de/wissen/jugendsprache-yalla-lan-bin-ich-kino-1.911134; and Wolfgang Krischke, "Sprache: 'Ich geh Schule'," *Zeit Online*, June 29, 2006, accessed January 7, 2010, http://www.zeit.de/2006/27/C-Kiezdeutsch.

27. Even though there are exceptions and special circumstances that impact legal decisions, the German citizenship law, generally, requires a choice between two nations. In many cases, in order to become legally German, an adult applicant has to give up the prior nationality; that is, he or she has to choose one nationality. This language example seems to be opposed to this legal notion of decision making. In the film, multiple affiliations are the norm or, at least, possible.

28. I do not mean to imply that people with an accent or different linguistic skills are not an integral part of Germany/Europe. It is precisely the diversity among the linguistic competences that reflects the diversity among Germany's and Europe's citizenry. However, on a localized reading of belonging, the regional dialects, more directly, mark people aurally as part of a region that might not have been considered theirs previously.

29. Göktürk points out that Cahit's line "She gives me love" is borrowed from a 1978 Grateful Dead song. Deniz Göktürk, "Sound Bridges: Transnational Mobility as Ironic Drama," in *Shifting Landscapes: Film and Media in European Context*, eds. Miyase Christensen and Nezih Erdoğan (Newcastle, UK: Cambridge Scholars Publishing, 2008), 155.

30. Ferruh Yılmaz intriguingly discusses the synonymous use of ethnicity and religion and the transformation from migrant to Muslim in the last thirty years of media and political discourse in his Danish case study, which can easily be applied to a larger western European context. Ferruh Yılmaz, *How the Workers became Muslims: Immigration, Culture, and Hegemonic Transformation in Europe* (Ann Arbor: University of Michigan Press, 2016).

31. Berna Gueneli, "Reframing Islam: The Decoupling of Ethnicity from Religion in Turkish German Media," "Framing Islam: Faith, Fascination, and Fear in Twenty-First Century Culture," special issue, *Colloquia Germanica* 47, no.1–2 (2014).

32. For a detailed historical discussion of guest workers in Germany, see Ulrich Herbert, *A History of Foreign Labor in Germany, 1880–1980* (Ann Arbor: University of Michigan Press, 1990); and Rita Chin, *The Guest Worker Question in Postwar Germany* (Cambridge: University of Cambridge Press, 2007).

33. Ludewig, *Screening Nostalgia,* 415.

34. Siewert uses the term discussing the extreme emotions of the protagonists in films such as *Head-On*: "The extreme emotional states denote the particular types of protagonists found in *Head-On,* as well as other contemporary European films such as *Trainspotting, Hate*, and *Inside Paris.* In these films, the protagonists escape the binary narrative of either succeeding or failing; they are neither rebels nor conformists; instead they can be seen as survivors, who live a life with risky cutting-edge experiences like racing at extreme speed in a car, dancing excessively, or taking drugs. Elsaesser also describes similar contemporary protagonists when he introduces them as 'abject heroes' (referring to Kristeva's famous term), here delineating a utopian dimension of double occupancy, because these abject heroes tell us something about 'the conditions of [the] possibility of a counter-image of what it means to be human.'" Siewert, "Soundtracks of Double Occupancy," 205.

35. On a similar note, Göktürk also notes, "Narrative structure as well as acting and staging in *Gegen die Wand* signal a self-confident mobility, that transcends conventional migration stories of leaving home and arriving in a new land." Göktürk, "Sound Bridges," 154.

36. Melissa Eddy, "Migrant Tide Bringing Out Europe's Best and Worst," *New York Times*, September 9, 2015, accessed September 11, 2015, http://www.nytimes.com/ 2015/09/10/world /europe/migrants-refugee-tensions-in-europe.html.

CHAPTER 3

The Sound of Music

TRANSNATIONAL SOUNDSCAPES

Music and sound have been intrinsically linked to films since the very beginning of cinema, even in the early years of silent film.[1] Film music, narration, and effects made sound visible, additionally live music often served to cover the noise of the projector, or to give dramatic and aesthetic sensations to audiences watching the first flickering images on the screen.[2] Nevertheless, up until the last decade or so, film sound has not received much attention in cinema scholarship. However, innovative work on film music is rapidly accumulating.[3]

The sound of Akın's cinema is an integral part of his aesthetics. For this reason, a discussion of his cinema must include a discussion of his films' soundtracks. The new European soundscape is most prominently played out by his use of music and dialogue. His film music highlights his aesthetic imagining of a diverse, transnational Europe. *The Edge of Heaven* is a prime example of how Akın's musical soundtrack invites the film's audience to aesthetically experience a heterogeneous European polyphony. One means by which this is achieved is through Akın's collaboration with Romanian German DJ Shantel. The sound of Shantel's dubbed/remixed music from northern, southern, and eastern European regions juxtaposed with the various languages, dialects, and accents of the characters testify to both a normalization of multilingualism and musical heterogeneity. At the same time, each sound element in Akın's cinema carries a multidirectional charge that leads to different histories (Turkish cinema history), politics (Kurdish and other minorities' treatment in Turkey), and geographies (Balkan, Black Sea coast), as the individual musical discussions below will demonstrate.

This chapter casts into relief Akın's aesthetic imagining of an acoustically heterogeneous Europe through a close reading of film sound, and in particular film music—although my analyses also include short discussions of the new voice and new noise in European cinema. Similar to Shantel, Akın creates a new aural experience for his audience through a mélange of sounds. These sounds of his imagined Europe mirror on an acoustic level the contemporary sociopolitical shifts and changes of a geopolitically defined Europe.[4] Daniel Goldmark et al. mention that film music follows a film's narrative and also has a life and identity of its own.[5] I suggest that Akın's entire polyphonic soundtrack is intrinsically linked to and interacts with the film's narrative and image to create an aesthetic of heterogeneity—what I call the overall audiovisual aesthetic in Akın's films—on multiple levels, and thereby normalizes the presence and experience of heterogeneity. The heterogeneity of sounds even goes beyond the contemporary and exhibits a connection between different, transnational film and music histories.

Film music as a point of departure for inquiry seems to be developing as a new path in Akın scholarship.[6] In fact, this aspect of his cinema has received some critical attention. For example, reading the technique of sampling as an overall structuring element, Senta Siewert provides initial observations about Akın's diverse sound in *Head-On*. She states that the music functions as sonic memory, as a means of enhancing emotions, and as a musical form of storytelling. Deniz Göktürk's enlightening work on *The Edge of Heaven* gives a complex account of the negotiation between the local and the global in Akın's and other European art films. Using examples from the musical soundtrack, Göktürk discusses how the local becomes globalized. One specific example Göktürk provides is the Turkish Black Sea musician and environmental activist Kazım Koyuncu. Roger Hillman and Vivien Silvey analyze the musical structure of Akın's *Soul Kitchen* (2009) by paying specific attention to soul music's function in the film. They observe, referencing an Akın interview, that musical traditions emerging from an African American experience (which reflect a historically minoritarian experience) become appropriated through global circulation in Hamburg in *Soul Kitchen*. Finally, Barbara Kosta offers an engaging analysis of Akın's music documentary *Crossing the Bridge: The Sound of Istanbul* (2005), in which she uncovers a differentiated depiction of "Turkishness" in Germany. Kosta reads the documentary to depict Istanbul as a complex polyphonic space. In conjunction with my work, these studies offer a variety of engaging observations about Akın's soundtrack. My analyses ultimately highlight the particularities of Akın's cinematic sound that contribute to the creation of an aural experience of a heterogenous European soundscape that simultaneously echoes different times and places.

The audience—whether at a public screening or at home—experiences Akın's unique musical and linguistic juxtapositions together with a nuanced view of characters and settings. Similar to his collaborator Shantel, Akın samples music and voices from a variety of European regions, urban and rural.

These sounds—the musical soundtrack and the diverse voices in the dialogue sequences—provide the audience with an aural experience of a filmic imagining of Europe, which accentuates multiethnicity and multilingualism, and gives a sensation of multidirectionality. While the mise-en-scène of *The Edge of Heaven* highlights different European landscapes through many long shots, the soundtrack specifically emphasizes diversity by providing musical heterogeneity with the highly eclectic songs in the film—which are in turn charged with various levels of meaning—and the accented speech of the six main characters. The eight very different songs in this contemplative film and Shantel's meditative original score place an emphasis on the particular selection of the songs and ask for specific scrutiny.

Shantel, responsible for the original score to the film, is known for creative musical mixes from seemingly disparate regions. As the recipient of the 2006 BBC Radio's World Music Award, Shantel was celebrated for his musical innovations blending Balkan sounds with predominantly western European electronic dance music. Shantel brings to electronic music, and thereby to his diverse audience in Germany and elsewhere, the rhythms and instruments from the Balkan region of Bucovina.[7] This culturally mixed region, with a rich Jewish folk music culture, stands for mixed populations in itself. Shantel's concept has been a critical and financial success. Touring from Turkey to Britain, from Italian fashion shows to rock festivals around Europe, Shantel not only brings together musical elements and instruments, but also audiences from various regions of Europe.[8] To be sure, Shantel, who calls himself a cosmopolitan, participates in a particular marketing of European sounds that has become very fashionable, and in doing so, he moves within the profit-driven industry that packages sound for mass media consumption. That said, Shantel's music creates an innovative, productive connection to the Balkan regions.

With *The Edge of Heaven*, Shantel extended his sampling to Karadeniz, the Black Sea coast of eastern Turkey.[9] Akın chose to work with Shantel for aesthetic reasons. The connecting link between the artists is the belief in the fundamental openness of music—that is, in the permeability and heterogeneity of music. Both artists share a curiosity about new musical creations. Ultimately, Akın's cinematic visions of a multiethnic and polyphonic Europe are matched with Shantel's musical visions of a pan-European dance floor, of a "boundary-free spirit of Balkan and South Eastern Europe music tunes."[10] These beliefs influenced the aesthetics of *The Edge of Heaven* in fundamental ways.

The Edge of Heaven is the second part of Akın's trilogy "Love, Death, and the Devil." Death is a central theme in the film and a motif that brings the protagonists into motion. *The Edge of Heaven* consists of three parent-child constellations: Nejat and Ali (a retired guest worker in Bremen and his second-generation Turkish German son, who works as a professor of German literature in Hamburg),

Yeter and Ayten (a Turkish sex worker in Bremen and her estranged daughter, who is a student activist in Istanbul), and Susanne and Lotte (a former 68-er, who is estranged from her daughter, a student in Hamburg, who falls in love with Ayten).[11] The film follows these six characters (later four, after Yeter and Lotte die) as they go through an emotional journey of reconciliation and love. All the characters are depicted traveling within Germany (Hamburg and Bremen) or to and from Turkey (several neighborhoods of Istanbul, and settings on the Turkish Black Sea coast). A polyphonic soundtrack accompanies their travels and interactions.

Musical Soundscapes in *The Edge of Heaven*

Shantel chose and sampled the music for *The Edge of Heaven* in close collaboration with Akın.[12] Akın is intimately familiar with the Black Sea region, which he visited during the filming of the documentary *Fatih Akın—Tagebuch eines Filmreisenden* (Fatih Akın—Diary of a Film Traveler, Monique Akın, 2007).[13] He is also familiar with the local music traditions as well as with urban classic and popular Turkish music. Further in the documentary, he states that his preshooting travel in Turkey was crucial for the visual (and musical) aesthetics of the film. These regional musical insights and Shantel's musical innovations are central to the creation of the soundtrack.

According to Michel Chion, the arrival of sound gave film a language, an ethnicity, and an identity.[14] Discussing film music, Chion goes on to say that in contemporary film, "each insistence of music in a movie fits into its own culture and stylistic cubbyhole. The various brands of 'world music' that have become popular in many recent films . . . juxtapose, without seeking to blend, harmonies, rhythms, melodic lines, and musical logics that we sense come from different places and should not be combined."[15] Both musically and visually, Akın clearly articulates in his films that there are no real isolated, distinct musical cultures. While there might be region-specific sounds, and different levels of familiarity with these sounds on the part of different film audiences, all of these sounds are mixed already. Akın works against the sense that different musical cultures should not be combined. In contrast, the musical soundtrack of *The Edge of Heaven* represents a highly productive blend of musical styles. The film's sound suggests that the act of blending, combining, and reassembling is the norm, and, in so doing, strives against essentialist categorizations.

The Original Score—Scenes of Transition

Based on a folkloric, regional Black Sea song, the film's original score is essentially one piece of film music. In creating the score, Shantel used nondiegetic music based on Kazım Koyuncu's "Ben seni sevduğumi" (That I love you) as a recurring song in the film;[16] it becomes a leitmotiv for the soundtrack. Akın explains in an interview that the individual tracks of the original song are used for different scenes, whereby each track highlights one instrument from the song (such as guitars, violins, and so forth) and is associated with a different figure in the film. Therefore, one piece of music becomes multiplied through its splitting into different tracks. That is, the nondiegetic music in the film is diverse, yet part of the same original song. The individual tracks are part of a larger entity, similar to the individual figures' roles as parts of a larger network of people within and beyond Europe. Through its appearance in various geographical settings, the original score creates an aural continuity that links different places in the film.[17] The score is used in scenes depicting settings of transition in Turkey or Germany. Transition scenes—scenes centered on movement, transportation, and the characters' travels (e.g., Ayten's, Ali's, and Susanne's border crossings, or the transnational repatriation of Yeter's and Lotte's bodies upon their deaths)—are matched with specific tracks of the score.

All these individual musical interludes—with titles such as "Ayten & Airport," "Road to the Funeral," or "Black Sea Trip"—sound contemplative and quiet, and together with the image, they create a meditative mood. Through the contemplative nature of these recurring musical interludes, juxtaposed with the calm images of travel, the film creates a connectivity of various scenes and local spaces. Akın invites the viewer to experience and retrace this connection aurally. The music in the transition scenes in Turkey, as well as in Germany, accentuates similarities, although, as mentioned previously, the songs differ slightly from one another, each featuring a different instrument. Thus, local places—the seemingly dispersed spaces of Akın's filmic European landscape—are juxtaposed and connected by means of the sonic continuity within the film.[18]

Besides using motifs from the original score to connect different geographical settings, Akın employs dialogues, voiceover narration, and diegetic/nondiegetic music as sound bridges to create a sense of continuity from one shot to the other. The film thus creates the illusion of spatial unity through sound, linking settings from Hamburg, Germany, to Trabzon, Turkey. While the characters in the film connect the places through their travels, the music lures the film's audience into experiencing these places as spaces that are in a dynamic relationship. The intertwining of the settings and the emotional searches of the characters is heightened through the film's original score. Discussing film sound, Randy Thom makes similar observations. "Movies are about making connections between things that couldn't possibly be connected in a single real life moment . . . . Sound is one of the best ways to make those connections. It's about making connections between characters and places and ideas and experiences."[19]

Soundscapes in Turkey

"Ben seni sevduğumi" and "Çamburnu"—Local Sounds of the Black Sea

The film's narrative begins in medias res in the Black Sea region. This opening sequence is significant for multiple reasons. First, it sets a tranquil and contemplative mood for the film, and second, it establishes an audiovisual connection between settings in northern Germany and the Turkish Black Sea. Deniz Göktürk and Barbara Mennel have both elaborated on this scene while discussing aspects of globalization in *The Edge of Heaven*, demonstrating the complexity and multilayered nature of this sequence.[20] To begin, the establishing shot is a long shot of a hut in a seemingly southern, rural area. The colors in the outdoor scene are warm and help to create a peaceful and calm exterior. The quiet diegetic sound of a song is heard from a distance. The camera slowly pans toward a long shot of an empty gas station, which is presumably the source of the music. A little later, the next scene shows the interior of the gas station shop. The diegetic sound is now louder, and the lyrics are more distinguished. The initially ambiguous setting and sound disorient the viewer at the beginning of the scene, while the subsequent panning and the explanatory dialogue in the second scene finally situate the film acoustically and geographically in the Turkish Black Sea region. The Turkish dialogue at the gas station between Nejat and the vendor explains the source of the music: Nejat (and the film's audience) is informed about the song and its singer, Kazım Koyuncu.[21]

This sequence introduces Nejat to the birthplace of his father and its musical and linguistic specificities, as we find out later in the film. Throughout the narrative, Koyuncu is the link to the Turkish Black Sea region through his local star persona, the musical instruments he employs, and his lyrics, all of which emphasize elements of the region's folkloric musical style and dialect. The vendor in the scene mentions that Koyuncu prematurely died of cancer as a result of Chernobyl, the nuclear catastrophe of 1986.[22] The opening sequence thus starts with the unfamiliar and gradually becomes familiar through the mentioning of names and locations (Koyuncu, Black Sea, Chernobyl).

Akın explains in an interview that he got to know the music of this artist during a preshooting trip: "During our trip, I fell in love with the music of Kazım Koyuncu. I was in an Internet café when I heard his song 'Ben seni sevduğumi.' I asked the owner of the café who the singer was. And what followed after that was pretty much the dialogue as it is in the beginning of the film."[23] "Ben seni sevduğumi," which was originally written and composed by Maçkalı Hasan Tunç, appears four times in the film's soundtrack, insisting on the song's relevance. Twice it appears as diegetic music: in the opening sequence, and when the scene is revisited at the end of the film's narrative (and is then interpreted by

Şevval Sam). The original version with Tunç's own interpretation is played while the final credits roll to the sights of the Black Sea. A long shot depicts Nejat sitting on the beach, waiting for his father, his back turned to the camera and facing the sea. We hear the fourth version as Shantel's original score, which we previously encounter in segments throughout the film's narrative. These songs function as aural experiences of contemplation and reflection throughout the film.

These scenes allow the film's audience to peacefully dwell in the Black Sea region.[24] Further audiovisual references to the Black Sea region are made by Yusuf Kaba's traditional song "Çamburnu," which features region-specific melodies played on the flute. Çamburnu is also the setting for the final scene of the film, where Nejat hopes for reconciliation with his father. The flute music accompanies touristic visuals of the Black Sea, though it is not clear whether the sound is diegetic or nondiegetic. The postcard images calmly display multiple long shots of the flute player himself, lush tea plantations, the folkloric costume of a tea cutter, country roads, and old bridges, each resembling an iconic still life of the region. These slow cuts of long shots and medium-long shots of picturesque Black Sea images in combination with the flute sound create a contemplative aural scene.

"Ölürsem yasıktr"—Sounds of Grieving and Turkish Yeşilçam Cinema

The Edge of Heaven also revisits Turkish cinema through its music. The more folkloric and local sounds of the Black Sea are juxtaposed with classical musical forms in Istanbul. In a dinner scene during the early stages of Nejat and Susanne's friendship, the urban setting and aural atmosphere recall classic Turkish Yeşilçam films, which I will introduce shortly.[25]

This scene opens with a bird's-eye camera angle, displaying colorful, individual Turkish *meze* dishes being placed on the dinner table. The sound accompanying the visuals of these culinary delicacies is the interpretation of the song "Ölürsem yazıktır" (If I die it would be in vain) by popular Turkish musician Sezen Aksu. Shots of *rakı* tables scored with a melancholic song like Aksu's are part of a Turkish cinematic iconography of grief. While the camera changes first to a medium shot of the couple eating and getting acquainted, and later to a shot/reverse shot, Susanne toasts with her *rakı* glass. Thereby, the Turkish lyrics, the music, and the characteristic table settings—recognized by those familiar with Yeşilçam films as depicting grief—are merged with Susanne's and Nejat's grief, mourning, and acceptance of death. The local elements of music and food are brought into relation with two melancholic persons from Germany, one mourning the loss of her daughter and the other his estrangement from his father. Incorporating references to Yeşilçam cinema, the scene thus becomes an audiovisual, aestheticized celebration of grief in Istanbul.

Through its sound and mise-en-scène, Akın's film makes clear references to Yeşilçam cinema. Sound thereby helps to create film-historical intertextualities. Let's briefly turn to this type of Turkish cinema that is so clearly evoked through film sound. Yeşilçam, which "produced cheap, low-quality films with large profit margins,"[26] derives its name from a street in the Beyoğlu district of Istanbul, and refers to the star-driven Turkish cinema that emerged in the 1950s and had its heyday from 1965 to 1975.[27] These films include popular genres such as comedies and gangster films, but a large majority of the films are melodramas. Among the melodramas, Dilek Kaya Mutlu differentiates the village melodramas of the 1950s—these have a rural setting in Anatolia, and the conflicts are played out within the same class—from the urban melodramas from the 1960s and 70s—here the protagonist is often a rural migrant in the city, who is confronted with the "westernized, urban" upper class. Frequently such class conflicts need to be overcome in the course of an urban melodrama.[28] Until the 1970s, Yeşilçam primarily had a mainstream Turkish target audience, and generally produced patriarchy-favoring, family-friendly films. In the 1980s, however, when the cinema sector lost its family audience, especially because of the increasing spread of television, Yeşilçam turned to soft porn. This was a strategy developed to cope with the declining numbers of mainstream cinema audiences.[29]

Classic Yeşilçam cinema was extremely popular with mainstream audiences. Intellectual film critics, however, rejected these films early on. According to Kaya Mutlu, the critics "not only viewed Yeşilçam films as undesirable and unacceptable but also condemned their viewers as 'passive,' 'irresponsible,' and 'mindless' masses. Gaining a more political tone, such criticisms sharpened in the 1960s. Overall, to the critical intellectual eye, Yeşilçam cinema was not only artless but uninterested in the 'real problems of Turkish society;' it was 'commercial,' 'exploitative,' and 'fake.'"[30] That is, critics read a "reproduction of patriarchal ideology" in the conservative content of Yeşilçam films, which they were quick to dismiss.[31]

Despite the critics' disregard for classic Yeşilçam cinema, however, this cinema still has an impact in Turkey today. Kaya Mutlu points out that the identification of stars and films from that era, the clichéd topics of Yeşilçam films, and their contemporary presence, are a common feature of today's popular culture, in commercials, TV shows, and other media.[32] Even Turkish Nobel Prize winner Orhan Pamuk refers to Yeşilçam. In *The Museum of Innocence*, Pamuk stages the suffering of his protagonist Kemal—who mourns the loss of his love interest, Füsun, a salesgirl turned Yeşilçam actress—against the backdrop of the *Yeşilçam* film industry.

Akın joins this community of Yeşilçam commemoration. His film similarly reiterates such classic Yeşilçam references. Thereby Akın allows Yeşilçam to claim a place in German cinema. That is, similar to Turkish media, he also partakes in revisiting and connecting to a transnational aspect of the cultural memory, imagery, and sound of Yeşilçam cinema.

A large body of immigrants and migrants in Germany and Europe watched Yeşilçam films on videocassettes and listened to the songs on music cassettes. An inexpensive way to view these films was to rent VHS cassettes through greengrocers in the 1980s and 1990s.[33] These audiences constituted a sizeable segment of the viewers across Germany. Some films were also screened on regional Turkish German TV channels such as TD1 Berlin.[34] Yeşilçam films and their iconic musical soundtracks, therefore, belong to the cultural memory of numerous Turkish German families and by extension have become a Turkish German filmic memory of the first and second generation of migrants.

This Yeşilçam cinema reappears in the above-mentioned soundtrack and mise-en-scène of "Meze in Istanbul." That is, the scene intertwines film histories through casting, setting, and soundtrack. This audiovisual intertextuality with Yeşilçam is made through two actors who are both fundamentally associated with German film history. Hannah Schygulla primarily stands for New German Cinema (NGC). Her roles as a Fassbinder muse and actor in many films of the NGC, most notably in *The Bitter Tears of Petra von Kant* (1972), *The Marriage of Maria Braun* (1979), and *Lili Marleen* (1981) are nationally and internationally renowned. Baki Davrak is an actor in contemporary Turkish German cinema and German theater. These actors become essential parts within the intertextual Turkish German entanglement.

It is noteworthy that by now, in other fields and in other artistic productions in Germany, artists have similarly engaged with the trend that Akın established within the cinema sector; that is, they commemorate and engage with Turkish cultural productions in productive ways and display cultural transfers. Turkish German DJ Ipek (Ipek Ipekcioğlu) for example, posted on Soundcloud, a social sound platform, a recording of Ajda Pekkan—a Turkish star closely associated with Yeşilçam cinema and Turkish music of the 1970s—singing a Udo Jürgens song, "Der groβe Abschied" (The big farewell). At the same time, in her shows in Berlin and around the globe, DJ Ipek herself covers popular Turkish musicians, including Pekkan's film songs from the 1970s, but she also features other famous musicians such as Bariş Manço on her Soundcloud website, thereby distributing widely cultural transfers across time between Turkey and Germany.[35] The multidirectional travels of cultural products of different origin and the synergies between them become ever more exposed in the contemporary media landscape in Germany. Setting an example, Akın was the first within the cinema sector to productively incorporate such links to Turkish musical and cinematic traditions within a popular format without exoticizing or romanticizing the artistic product.

Bach on the Banjo—Transatlantic Travels of a Classical Composition

To be sure, the sounds scoring the scenes in Turkey are not limited to Turkish musical styles reminiscent of Yeşilçam films, but include, for example, classic German music as well as the voice of a muezzin, who sings a religious prayer (*ezan*) in Arabic. In one scene, Nejat enters a German bookstore in Istanbul. A handheld camera follows him as he gazes at and touches the books and walks through the dark narrow aisles crowded with stuffed wooden bookshelves. The diegetic music that accompanies his stroll is Bach's "Minuet in G Minor/ Polonaise in G Minor" arranged for banjo by US musician John Bullard. Marcus, the current German owner of the Istanbul bookstore, orders tea in Turkish for Nejat and himself. Both characters first stand and later sit across from each other, divided—or united—by both a small German and a Turkish flag. The camera emphasizes the similarities of both men: Nejat and Marcus (Lars Rudolph) are both dressed in brown jackets, have dark hair, are of a similar height and are passionate about German literature and language.

In his discussion of film music in New German Cinema, Roger Hillman examines the image/sound imbalance created for the audience through the implementation of preexisting (typically classical) songs. These familiar pieces of music, which already occupy a cultural space, create unevenness when combined with new images that are free of preexisting associations.[36] At the same time, classical music provides a "historical montage," states Hillman: a "simultaneous presence of different time layers via the soundtrack."[37] Akın's diegetic (classical) music references multiple layers of time, but it also alludes to cultural shifts that classical music can undergo, as is the case with Bach and the "Minuet in G Minor/Polonaise in G Minor."

Bullard's CD *Bach on the Banjo*, which sets the general mood for the aural space of the bookstore, helps break essentialist and elitist conceptions of culture and cultural master narratives: A cultural icon of German Baroque *E-Musik* (so-called *ernste Musik*, the traditional German definition of highbrow music), Bach is transformed through a new-world musician who plays the piece on an instrument that is generally associated with Irish or American folk music, which is *Unterhaltungsmusik* (entertainment music) in the German traditional cultural binary. Lastly, this musical transformation reveals itself to the listener/ viewer in Istanbul, making the music both familiar and new at the same time. New constellations and possibilities of musical and linguistic sounds are delicately introduced in this scene. The impermeability and fixity of German *Leitkultur* (hegemonic high culture) is subtly and almost ironically penetrated. Akın implements his aesthetic of heterogeneity, subverting German *Leitkultur* by playfully beginning with a fake Goethe quote by the Turkish German professor in Hamburg[38] and ending in a bookstore with many examples of German "high

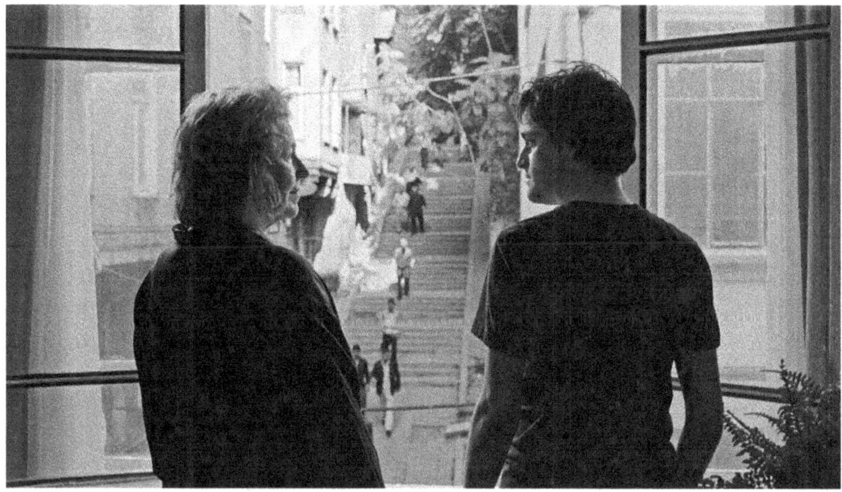

Figure 3.1. Nejat (Baki Davrak) and Susanne (Hannah Schygulla) talk about the men passing by Nejat's apartment in Istanbul. *The Edge of Heaven* (2007). With kind permission of Corazón International.

culture" on the bookshelves exported to Istanbul and surrounded by an Americanized Bach.

Juxtaposed with the new, multidirectional sound of Bach is the sound of an Arabic prayer in Istanbul. The images of various mosques and minarets paired with the sound of prayer in Arabic connect two different scenes: The first scene depicts Ayten in her (secular) prison cell looking into the sky (which cuts to the images of the mosque), and the second scene shows Susanne and Nejat looking down from the window of their apartment, talking in German about the men going to morning prayer (fig. 3.1). The figures of the German mother, the Turkish German son, and the Turkish daughter are linked through the sounds of Arabic prayer and the visuals of Muslim men going to the mosque; Özkan Ezli even recognizes church towers in the scene.[39] The sound of the Arabic prayer as well as the crosscut of chatting men are not displayed as foreign or alien, but as a peaceful act of religious piousness. The calm dialogue between Nejat and Susanne in soft-spoken German, which follows the imam's voice, underscores the unthreatening sounds and sights of Islam in this sequence. Explaining the religious holiday, Nejat starts talking about the Koranic story of Ibrahim and his son, which Susanne knows through the Christian tradition. Yet this religious story does not serve to create a dialogue between different cultures; in fact, that kind of benevolent dialogue is rejected. Instead, the story of Ibrahim initiates the possible reconciliation between Nejat and his father.[40] The juxtaposition of Koyuncu, Aksu, Bach, and so forth suggests that these sounds and sights are not isolated, but rather exist simultaneously and in exchange with each other. Arabic prayers and Bach on a banjo do not have to be mutually exclusive but can be part of the same, overlapping geographic space.

Soundscapes in Germany

The polyphonic musical soundtrack for the parts of the plot set in Germany ranges from stereotypical German marching bands, to classic Turkish film music, to Shantel's remixes of a Romanian song. Similar to the scenes set in Turkey, these complex sounds help to create a heterogeneous European soundscape—an aural space that references different times and geographical settings—and to give insights into the diverse characters, who at times actively listen to—but are always closely identified with—the music.

"Son hatira"—Revisiting Sounds of Yeşilçam Cinema in Germany

The sequence introducing Ali and Yeter at the red-light district in Bremen follows the opening of the film set at the Black Sea. In contrast to the long shots, slow camera movements, and quiet musical soundtrack of the film's opening, this sequence opens with fast-cut images of a May Day demonstration in Bremen. The visuals of street demonstrators are accompanied by the diegetic sound of a *Spielmannszug* (marching band), a typical German tradition for street festivities. The medium-long shot and sound of the marching band sets the mood for Ali's adventures. Ali, a man in his sixties, is smiling as he approaches the camera. He moves in the opposite direction from the marching band and demonstrators. Once the elderly man is in focus, the film cuts to the infamous Helenenstrasse—a red-light district since the early nineteenth century—into which he has turned. The scene is now silent, and city noise is absent. The only sound featured is of the man walking by the sex workers' colorful *Gründerzeit* houses.

Yeter/Jessy, a sex worker, invites Ali into her workspace. Yeter is in her forties and dressed in a red-and-black latex outfit.[41] The static camera shows two adjacent rooms, with the furniture, faucet, refrigerator, and other items placed against the walls of the square rooms. The colors of Yeter's workplace are rendered in red and yellow, creating a conventional erotic atmosphere. Once Ali enters Yeter's place, she turns on the music. The voice of Neşe Karaböcek, a Turkish pop star frequently featured in the Yeşilçam films of the 1970s, appears.

Yeter plays Karaböcek's 1972 interpretation of "Son hatıra" (Last memory) on a cassette recorder. The song is a tango written by Fehmi Ege (1902–78), a composer of Turkish tango. The soundtrack in this scene highlights transnational intertextualities and motives of travel and migration: Having roots in the colonial experience in the Americas and the Caribbean, the Argentinian tango was created by European immigrants in Argentina/Uruguay in the nineteenth century.

The Turkish tango calls to mind the Yeşilçam films of the 1970s, foreshadowing the meze scene in Istanbul. The song's introduction in this scene functions as an intertextual reference to this hybrid musical text and its transatlantic, multidirectional travels and, within the scene, emphasizes the melancholy prevailing in the sex worker's room. After Yeter plays the song, Ali inquires about her nationality. The song reveals Jessy/Yeter to be of Turkish origin and thus connects the two Turkish German characters. Karaböcek's rendition of the song creates a nostalgic space for the two émigrés, who get increasingly familiar with each other. The medium of the antiquated cassette player, with its characteristic noise, as much as the melancholic film song itself, creates a specific aural setting, an intermedial experience of exile and nostalgia for Turkey of the past decades that generates a connecting element between the two protagonists, who, although different in age, represent the first (non-German-born) generation of guest workers or political migrants who left Turkey many decades ago.[42] However, in addition to a cultural connection between the two characters, the diegetic song in the soundtrack helps to establish a direct connection to Turkish cinema history, such as Yeşilçam cinema. The combination of the song with the actor Tuncel Kurtiz in this scene, however, creates more complicated references to Turkish cinema history, as I will elaborate on below by taking into account the casting of Turkish actor Kurtiz and his link to Young Turkish Cinema.

The casting of Turkish cinema legend Tuncel Kurtiz (1936–2013) reveals the politics of casting in *The Edge of Heaven*. It opens up new archives and mandates further scrutiny in the context of Akın's work. This Turkish stage, film, and television actor made important contributions to Akın's cinema through the references to his life and work. Kurtiz's career began in the 1960s with the writing and directing of political satire. He further acted and directed theater, which included plays by Bertolt Brecht, Tennessee Williams, and Eugene O'Neill. As an actor, Kurtiz became nationally famous for his role in *Umut* (*Hope*, 1970), an early film by acclaimed Turkish director Yılmaz Güney, the creator of the Young Turkish Cinema of the 1970s.

Being involved in Turkish political and leftist filmmaking and artist circles, and critical of the government, Kurtiz lived in exile in the 1970s and 1980s. In exile, he collaborated with the productions of international/transnational film and theater, including those for the Schaubühne in Berlin.[43] While in Sweden, Kurtiz also directed a film about "immigrants in the West," the award-winning Swedish-Turkish low-budget coproduction *Gül Hasan* (*Hasan the Rose*, Turkey/Sweden, 1979).[44] Critical of capitalism, *Hasan the Rose* is a film guided by a Brechtian-style narrator, depicting the exploitations of guest workers, their dreams of becoming rich by becoming film stars, and their exploitation by the film and porn industry. Additionally, as an actor, throughout the 1970s and 1980s, Kurtiz played in international films, such as in the Israeli *Jiuch HaGdi* (*The Smile*

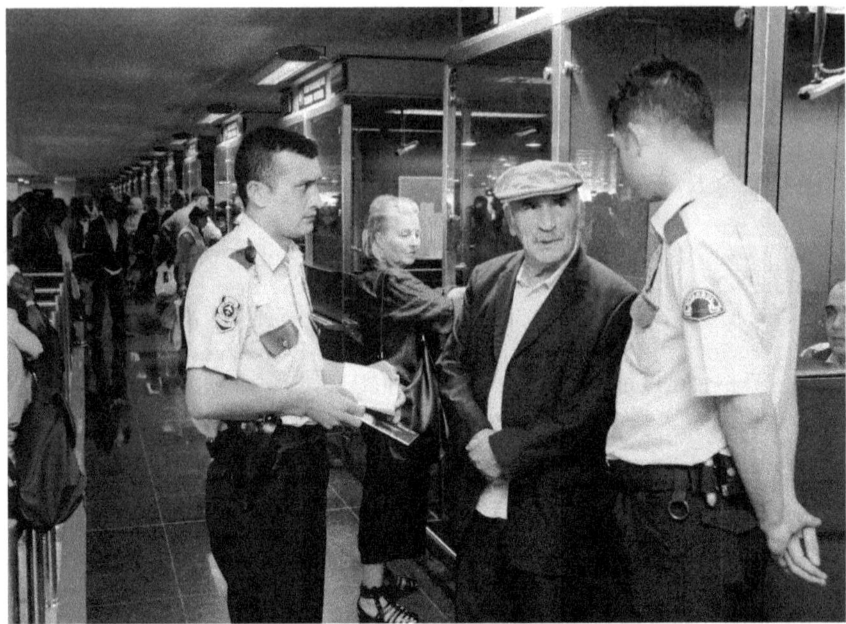

Figure 3.2. Ali Aksu (Tuncel Kurtiz) at the Turkish border. Photo: Kerstin Stelter/Corazón International. With kind permission of Corazón International.

of the Lamb, 1986) by Shimon Dotan, for which he received the best actor award at the thirty-sixth Berlin International Film Festival.

Later in his career, he took a role in *Tabutta Rövaşata* (*Somersault in the Coffin*, dir. Derviş Zaim, 1996), one of the first films that launched the New Turkish Cinema, also referred to as the "new wave cinema" of Turkey.[45] This casting of the 1990s connected to Kurtiz's socially critical films from the 1970s. Finally, with his subsequent role in *The Edge of Heaven* (fig. 3.2), Kurtiz lived through an international reawakening that brought him to Cannes in 2007, accompanying Akın.

Through the casting of Kurtiz, we get an extensive connection to predominantly leftist Turkish and international theater, television, and cinema history, including to Turkish cinema legend Güney. Considering Güney's filmography and biography, these elusive Güney associations in Akın's film are equally important for their political implications. Güney began with commercial films and was associated with the popular cinema of Yeşilçam in the early years of his career. His own production company, Güney Filimcilik, founded in 1968, began with a less commercially driven and more politically oriented filmmaking. Kurtiz starred in Güney's important film *Hope*, a political film about a man with socioeconomic problems in Turkey. *Hope* set the stage for a new Turkish cinema, which initiated the artistically motivated Young Turkish Cinema[46] that had a "leftist social realist perspective."[47] In 1972, Güney was sentenced to several years in prison, due to allegations that ranged from "sheltering anarchist refugees"[48] to "killing a judge."[49] In prison, he wrote film scripts, including *Yol* (*The Way*, 1982), which had to be filmed by his associates. The film, prohibited in Turkey, was smuggled out of the country and won the Palme d'Or at the 1982 Cannes Film Festival. According to Suner it is "the most internationally acclaimed Turkish film ever made to date."[50] Güney himself managed to escape from prison in 1981 and lived his remaining years until 1984 in French exile. In France, he directed his last film, *Duvar* (*The Wall*, 1983).[51]

While Karaböcek's song references the more popular, less political Yeşilçam cinema, the references to Güney establish political connections in Akın's film. The Güney/Kurtiz references open new historic archives and foreground thematic continuities between Young Turkish Cinema and Akın's contemporary transnational cinema. Through the Güney allusions, *The Edge of Heaven* relates to and commemorates a Cannes Film Festival winner, social-justice seeker, refugee, and socially critical filmmaker in exile. Güney's quest for social justice from the 1970s and 1980s seems to endure in Akın's stories about Yeter and Ayten. The narrative in *The Edge of Heaven* informs the audience that Yeter's husband was killed in the seventies in Maraş, suggesting that he was possibly a Kurdish political activist. The viewer can further assume that Yeter fled Turkey because of sociopolitical problems. Additionally, Yeter's daughter Ayten (Nurgül Yeşilçay) tells Susanne (Hannah Schygulla) about her quest for "one hundred percent human rights." This goal seems to be a direct, and rather blunt continuation of Güney's political inquiries from the 1970s and 1980s.

Akın himself alludes to these politically tumultuous times in an interview and hopes that his films might provoke political consciousness and humanitarianism in his audiences: "There is also a political thrust. In the '80s, a lot of left wing people came to Germany, but the problem we have in Germany is that young people today are less interested in changing anything. Young people are really not interested in society, nor do they feel responsible for their society. My film is to provoke people to feel responsible for other humans."[52]

Daniela Berghahn states that Akın and Fassbinder are not truly political filmmakers, but that both "try to marry the popular with the political" in their films.[53] While I agree with Berghahn that Akın manages to bring together the popular and the political, I maintain that Akın's sound and cast are explicitly political. More specifically, the Kurtiz/Güney reference in his film represents an intervention that reveals an overt, political dimension.

By casting Kurtiz, Akın links his own film to an actor who is simultaneously associated with leftist art and political cinema of the 1970s, with contemporary, socially critical New Turkish Cinema, and with popular television shows.

The intertextual references to these cinemas are not merely superficial allusions, but work in different layers within *The Edge of Heaven*. The political criticism of Young Turkish Cinema of the 1970s is revisited thematically and is connected to the sociopolitical complications in Turkey's past and present—for example, regarding the position of the Kurdish minority in Turkey. Furthermore, depictions and experiences of exile, deportation, forced migration, and political injustices in *The Edge of Heaven* create intertextual references to Kurtiz's and Güney's lives and work as mentioned above. These themes echo the Turkish politicized films of the 1970s. By producing such intertextual links to Kurtiz and Güney, Akın establishes a political and aesthetic connection to Turkish cinema and creates new layers of meaning for his own films.

The character of Yeter, in combination with the musical track, similarly represents a connection to Turkish and even to New German Cinema. Within Turkish cinema this figure of the sex worker is known, for example, through Ömer Lütfi Akad's classic melodrama *Vesikalı Yarim* (*My Prostitute Love*, 1968). *Vesikalı Yarim* tells the story of an unfulfilled love between Sabiha (Türkan Şoray), a nightclub singer and sex worker, and Halil (Izzet Günay), a green grocer and married family man. In relation to the figure of the sex worker, Akın states, "The aging prostitute is a popular figure in Turkish cinema. However, she is always romanticized . . . in that regard, the figure of Yeter can also be seen as my personal view on Turkish cinema. I like the figure, but not the realization of it. It needs some more realism, some more dirt. A little less mainstream. For me, Nursel plays that perfectly."[54]

The theme of the Turkish sex worker was also addressed in New German Cinema. Despite their differences, it could be argued that the figure of Yeter alludes to Helma Sanders-Brahms's Shirin in the 1976 film *Shirins Hochzeit* (*Shirin's Wedding*). In Sanders-Brahms's film, the female protagonist, played by Ayten Erten, is a Turkish guest worker who is raped, forced into prostitution, and eventually killed. However, Shirin does not have the same self-confidence as her sibling Yeter.

The soundtrack, Karaböcek's Turkish tango, befitting the nostalgic atmosphere enjoyed by the two Turkish expatriates, aids in underscoring the strong sense of melancholy prevalent in the sex worker's work environment. The song provides a connecting element between the two protagonists and helps reveal Jessy/Yeter to be of Turkish origin. It serves to create a transitory nostalgic home for the expatriates by aurally recreating Yeşilçam cinema. The increasing familiarity between the two characters, which is initiated through Karaböcek's song, is further emphasized through the shifts in the names that Ali uses to address Yeter: from Jessy to Yeter, her Turkish name, to Gülüm (my rose), a name of affection.

However, paradoxically, this nostalgic Turkish refuge does not feature a romantic, uncontested, or even Islamic setting, but, in a very matter-of-fact style, the workplace of a Turkish sex worker in northern Germany. In this way, Akın constructs new filmic images for Turkish German figures. The complex staging of two first-generation migrants creates productive tensions. First, Akın's scene alludes both to the low-budget, less artistic, but highly popular Yeşilçam cinema through the music of Karaböcek as well as to critical Turkish art cinema through the actor Kurtiz. Second, the film alludes to the figure of the aging prostitute of Turkish cinema, whom Akın strips of its romanticized veil and transforms into an edgier figure.[55] Third, the film opposes the stereotypical portrayals of first-generation Turkish German migrants as miserable and sympathetic characters in West German film of the 1970s and 1980s by showing the self-confident, multilingual characters of Ali and Yeter. Ultimately, Akın creates a completely new and complex audiovisual display of two first-generation Turkish Germans. Their language and their musical and cinematic heritage become a part of Akın's new European soundscape.

"Inel Inel de Aur—Bucovina Dub"—
Remixing Sounds of Eastern Europe

The scene in a Hamburg nightclub with Ayten and Lotte highlights a young, multilingual, and urban generation. This sequence offers an audiovisual experience of a cosmopolitan urban space as it portrays a blossoming emotional relationship between two cosmopolitans. People are drinking, smoking, and dancing to music DJed by Shantel himself in a cameo appearance. The sequence starts with a close-up of the DJ's arm and moves up to his face and headphones. The next cut shows a long shot of the dance floor, displaying people dancing in slow motion, intoxicated by the music. Shantel's music brings the protagonists emotionally and physically closer. Next, we see a sensual close-up of Lotte's and Ayten's faces. The two proceed to kiss passionately. All the camera shots are in slow motion, yet the music is in real time throughout the entire sequence, leaving one with the ambiguous impression that it could be diegetic or nondiegetic. The sequence is thus highlighted for the viewer as important through its camerawork and sound.

The sequence's featured song, the "Inel Inel de Aur (Ring oh golden ring)—Bucovina Dub" dance hall mix by Shantel, slyly and compactly signals the plot's future direction and the director's vision of movement and connectedness. The Romanian song about the travels of a lover[56] is a remix of French DJ Click and German Romanian singer Rona Hartner. Hartner is an actress/singer whose life and artistic work are marked by travel and migration. Her music is characterized by the fusion of so-called gypsy music and electronic music: "électro tzigane" (electro gypsy). Not surprisingly, her music and background accentuate popular connotations of nomadic migration with a romanticized idea of a Romani lifestyle. Hartner has become a symbol of Romani and Balkan music.[57] In the lyrics, the singer, the song, and the film's characters share a connection through the theme of travel. Just as in the song, Ayten and Lotte are in constant movement. The song also foreshadows Lotte's travels to Istanbul to see Ayten.

Ultimately, Akın's selection of artists, actors, and songs is the foundation for his aesthetic of heterogeneity. The songs have different backgrounds, are themselves fused with new sounds, and accompany the visuals of ethnically diverse characters. A Turkish human rights activist and a German student of languages fall in love in Hamburg dancing to a song that merges variations of Balkan, Romani, French, and German musical traditions. This scene clearly demonstrates the networks within the European music industry and between musical artists. The musical art forms of sampling, remixing, and dubbing, as well as the Romanian lyrics, become symbols of the permeability of musical and linguistic borders.[58] This musical heterogeneity ultimately becomes personified in the sensual/physical encounter between Ayten and Lotte.

Finally, Akın's musical insights and Shantel's dubbing and sampling display the permeable and fluid characteristic of the European soundtrack in *The Edge of Heaven*. The songs reflect on and, in fact, become an integral part of the Europe displayed. The songs are from different locally influenced musical settings stemming from Turkish, German, French, and Romanian contexts. The music is diverse yet linked through Shantel's dubbing/sampling treatments. Individual songs do not exist side by side in isolation but are in direct exchange and share a relationship as the various versions of Hartner's song exemplify. Turkish commodities such as a cassette of Neşe Karaböçek, the music of Sezen Aksu, or Shantel's remixes of a Romanian song become familiar examples of the new soundscapes in Europe. That is, eastern European sounds, as well as sounds traditionally considered non-European, permeate both private and public spheres in the film. This filmic soundscape subtly includes sounds from different times (Bach and Karaböcek) different European places (the Balkans, the Black Sea, and so on), and different film histories (Yeşilçam, Young Turkish Cinema). Thus, the musical elements in *The Edge of Heaven*—whether contemporary or from other time periods—are not portrayed as exotic or foreign but are smoothly integrated into the general soundtrack of the film and its narrative.

Linguistic Soundscapes in *The Edge of Heaven*

Akın emphasizes that the sound of his imagined Europe is as diverse as its people. The complex function of music in *The Edge of Heaven* is intrinsically intertwined with the sound of languages to construct a European polyphony. The film's characters are highlighted as speaking numerous languages, dialects, and accents in geographically different settings. Through their travels, German and Turkish dialects and accents are heard in Istanbul and the Black Sea region as well as in Hamburg and Bremen. A survey of scenes shows that variations of languages, accents, and dialects become the aural norm in his film and replace the idea that "strange" sounds and languages are limited to the alien, "other" immigrant in the Western city, as urban sociologist Fran Tonkiss has observed in a different context on urban sound.[59] In fact, one could even go so far as to say that, speaking globally, the monolingual subject becomes the minority. In the context of the written and performed word, Yıldız has made a similar argument.[60]

Akın democratizes accented languages in his depiction of linguistic sounds. In his films, be it in *In July*, *Head-On*, or *The Edge of Heaven*, protagonists from all cultural backgrounds speak with accents or dialects.[61] Here, too, Akın's cinema differs from Hamid Naficy's conception of "accented cinema." Naficy argued for the importance of the protagonists' accents, stating that such alteration of sound is relevant in order to make the migrant, the "other," audible and to force the "dominant cinema to speak in a minoritarian language."[62] However, Naficy's interventions, while crucial, are limited to the (literally) accented language of the migrants moving into the West; although he states himself that "it is impossible to speak without an accent."[63]

In *The Edge of Heaven*, Ali and Yeter are representatives of the first generation of guest workers in Germany. They speak Turkish as their first language. Both characters have Turkish accents when they initially address each other in German. Once their Turkish background is established, Ali and Yeter switch to Turkish. It is now their regional dialects that distinguish their language and provide a diversified sound of Turkish. With this differentiation, Turkish is acoustically revealed to be different for every speaker.

Similarly, Nejat and Markus, and Susanne and Lotte speak their own dialects and sociolects of German. When they speak other languages, their accents are made explicit. For example, when Nejat or Markus speak Turkish, or when Lotte and Susanne speak English, these characters carry over a variation of their German accents into the other language. Therefore, all characters, depending on which languages they speak, have accents. Many films portraying Turkish German characters have focused on the differentiation of the migrants or foreigners (from the native population) by accentuating their language accents. In Akın's films, the viewers and listeners are presented with a democratization of accents and dialects. All characters speak "differently," and, therefore, migrants and foreigners are not singled out, but are integral to the film's multifaceted European soundtrack. Appearing in settings in Germany and Turkey, these sounds help to create a similar aural space featuring multilingualism and accented languages across borders.

Such linguistic differences are not solely displayed in the use of accents, but also in the use of dialects. Barbara Mennel suggests that dialects are generally locally specific and immobile as opposed to the multiplicities of accents.[64] At the same time, in Akın's film, this local specificity of dialects seems to become mobile in certain aspects. I will take Ali Aksu's language use as an example.

Dialects establish regional differences within languages, thus Ali's actual language of communication is not only marked by a Turkish accent (when speaking German) but also by a specific regional Turkish dialect. In Turkish, he asks his son: "Eh, sen şimdi kimi dizisin? Kimi bum bum *edisin*" (colloquial for "With whom are you sleeping at the moment?"). Ali's use of "edisin" instead of the standard Turkish verb conjugation "ediyorsun" (to do, second person singular) refers to a very specific regional dialect of the Black Sea region. Ali uses signifiers of this dialect in both Turkish and German. For example, often he adds "da" to the end of the sentences in German as well as Turkish. Talking to his son, he says: "Ich trinke gar nicht so viel, da" ("I do not drink that much, da"). "Da" does not seem to have specific semantic implications, other than the reference to this particular dialect. Later in the film, we see Ali's nephew (Erkan Can), who is typecast for his role. Can is known to Turkish audiences as Temel, a Black Sea character he played in the popular TV show *Mahallenin Muhtarlari* (*Headmen of the Parish*, 1992–2002).[65] In this show, which takes place in Istanbul, Temel represents the large community of migrants who came from the Black Sea to Istanbul in the course of the twentieth century. Thus, *The Edge of Heaven* portrays the travel of a certain dialect to the city of Istanbul, as well as to Bremen, a northern German port city, where it is also integrated into the German language. Through Ali, a particular dialect is shown in direct contact with another language. By merging the Black Sea dialect with German in *The Edge of Heaven*, Akın characterizes languages as permeable, flexible, and in constant change.

To be sure, these minute differences are not discernible to all viewers of the film. These language differences might be a result of the realism of Akın's films, which is also reflected in Akın's international cast and their use of languages. Yet these linguistic differences are important in making a democratized, accented way of life in a globalized world audible: filmic figures are not characterized as "others" simply by their use of languages, dialects, or accents. Instead these diversified linguistic sounds allow for an aural experience of Akın's vision of a multiethnic and multilingual contemporary Europe. In this context, the film's subtitles are important. Because subtitles are used for most of the spoken languages in the film, various viewers have to read different sections of the film. Thereby, the democratization of the languages extends to the audiences. Ignorance of a language does not need to lead to feelings of fear, but can be part of an aural experience of Europe with its multiple languages and dialects.

The New Noise of Europe

The larger arguments in my book, and especially in this chapter, about the heterogeneity of Akın's sound and its multiple connections to diverse images, politics, histories, and geographies, draw on the music and voices from his films.

It is, however, certainly important to note that a film's soundtrack consists of more elements than these. According to Gianluca Sergi, the soundtrack "is a highly complex combination of four elements—effects, music, dialogue, and silence—whose qualities are inextricably blended. Indeed, it is the relationship of these four elements that . . . [the author regards] as the core of the soundtrack."[66] While I agree with Sergi about the collaborative nature of these different sound elements, for my study on the diversity of European cinema, the focus on music and dialogue has proven to be most fruitful. I do not discuss the other two elements—effects and silence—directly, as they seem, at first sight, less significant for my argument. However, I would like to briefly mention these other two elements, as they certainly support *The Edge of Heaven's* general aural composition.

For silence, it shall suffice to say that the music in *The Edge of Heaven* is particularly foregrounded through the use of silence. The silent scenes that allow us to dwell in the different geographic settings and with the different multiethnic characters support the rather contemplative mood of the film. At the same time, this silence allows for the diegetic and nondiegetic music to be noticed more meaningfully, once it is introduced. The same applies to the "collaboration" between silence and sound effects and noise. The lack of music and voice heightens the sensibility of the audience to hear noise more clearly—noises such as unwrapping a lunch bag, opening a door, or starting a car.

A brief focus on the new noise of Europe (foley and ambient noise) in this context shows that this sound element in Akın's work also carries a multidirectional charge, displaying a connectivity between scenes, similar to the dialogue and music in *The Edge of Heaven*. Watching the film with attention to noise, we find that especially city noise and culinary noise are foregrounded. The city noise in Istanbul, Hamburg, and Bremen, for example, provide an impressive array of aural experiences of mobility, urbanity, and multidirectionality. Everyday traffic sounds such as light rail, trains, buses, cars (the opening of car doors, the starting of engines, and an orchestra of car honks) are heard in the cities (with the car honks being more specific to the setting in Istanbul). Such traffic sounds are the predominant sounds in most, if not all, the frequent outdoor scenes, whether these occur on balconies, patios, train stations, prisons, or on the street. Other urban sounds include the combined sound of police sirens, footsteps (running and walking), skateboards, and the chanting and speaking of a multitude of indistinct voices.

However, as several scenes in Istanbul demonstrate, traffic/commuting sounds are not always mechanical or machine related. In Istanbul, the sound of water and waves, as well as the foghorns of the commuter ferries, are less harsh mechanical sounds. Distinctly a sound of Istanbul, the sounds of the Bosporus (waves and ferries) are partially repeated at the end of the film at the Black Sea coast, where Nejat is waiting for his father to return from his fishing trip while he listens to the waves. Such sounds of water can be located only marginally in Bremen: although Bremen is not far from the North Sea, we do not hear the sound of the sea; rather, it is the sounds of water pouring into glasses or the watering of tomatoes on Ali's balcony that operate as a possible link to the waves in Istanbul.

A second noticeable sound element is what I call culinary sound. In addition to water and Coke being poured into glasses, in Istanbul as well as in Bremen and Hamburg, we hear the sound of mocha pots being prepared, mocha cups being placed on tables, teaspoons swirling Turkish black tea, the unwrapping of *börek* (Turkish pastry), and the clanging of plates and silverware indicating active meal time, whether at home or in a restaurant. These culinary sounds occur on different occasions (festive, mourning, everyday settings) signaling the unifying and quotidian human element present when enjoying meals and drinks. Coffee and tea especially, as cherished beverages in Germany and Turkey, appear in both sight and sound, replicating the familiar sounds associated with tea houses and coffee shops, or with guests in a private home.

In sum, the new noise of Europe is all of these: urban, mobile, and impersonal, as well as quotidian and familiar. Even though the film is rather tranquil, creating a contemplative mood, the noise of the cities (traffic, voices, footsteps) is noticeably present almost all the time, indicating a multitude of impersonal sound and mobility. For example, while pensive Nejat might be depicted in rather silent lecture halls, university offices, or train cabins, the places and people around him create the noise of a globalized, mobile, vibrant, and lively urbanity, be this in Germany or Turkey. At the same time, in the midst of all these rather impersonal sounds, culinary noises provide the context for a personal, friendly, cultural noise, since culinary noises often indicate companionship and conviviality.

As sound elements, silence and noise support the musical and linguistic sounds in *The Edge of Heaven*. While silence activates an attentive listening to other sound elements, the new noise of Europe indicates a fast and mobile lifestyle (city and traffic noise) on the one hand, and, on the other hand, it focuses attention on the cultural culinary experiences (coffee, tea, *rakı*) capable of uniting people and providing a space for tranquility and camaraderie, for personal encounters, and for emotional outbursts.

The New Sound of Europe in *The Edge of Heaven*

The analyses of Akın's film music have two preliminary results: First, a new, nonexoticizing portrayal of sonic diversity extending well into southern/eastern Europe and beyond has made its way into German film sound. Not only does this new, diverse sound of Europe become an aurally pleasant soundtrack to *The Edge of Heaven*, but more important, as a sonic dimension of Akın's cinema, it plays a crucial role in the construction of a diverse and multiethnic European space as imagined in film. Second, the film triggers a new commemoration of Turkish and German film history. New German Cinema, Young Turkish Cinema, and Yeşilçam cinema are revealed as cinematic heritages that influence Akın's filmmaking and are thus posited as being central to the Turkish German filmic discourse. These film histories are evoked through film music, but also through casting; through iconographic, intertextual mise-en-scènes; and even through specific Turkish cinema stock figures. Furthermore, the additional discussion of silence and noise in this chapter has shown that musical and linguistic sounds are enhanced through the use of silence and augmented through the use of noise. Noise indicates a fast and mobile lifestyle in the urban sounds of traffic and people, while also gesturing toward slowed-down personal encounters in the noises associated with culinary experiences.

Ultimately, through his soundtrack, Akın showcases examples of a fundamentally changed soundscape of post-1989 Europe and emphasizes that these sounds transcend traditionally defined European borders by including eastern European as well as Turkish sounds from the past and present. The particularity of sound allows the film's audience to subtly experience the heterogeneity prevalent in Akın's work. Similar to Shantel's musical imaginations, Akın's filmic visions challenge competing conceptions of a geopolitical Europe that exists as an agglomeration of monolingual nation-states. Akın's acoustic creation of a diverse European soundscape strives to make alternative conceptions of Europe (aurally) palatable for the viewers and listeners of his cinema. Although themes of illegal immigration, deportation, manslaughter, and terrorism—all of which allude to problematic aspects of contemporary Europe's multiethnicity—are part of the film's narrative, the acoustic composition of the film seems to suggest that a harmonious and productive diversity already is and should be possible.

To be sure, Akın's artistic visions of a post-1989 Europe contrast with simultaneously existing, complex European realities and debates. The aforementioned Islamophobic protest movements juxtaposed with violent Islamists' attacks show a more complicated European reality. Additionally, state regulations such as the minaret ban in Switzerland, the critical discussion in northern Germany about the muezzins' call to prayer, as well as the visual ban of an orthodox Islam in public spaces in France and Belgium, all stand in sharp opposition to the aestheticized sounds and sights in Akın's films. Yet, as a public figure, Akın frequently comments on such debates.[67]

To conclude, despite, or maybe because of a focus on more problematic portrayals of (Muslim) immigrants in film and media, as well as in public and political discourse in the last few decades, Akın does not shy away from his heterogeneous imaginations of Europe.[68] About a decade after the release of *Head-On*, Akın's visions have earned him the Bundesverdienstkreuz (Federal Cross of

Germany), the Peter-Weiss Award in 2012, and more than twenty other awards for *The Edge of Heaven* from across Europe. Journalists have named him the most "European German director" and he is praised as a talented *auteur* with a unique style in international film festivals.[69]

Akın's films seem to be experienced as intrinsically European and contemporary. Akın's signature style rests heavily on his aesthetics of heterogeneity; his audiovisual style and composition mix and juxtapose a variety of European and non-European sounds and images, which by default promote a diverse Europe. In an interview about *Soul Kitchen*, Akın stresses that he does not have a "message of tolerance," but that he simply depicts "his reality," which in his films is manifest as an audiovisually diverse, European space. His films' narratives unravel in a multiethnic context, which he describes as something "normal."[70] The sonic diversity in *The Edge of Heaven*, together with his collaboration with Shantel, whose work equally transcends ethnic boundaries, complements the diverse settings, cast, and characters of Akın's films. His artistic vision of Europe is decidedly multiethnic and polyphonic. This aesthetic of heterogeneity lies at the heart of Akın's captivating stories. Rather than being a utopia, Akın's multiethnic Europe is presented to the viewer as lived experience of his protagonists. This Europe is already in existence; it is revealed to the viewer through Akın's unique audiovisual aesthetics.

Notes

1. Parts of this chapter have been previously published in Berna Gueneli, "Remixing Film Histories: Fatih Akın and the Creation of a Transnational Film History," *Colloquia Germanica* 44, no. 4 (2011, publ. 2014); and in Berna Gueneli, "The Sound of Fatih Akın's Cinema: Polyphony and the Aesthetics of Heterogeneity in *The Edge of Heaven*," *German Studies Review* 37, no. 2 (2014). All translations (newspaper articles, film subtitles, and so on) from Turkish, German, Spanish, and French into English are the author's, unless translations existed previously.

2. Michel Chion briefly discusses sound effects used in silent film. Michel Chion, *Film, A Sound Art*, trans. Claudia Gorbman (New York: Columbia University Press, 2009), 6–7, 9.

3. Roger Hillman's 2005 *Unsettling Scores*, on classical music in New German Cinema; Claudia Gorbman's seminal 1987 *Unheard Melodies*; Anahid Kassabian's 2001 book *Hearing Film*, on contemporary Hollywood films and the function of film music; Amy Herzog's 2010 study of musicals, *Dreams of Difference, Songs of the Same*; and anthologies on film music such as *European Film Music* (2006), *Movie Music: The Film Reader* (2003), and *Sound: Dialogue, Music, and Effects* (2015) provide a broad array of original scholarship.

4. Changes include the accession of several eastern European countries to the EU and the increased east-west and south-north migration of European/non-European citizens.

5. Daniel Goldmark, Lawrence Kramer, and Richard D. Leppert, "Introduction: Phonoplay: Recasting Film Music," in *Beyond the Soundtrack: Representing Music in Cinema*, eds. Daniel Goldmark, Lawrence Kramer, and Richard D. Leppert (Berkeley: University of California Press, 2007), 3.

6. Deniz Göktürk, "World Cinema Goes Digital: Looking at Europe from the Other Shore," in *Turkish German Cinema: Sights, Sounds, and Screens,* eds. Sabine Hake and Barbara Mennel (Oxford: Berghahn, 2012), 198–211; Roger Hillman and Vivien Silvey, "Remixing Hamburg: Transnationalism in Fatih Akın's *Soul Kitchen,*" in *Turkish German Cinema in the New Millennium*, eds. Sabine Hake and Barbara Mennel (Oxford: Berghahn, 2012),190–191; Barbara Kosta, "Transnational Space and Music: Fatih Akın's *Crossing the Bridge: The Sound of Istanbul* (2005)," in *Spatial Turns: Space, Place, and Mobility in German Literary and Visual Culture,* eds. Jaimey Fisher and Barbara Mennel (Amsterdam: Rodopi, 2010), 343–360; Senta Siewert, "Soundtracks of Double Occupancy: Sampling Sounds and Cultures in Fatih Akin's *Head On,*" in *Mind the Screen: Media Concepts According to Thomas Elsaesser*, eds. Jaap Kooijman, Patricia Pisters, and Wanda Strauven (Amsterdam: Amsterdam University Press, 2008): 199.

7. This musical combination brought a new sound onto European dance floors. "Shantel called his night Bucovina because his maternal ancestors have roots in the region, once part of the mighty Habsburg Empire but now partly in Romania and partly Ukraine. Bucovina Club Volume 2 features Balkan heavyweights Goran Bregovic and Fanfare Ciocarlia alongside a Gypsy take on North African anthem Ya Rayah and other material." Garth Cartwright, "Awards for World Music: Winner 2006 DJ Shantel (Germany)," BBC Radio, February 2007, http://www.bbc.co.uk/radio3/worldmusic/ a4wm2006/a4wm_ shantel.shtml.

8. The official page of Shantel's recording company states: "Shantel's vision is to create a pan-European pop music with global appeal." "Essay Recordings New Releases: Shantel Authentic e.p.," Essay recordings, http://www.essayrecordings.com/ essay_authentic.htm; Cartwright, "Awards"; "Shantel Biography," Last.fm, http://www.last.fm/music/Shantel/+wiki.

9. Next to tracks inspired by the Balkans such as "Inel Inel de Aur—Bucovina Dub," he also produced tracks such as "Ben Seni In Dub." "CD Release Auf der anderen Seite," Essay recordings, http://www.essayrecordings.com/essay_adas.htm.

10. "Essay Recordings New Releases."

11. The casting is a mix of actors/actresses known from Turkish, Turkish German, and German cinema: Nejat (Baki Davrak), Ali (Tuncel Kurtiz), Yeter (Nusel Köse), Ayten (Nurgül Yeşilçay), Susanne (Hanna Schygulla), and Lotte (Patrycia Ziolkowska).

12. Klaus Maeck, email message to author, May 26, 2010.

13. Akın mentions and displays specifically the birthplaces of his father (in Filyos) and grandfather (in Çamburnu) in this documentary, which is in the extra features on *The Edge of Heaven* DVD. *Fatih Akın—Tagebuch eines Filmreisenden* (Fatih Akin—Diary of a Film Traveler, directed by Monique Akın, 2007).

14. Chion, *Film: A Sound Art*, 85.

15. Chion, *Film: A Sound Art*, 104–105.

16. For a discussion of Kazım Koyuncu's music in this film, see Göktürk, "World Cinema," 204–205.

17. *Fatih Akın—Tagebuch.*

18. Discussing film sound, Chion elaborates on temporal and spatial continuity that can be established through songs. Chion gives the example of Alfred Hitchcock's *The Birds*, where the same song is used in different scenes in order to create continuity and unity of space for the viewer. Chion, *Film: A Sound Art*, 168–169.

19. Randy Thom and Philip Brophy, "Randy Thom in Conversation: Designing a Movie for Sound," in *Cinesonic*, ed. Philip Brophy, (New South Wales, Australia: Southwood Press, 2000), 10.

20. Göktürk has highlighted this scene in her discussion of the complicated relationship between the local and the global in the film. Mennel also uses the opening scene to discuss

aspects of globalization in the film. Göktürk, "World Cinema," 199–202; Barbara Mennel, "Criss-Crossing in Global Space and Time: Fatih Akın's *The Edge of Heaven* (2007)," *TRANSIT* 5, no.1 (2009): 9–10, http://escholarship.org/uc/item/ 28x3x9ro.

21. Koyuncu is established as a local Black Sea artist who died prematurely as a result of the nuclear accident at Chernobyl that had global effects. Göktürk, "World Cinema," 204–206.

22. This accident in the Ukraine had a major impact on the agriculture and health of the people from the Black Sea region. Akın is indignant about the Turkish government's reaction to Chernobyl, as it did not take the Soviet nuclear accident seriously. Until today there has been no official report on the effects and dangers of Chernobyl on Turkey's northeast cost. *Fatih Akın—Tagebuch.*

23. *Fatih Akın—Tagebuch.*

24. Akın states that this film is a collection of memories and works like a photo album. These scenes of the Black Sea in particular remind one of a photo album. Karin Luisa Badt, "Fatih Akin '*The Other Side of Heaven*,'" *Parisvoice*, 2010, accessed on March 20, 2014, http://www.parisvoice.com/movies/427-fatih-akin-qthe-edge-of-heavenq.

25. Yeşilçam, named after a street in Beyoğlu, Istanbul, is a commercially oriented popular cinema that emerged in the 1950s.

26. Ekkehard Ellinger and Kerem Kayi, *Turkish Cinema: 1970–2007* (Frankfurt am Main, Germany: Peter Lang, 2008), 582.

27. Dilek Kaya Mutlu, "Between Tradition and Modernity: Yeşilçam Melodrama, Its Stars, and Their Audiences," *Middle Eastern Studies* 46, no. 3 (2010): 417; Asuman Suner, *New Turkish Cinema: Belonging, Identity and Memory* (London: I.B. Tauris, 2010), 3, 7.

28. "In Yeşilçam melodramas the tension between tradition and modernity is reflected also as a tension between different social and economic classes, while modernization is associated with the westernized upper class urbanites and upward class mobility." Kaya Mutlu, "Between Tradition and Modernity," 419.

29. "During the turbulent 1970s, at the height of political oppression and censorship, Yeşilçam resorted to soft porn to attract the migrant male audience and compensate for its loss of women and family audiences to television." Gönül Dönmez-Collin, "Women in Turkish Cinema: Their Presence and Absence as Image and as Image-Makers," *Third Text* 24, no.1 (2010): 99.

30. Kaya Mutlu, "Between Tradition and Modernity," 418.

31. Kaya Mutlu, "Between Tradition and Modernity," 418.

32. Kaya Mutlu, "Between Tradition and Modernity," 417–18.

33. For a discussion of Turkish film and music in Germany, see also Andreas Goldberg, "Medien der Migrant/Innen," in *Interkulturelle Literatur in Deutschland: Ein Handbuch*, ed. Charmine Chiellino (Stuttgart, Germany: Metzler, 2000), 420; and Mine Eren, "Cosmopolitan Filmmaking: Fatih Akin's *In July* and *Head-On*," in *Turkish German Cinema in the New Millennium: Sights, Sounds, and Screens*, eds. Sabine Hake and Barbara Mennel (Oxford: Berghahn, 2012), 176–177.

34. Kira Kosnick, *Migrant Media: Turkish Broadcasting and Multicultural Politics in Berlin*, (Bloomington: Indiana University Press, 2007), 28.

35. Dj Ipek's SoundCloud includes a variety of other global musicians. SoundCloud, "djipek," accessed May 20, 2016, https://soundcloud.com/djipek.

36. Roger Hillman, *Unsettling Scores: German Film, Music, and Ideology* (Bloomington: Indiana University Press, 2005), 26.

37. Hillman, *Unsettling Scores*, 25.

38. Hillman quoted in Mennel, "Überkreuzungen in globaler Zeit und globalem Raum in Fatih Akıns *Auf der anderen Seite*," in *Kultur als Ereignis*, ed. Özkan Ezli (Bielefeld, Germany: Transcript, 2010), 106.

39. Özkan Ezli, "Von Lücken, Grenzen und Räumen. Übersetzungsverhältnisse in Alejandro Gonzáles Iñarritus *Babel* und Fatih Akıns *Auf der anderen Seite*," in *Kultur als Ereignis*, ed. Özkan Ezli (Bielefeld, Germany: Transcript, 2010), 85.

40. Ezli, "Von Lücken," 83. Levent Tezcan, "Der Tod Diesseits von Kultur—Wie Fatih Akın den Großen Kulturdialog umgeht," in *Kultur als Ereignis*, ed. Özkan Ezli (Bielefeld, Germany: Transcript, 2010), 63–64.

41. Akın said that Nursel Köse has the faith of many Turkish actresses over forty in Germany; they are left to play the "Kopftuch-Mutti" (headscarf mom). Yet she is "too sexy" to do that. He states about Köse: "I think she is a great actress, whose presence reminds me of the divas of Italian cinema of the 1950s and 1960s." *Fatih Akın—Tagebuch.*

42. Yeter's husband was killed in the seventies in Maraş. He was possibly a Kurdish political activist. Yeter talks about this incident during her first evening at Ali Aksu's house. The audience can infer that Yeter left the country due to political and economic reasons, after the death of her husband. Akın references this politically active time in an interview about *The Edge of Heaven* and hopes that through his films he might provoke political consciousness in his audiences: "There is also a political thrust. In the '80s, a lot of left wing people came to Germany, but the problem we have in Germany is that young people today are less interested in changing anything. Young people are really not interested in society nor do they feel responsible for their society. My film is to provoke people to feel responsible for other humans." Badt, "Fatih Akin."

43. The archive of the Schaubühne Berlin has several documents about Kurtiz's engagement with the theater as director and actor. For other details about Kurtiz, see Yavuz Baydar, "Death of a Great Actor—Tuncel Kurtiz," *Today's Zaman*, September 29, 2013, modified September 30, 2013, accessed on February 5, 2016, http://en.dunyatimes.com/article/death-of-a-great-actor-tuncel-kurtiz-24135.html.

44. Baydar, "Death of a Great Actor."

45. Suner, *New Turkish Cinema*, 143.

46. Ekkehard Ellinger and Kerem Kayi, *Turkish Cinema: 1970–2007* (Frankfurt: Peter Lang, 2008), 598-99.

47. Suner, *New Turkish Cinema*, 8.

48. Suner, *New Turkish Cinema*, 5.

49. Alison Kenny, "Coming to Terms with Turkey through Films: *Yol*—by Yılmaz Güney," *Today's Zaman*, September 20, 2010, accessed on April 12, 2014, http://www.todayszaman.com/news-222104-coming-to-terms-with-turkey-through-films-yol-by-yilmaz-guney.html.

50. Suner, *New Turkish Cinema*, 5.

51. Suner, *New Turkish Cinema*, 5–6.

52. Badt, "Fatih Akin."

53. Daniela Berghahn, "Seeing Everything with Different Eyes: The Diasporic Optic of Fatih Akin's *Head-On* (2004)," in *New Directions in German Cinema*, eds. Paul Cooke and Chris Homewood (London: I.B. Tauris, 2011), 255.

54. *Fatih Akın—Tagebuch.*

55. This transformation is also verbally hinted at in the introductory sequence between Nejat and Yeter. Yeter explains to Nejat that she is a prostitute. She uses the word "Hayat kadını" (literally, woman of life), which is a Turkish euphemism for sex worker, also commonly used in Turkish cinema. Since Nejat does not understand the meaning of the word, she has to be more precise: "Bildiğın orospu işte" (A whore as you know it).

56. Rona Hartner, email message to author, July 26, 2010.

57. Hartner, who has a Greek/Hungarian background, moved from Romania to Paris in the late 1990s. Her collaboration with DJ Click began her musical career, throughout which she has emphasized the themes of movement and migration. Her recent 2007 album continues

the musical fusions and ideas of migration and movement that the musician herself represents. "Nationalité Vagabonde" (Vagabond nationality) is a "true fusion between electro gypsy and Afro-Jazz arranged by Jérémy Demaesmaker and Mike Aube." Stéphanie Griguer, "Rona Hartner bio," 2009, http://ronahartner.com/ contactpro/attachment/rona-hartner-bio/.

58. In a different context, Akın highlights and connects the method of mixing and sampling also to his filmmaking in general. He suggests, for example, that his creation of a mixed aesthetic through filmic references resemble the art of DJing. "I try to find the right information for the image. I try to find the right images. The music in my film is also important. I am still doing my DJing in Hamburg. I am a cinema DJ. I can mix Fassbinder with Fellini. Cinema reminds me of sampling. Costa Gavras's movie *Missing* influenced me. I tried to shoot the runaway scene like Polanski would do it. I try to watch a movie a day. I watched a lot of silent movies before this. I really tried to tell the story in the form of a silent movie, without language. This is DJing." Badt, "Fatih Akin."

59. Fran Tonkiss, "Aural Postcards: Sound, Memory and the City," in *The Auditory Culture Reader*, eds. Michael Bull and Les Back (Oxford: Berg, 2003), 303.

60. In her book *Beyond the Mother Tongue: The Postmonolingual Condition*, Yıldız traces literary texts from Kafka and Adorno to Yoko Tawada and Feridun Zaimoğlu and astutely examines literary multilingualism. Introducing her concept of the postmonolingual condition, Yildiz unravels the origins of the creation of monolingualism in the eighteenth century. She states, "The notion of monolingualism rapidly displaced previously unquestioned practices of living and writing in multiple languages. . . . With the gendered and affectively charged kinship concept of the unique 'mother tongue' at its center . . . , monolingualism established the idea that having one language was the natural norm, and that multiple languages constituted a threat to the cohesion of individuals and society." Yasemin Yıldız, *Beyond the Mother Tongue: The Postmonolingual Condition* (New York: Fordham University Press, 2012), 6.

61. Analyzing Akın's response to globalization in *The Edge of Heaven*, Mennel also highlights the use of characters' accents, which marks their mobility. Mennel, "Criss-Crossing," 7.

62. Naficy, *An Accented Cinema: Exilic and Diasporic Filmmaking* (Princeton, NJ: Princeton University Press, 2001), 25.

63. Naficy, *Accented Cinema*, 23.

64. Mennel, "Criss-Crossing," 7–8; Mennel, "Überkreuzungen," 98.

65. "Mahallenin Muhtarlari 1992-2002," IMDB, http://www.imdb.com/title/ tt0299348/.

66. Gianluca Sergi, *The Dolby Era: Film Sound in Contemporary Hollywood* (Manchester, UK: Manchester University Press, 2004), 6–7.

67. In reaction to the minaret ban in Switzerland, for example, which I mentioned in chapter1, Akın writes in an open letter: "This referendum goes against my understanding of humanism, tolerance, and the belief that a harmonious coexistence among people of different background, race, and religion must be possible. Since I am a child of Muslim parents, who do not see a political Islam in minarets, but a completeness of the architecture of their religious buildings, I feel personally offended by the referendum. . . . My only explanation for the Swiss referendum is fear. Fear is the source of all evil. *Fear Eats the Soul* is the title of a film by Rainer Werner Fassbinder. Maybe fear has eaten too many souls in Switzerland already." "Offener Brief: Fatih Akin boykottiert Filmpremiere in der Schweiz," *MIGAZIN. Migration in Germany*, December 4, 2009, http://www. migazin.de/2009/12/04 /fatih-akin-boykottiert-filmpremiere-in- der-schweiz/.

68. *In July* might be read as a less critical portrayal of European mobility/border crossing compared to *Head-On*. Eren, "Cosmopolitan Filmmaking."

69. "48 FIC XiXÓn: Festival International de Cine de Gijón 19–28 Noviembre de 2009," *Gijon Film Festival*, accessed on July 22, 2010, http://www.gijonfilmfestival.com

/noticias.asp?idioma= 3&idmenu=2&idnoticias=73; "Akin, Fatih," *hamburg.de*, accessed on July 22, 2010, http://www.hamburg.de/ magazin/8204/hamburg-von-a-d.html; "Fatih Akin: 'El cine y la cocina tienen muchos elementos en común,'" *El Mundo*, March 30, 2010, http://www.elmundo.es/elmundo/ 2010/03/29/cultura/12698612 36.html.

70. "For me it is something automatic. Multiculturalism is something so normal for me that I do not purposefully emphasize it. There is no message, I am not talking about tolerance. I am talking about my reality." Badt, "Fatih Akin."

CHAPTER 4

Expanding the Scope of European Cinema

AKIN'S CINEMATIC IMAGINING OF A DIVERSE EUROPE IN CONTEXT

HAVING READ AKIN as a transnational auteur with European sensibilities in the previous chapters, in this chapter I contextualize his work with that of other contemporary European filmmakers. These directors are global auteurs, who, like Akın, contribute to the creation of a new transnational, cosmopolitan Europe on the screen. Either they have directly influenced Akın, or they share stylistic and/or political similarities. My selection of European films discussed here includes the work of Philippe Lioret, Mathieu Kassovitz, and Yamina Benguigui (France); Michael Haneke (Austria); Stephen Frears (UK); Emir Kusturica (FRY); and Nuri Bilge Ceylan (Turkey). These filmmakers and their films either depict a similarly transnational makeup of European cinema, raising questions comparable to Akın's work, or they engage in other ways with questions of diversity and sociopolitical, socioeconomic inequalities in Europe. That is, not only minority filmmakers (Akın or Benguigui), but also filmmakers who are not solely associated with minority cinema partake in the creation of a cinematic European multiethnicity and diversity, however divergent their cinema might be thematically, artistically, and stylistically. Frears, who directed *High Fidelity* (2000) and *The Queen* (2006), also made the multiethnic London classics *My Beautiful Laundrette* (1985) and *Dirty Pretty Things* (2002); and Kassovitz, who directed the internationally known thrillers *The Crimson Rivers* (2000) and *Gothika* (2003), is still primarily remembered for his critically acclaimed Parisian *banlieue*[1] thriller *La Haine* (1995).

In these films, diversity becomes the core of a cosmopolitan, transnational Europe, as embodied in the phenomenon "global cities."[2] This chapter then shows how Akın's films encapsulate general thematic and stylistic tendencies within contemporary European cinema. It shows that European cinema has adapted to the ever-changing, highly dynamic diversity of the twenty-first century. My analysis includes New Turkish Cinema, which is most often categorized separately from European cinema although it is frequently funded through the same European sources (e.g., Eurimages, MEDIA) and engages with similar aesthetic or thematic questions, or produces a contemplative cinema that could equally be qualified as "European" in its style and form. Yet what constitutes, or what has been seen as constituting, European cinema? How do Akın and his contemporaries navigate within this category and simultaneously expand and transcend its borders?

European cinema, like Europe itself, has had a plethora of definitions since its inception. Elsaesser succinctly summarizes his observation about the current state of European cinema by stating that it "does not exist, except as a bureaucratic dream or a promotional tool for national producers and distributors of art house films."[3] Yet Elsaesser previously also stated, "Any book about European cinema should start with a statement that there is no such thing as European cinema, and that yes, European cinema exists, and has existed since the beginning of cinema a little more than a hundred years ago."[4] In an assessment of contemporary European cinema and its themes, Luisa Rivi states that recent EU coproductions reflect on a new diversity and hybridity in European filmmaking.[5] In a more specific context, Göktürk declares that the films of Akın, like the work of Michael Haneke and Krzysztof Kieślowski, are examples of a decentralized and multilocal Europe.[6]

The filmic depiction of a decentralized, multilocal, diverse, and hybrid Europe is most certainly connected to the effects of globalization on European cinema. At the same time, contemporary European cinema, especially the coproductions, seems to draw from a variety of cinematic influences, including eastern and southern European, cross-Atlantic, and other non-European inspirations. Yet these are newer—if by now increasingly accepted—insights. They had not been fully acknowledged at all times in European cinema scholarship. For the longest time, the discourse on European cinema has been defined and analyzed in an isolated and elitist approach, separating and elevating it from, for example, the cinemas of Hollywood, eastern Europe, or any other cinemas of the world. However, contemporary film productions, especially supranational coproductions in the unified and unifying European Union once more force us to see the connectedness of the globalized film industry, linking today's global structures of cinema to its aesthetics and content.[7]

With Akın, we encounter a filmmaker whose work receives transnational—that is, regional, national, and supranational—funds, a phenomenon also reflected in the reception, style, and composition of his cinema. Awarded with European, Turkish, and German film prizes, and selected to represent Germany and Turkey at the 2008 Academy Awards, Akın remains hard to categorize. In terms of film genre and style, as well as regarding cultural affiliations, his work challenges any kind of one-dimensional categorization. Located at the nexus of the so-called Hollywood, European art house, and European popular cinemas, Akın complicates traditional cinematic categories that often have been kept apart in European cinema scholarship. Taking a critical approach to such restrictions, Jill Forbes and Sarah Streets elaborate on the deeply inflected mutual influences that films and filmmakers across the Atlantic have had over many decades. An intriguing example they reference is Mathieu Kassovitz's 1995 *La Haine*, which was inspired by Martin Scorsese, who, in turn, has been inspired by the European art cinema of the 1960s for his own cinematic oeuvre.[8] Complicating the web of cinematic exchanges even more, Akın's *Short Sharp Shock* is inspired by *La Haine*, and Akın himself mentions Scorsese in his credits. According to Everett, European cinema has a "multiple, diverse, and complex identity," something which should be considered more in European cinema scholarship.[9] With Akın's cinema, these complexities are laid out on the screen with a director whose work links elements of Turkish, German, European, and global cinema, as well as entertainment and art house cinema. Concerned with Akın's cinema and its relationship to the work of other contemporary European directors, I will now investigate contemporary cinematic imaginings of the continent. Drawing on films from eastern, central, western, and southern Europe, I will highlight this new European cinema.

A Decentralized, Multilocal, and Diverse Europe in European Cinema

The films to be discussed in this chapter create decentralized and multilocal imaginings of Europe, while they simultaneously expand and diversify the category of European cinema itself. Yet what does "decentralized" mean in the context of European cinema? If we take "central" to mean "dominant, important, and relevant" in terms of cultural and economic power dynamics as played out in Europe and European cinema, and if we were to look at the dominant cinematic scholarship and film distribution, we would likely find it to refer, very limitedly, to the northern/western European countries and their national art house cinemas. These cinemas also have dominated the film circuits and college courses of the twentieth and twenty-first centuries. Both have only seldom included cinemas outside this geographical region. A similar elitism can be traced in *The International Journal of Film*. Rosalind Galt and Karl Schonoover refer to the films that the journal has surveyed annually since 1964 and show the gradual and very slow opening of cinema's reception and distribution beyond western Europe (and North America). In 1964, Galt and Schonoover observe, the "World Survey" section of the journal included only thirteen countries, compared to sixty national cinemas in 1989, and more than a hundred in 2006. Finally in 2008, the journal presented itself as "the definitive annual survey of contemporary global cinema,"[10] including a wide-reaching survey and discussion of cinemas from around the world.

Centrality thus has always been a discursive centrality in the first place. European cinema scholarship has slowly recognized and destabilized this "centrality" by attending to the cinemas of a larger geographical region, including points of reference in Turkish, North African, eastern, northern, and southern European regions; by incorporating the cinemas that are situated beyond the mainstream and the art circuits (including internet films, less bankable and profit-driven cinemas); and by discussing topics and themes (made) relevant to a diversity of audiences (including topics such as migration, diaspora, and class, gender, and race inequalities). Investigating beyond the "centrality" of traditional European cinema studies, such scholarship invites a critical regionalism in cinema studies (Mike Wayne); it suggests a study of the so-called European *interzones*, engaging productively with a decentralized European cinema (Randall Halle); it discusses regional film festivals and their impact on the funding and distribution of films from eastern and southern Europe (Kristine Kotecki); it foregrounds eastern European and Balkan cinematic traditions and aesthetics (Dina Iordanova); it urges critics to acknowledge the continuous processes of shifting centers and margins in European cinema and its discourse (Michael Gott and Todd Herzog), and finally it focuses on the impact the cultural shifts and changes in post-1989 Europe have had on cinema's engagement with its postwar memory across the New Europe (Rosalind Galt).[11] Chapters 1 to 3 in this book are in dialogue with such scholarship, and make ample references to the decentralizing aspects of Akın's multilocal cinema by discussing the audiovisual composition of local sights and sounds from eastern and central Europe, and particularly from Turkey, in his films. At this point in the study, it is very illustrative to juxtapose these results with select examples from European cinema.

In the next section, I focus on a variety of audiovisual elaborations on European diversity, decentrality, and multilocality in order to show how Akın's dedication to these topics appears in numerous contemporary filmmakers' work. Akın's cinema is, in fact, part of a trend in a new European cinema. This book started by laying out Akın's audiovisual construction of a cinematic European space in *In July* (2000). To review, Akın's road movie moves, geographically, from the European North (Hamburg), accompanying its protagonists across Europe, traversing central and eastern Europe from Austria, Hungary, Bulgaria, and Romania, to places beyond the European Southeast—that is, Istanbul and the South of Turkey. While the film manages to portray the continuity and connectivity of the

European landscape and its urban centers, as discussed in chapter 1 and further elaborated in chapters 2 and 3, the film also aurally introduces viewers to a mixed European sound of languages, accents, and music, including east European sounds. The analysis of *In July* at the beginning of this book offers an invitation to move toward the comparative section, featuring Emir Kusturica's *Crna macka, beli macor* (*Black Cat, White Cat*, 1998), which clearly influenced the audiovisual style of Akın's *In July*, and perhaps other European films of the late twentieth century, marking the increasing decentrality and multilocality of European cinema years before cinema scholarship engaged with this topic.

Emir Kusturica

This section on Kusturica will primarily highlight the similarities between Akın's and Kusturica's filmic atmosphere. Kusturica's cinema represents a multiethnic and diverse Europe—Kusturica himself is a part of this diverse Europe. On the claim of having "emerged as one of the last examples of a European auteurist tradition,"[12] Kusturica is a Sarajevo-born Serbian Bosnian filmmaker and musician, who studied film in Prague and, in addition, resided in cosmopolitan cities, such as Sarajevo, Belgrade, New York, and Paris, over the course of his career. During the early tumultuous post–Cold War years in the Balkans, he "dissociated himself from the Bosnian Muslim government . . . and refused to endorse any nationalistic doctrine."[13] His family history personifies the Yugoslav project: an Orthodox (he converted from Islam), he is married to a woman of Bosnian Serbian and Slovenian Croatian heritage.[14] According to Dan Halpern, his *New York Times* interviewer in May 2005, Kusturica himself is a believer in the Yugoslav project, like many other Sarajevens. This is a region Halpern defines as "a complex cultural brew of Catholics, Orthodox Christians, Muslims, Jews, gypsies—a mix of religions and ethnicities and historical nationalities that together formed a single nation."[15] Kusturica believed in that nation, but it did not last. In fact, the Balkan region had been referred to as a powder keg already in the pre–World War I period. During the separatist nationalist movements in the Balkans of post-Soviet Europe, political unrest erupted again violently. These tensions also mark Kusturica's controversial, overtly political film *Underground* (1995).[16]

Focusing on the influences on Akın's cinema, I will concentrate my discussion on Kusturica's *Black Cat*.[17] Moving away from the polarizations of his previous film, *Black Cat* is a seemingly nonpolitical comedy. Winner of the Venice Film Festival in 1998,[18] it is a typical coproduction funded by European film companies (French CIBY 2000, France 2 Cinema, German Pandora Film, and Serbian KOMUNA) with additional support and collaboration coming from France (Canal+), Germany (Bayerischer Rundfunk, Filmförderung Hamburg, Filmstiftung NRW), Austria (Österreichischer Rundfunk), and Greece (Stefi S.A.).

Black Cat is a Romani-gangster romantic comedy. Choosing an entirely Romani setting and cast—that is, drawing from a group of people generally associated with movement and migration, rather than fixed, bordered nationalistic spaces—Kusturica purposely refrains from explicit nationalist politics. Although intended as a documentary on the Romani and their music, *Black Cat* developed into a fictional comedy, set at the Romani settlements along the Balkan banks of the Danube.

Just as Akın does with his use of a multiethnic cast, heterogeneous sounds, and settings, Kusturica diversifies European cinema in similar ways through his cast (Romani actors), setting (Balkan), and sound (Romani languages and music). This diversification first and foremost attracts attention through its Romani cast. While Romani figures are not very common in western European cinema, the use of Romani subjects in film, more so than other minorities, accords with Balkan cinematic traditions. Dina Iordonova states that in the history of Balkan cinema the figures and lives of Romani ("gypsies") have been a constant subject of cinematic interest, unlike other minorities, such as the Gagauz (Turkish-speaking Christian minority), Vlachs (Aromanian-speaking minority), and Sarakatsani (Greek-speaking minority).[19] Notwithstanding the clichéd representation of Romani in films as exotic, marginal, or poor, they have generally not been represented as hostile dangers, presumably because of their "transnational minority" status and because they do not "belong" to any existing nation-state, unlike the Muslim minorities who are perceived as an extension of the Islamic threat and have often appeared as "hostile and paternalistic" in Balkan films.[20]

The post–Cold War anti-Romani discrimination in the Balkans resulted in two major trends in their cinematic portrayal: one foregrounds a "social concern," documenting and countering negative media portrayals, and the other, an "exoticism," celebrating the unconventional lifestyle of Romani.[21] Kusturica's *Black Cat* can be interpreted as visualizing aspects of both cinematic trends; but at the same time, his film also operates beyond ethnographic representation and exoticization, as will be briefly discussed further below.

Set in a Romani settlement on the Serbian banks of the Danube, *Black Cat* introduces and visualizes a new European cinema setting in the Balkans. The film engages with the petty criminal activities, family bonds, rivalries, and friendships of the families of Zarije Destanov and Grga Pitic, and the disco-loving, cocaine-snorting gangster, Dadan. While the film has a fairly fixed setting, the multilingualism of the script, the changes of scenery (woods, the Danube river, train stations, different settlements, and private homes), the unusual, self-crafted vehicles of transportation, as well as the energetic brass band and other frequent lively musical interludes—in combination with the fast cutting of sequences—imbue the film with a fast pace, a sense of mobility, and narrative openness. This multilingual film—the script was written in Serbo-Croatian and Romani, and Bulgarian is spoken, for example, by the Bulgarian border official (Stojan Sotirov)—takes its audience on a vibrant and tumultuous ride across the Balkans. In this aspect, several Balkan scenes in Akın's *In July* are reminiscent of *Black Cat.*

Akın's *In July* revisits several audiovisual tropes that *Black Cat* introduced to a predominantly European (if also global art house) audience. Apart from individual cues, such as large eccentric buses moving across rural regions of the Balkans or certain casting choices (Branka Katić), the film highlights specific Balkan sounds and settings. First and foremost is the setting of the Danube. Functioning as a natural element that links various regions of Europe, it is also a place for romance, commerce, tourism, and traffic, and it symbolizes a source of life. In *In July*, Juli and Daniel's castaway travel on a cargo boat on the Danube recalls Kusturica's setting along the Danube, which is crossed by large and small vessels, with Russian and other (legal and illegal) vendors selling items from their boats, tourist boats traversing the Danube, and commercial enterprises on the shores, such as restaurants and ice cream vendors. In this regard, it is especially Daniel's and Juli's awakening on a Slavic cargo boat after a night of romantic hallucination (smoking marijuana) on the Danube, that recalls the happy ending of *Black Cat,* with the Romani Ida and Zare embarking on a journey leading to an unknown future elsewhere as stowaways on a tourist boat.

Akın's Balkan sequences not only reuse the actual setting of the Danube but also the scenes at the Bulgarian-Serbian border. The opening of *In July* "somewhere in Bulgaria," as well as the Hungarian-Romanian border crossing, which both depict wide and open fields and landscapes that transcend the frame, recall Kusturica's Serbian-Bulgarian border crossing in the countryside. Additionally, as discussed in chapter 1, a border pole that is staged as a death pole for the corrupt Bulgarian border official in *Black Cat,* comes up as an actual (arbitrarily used) pole in Akın's border-crossing scene. Both films thus provide border imageries that seem to be taken out of their usual context or purposefully dysfunctionalized, and landscapes that seem to continue seamlessly across the Balkans, despite the relics of physical borders. In sum, the atmosphere created by Akın and Kusturica reveals stunning similarities. Akın's mise-en-scène of the Balkan countryside and the Danube is almost a one-to-one replica of Kusturica's visual scenery.

The multilingualism of the films—in particular the foregrounding of lesser-known languages and accents—demands further attention. That is, Akın's and Kusturica's musical and linguistic soundtracks mark further resemblances between the two films. In Kusturica's case, this includes variations of Romani, the language of the marginalized Romani in the Balkans (and elsewhere in Europe),[22] contrasted with eastern European languages, such as Serbo Croatian and Bulgarian, that populate the European cinema screens, while Akın adds Turkish and eastern European languages and accents.

Kusturica and Akın augment and diversify the sound of European cinema through their international cast, and through their soundtrack (music and dialogue), thereby normalizing this specific film sound, while captivating their audience with visual spectacles, narrative complications, and musical enchantments. In other words, their filmic narratives tell stories using the sound and images of lesser-known European subjects. These subjects (actors and characters) thereby become not the ethnographic interest of a documentary, but normalize, and grant validity to an aestheticized, fictionalized depiction of an individual subject, whose ethnicity, marginality, nationality, or regional affiliations have been either ignored, left out, or used for minor, stereotypical, or romanticized roles in earlier European cinema. Through their films, Akın's and Kusturica's characters, with their possible linkages to more than one category, begin to populate European cinema screens; for example, they may have eastern European, Russian, Serbo-Croatian, Hungarian, Bosnian, Bulgarian, Slavic, Muslim, Orthodox, and Romani affiliations.

Yet some critics highlight, with good reason, the complications that arise when non-Romani filmmakers use Romani characters in films.[23] Certainly, to some degree such interpretations and complications might also be true for *Black Cat*, yet I argue that one of the additional effects of Kusturica's film is that it grants validity—on a European and global scale—to the Romani as filmic subjects by portraying them in a feature-length gangster comedy, rather than as affective objects of documentary, or using them solely in the context of a naïve celebration of the unconventional Romani lifestyle. That is, in echoing Russian critic Plachow's comments about Akın, I would like to similarly stress that Kusturica makes the perceived "nationally marginal" the subject of Balkan cinema, of Balkan culture, without necessarily obscuring its subjectivity.

The scholarship on Balkan music and on Kusturica has credited Kusturica with popularizing Balkan musical traditions, especially the so-called gypsy music, including brass bands. Some scholarship, though, has been critical of the stereotypical and one-dimensional portrayal of gypsy music, which, as Ioana Szeman reminds us, is much more complicated than the cinematic, romanticized, even "Orientalized" version of the music and its players. Often music subsumed under the moniker "gypsy" is also taken as an overgeneralized representation of the "Balkans," even though there are a multitude of differences and influences within Romani music (Ottoman influences in Mana and Manele) and other Balkan musical traditions (which also include a variety of other styles and sounds).[24] Within the Balkans, especially among the Romanian elite, for example, Szeman states, Romani music is stereotypically associated with "bad taste," "kitsch," and the marginalized Romani as well as with the Ottomans and Turks, and it therefore falls short of garnering general praise among all of Romanian audiences.[25] This observation of course complicates the generalizing (western European/global) assumption that "gypsy music" equals "Balkan music."

These important critical engagements with romanticized depictions and disseminations of Romani music and language notwithstanding, *Black Cat* works toward a diversification of European cinema in the long term. While it could be argued that Kusturica to some extent depicts stereotypical and romanticized images and sounds of the Romani (criminal, lazy characters, who continuously sing and dance to Romani music, speak Romani, and are dirty, unkempt, unstable, and homeless, living in makeshift camps, and so forth),[26] it could also be argued that his audiovisual imagining of a Romani settlement precisely through its *excess* of stereotypes, which is a common element in comedy, reminds the audience of the artificiality of such stereotypes in the first place, and, I suggest, loses most of its discriminatory potential in Kusturica's case.

It is curious, however, that the one love story we follow from the beginning to the end of the narrative depicts the only two conventionally attractive figures in the film. One figure embodies a clean-cut Romani masculinity: in the opening sequence, Zare Destanov (Florijan Ajdini) is dressed in a blue-and-white striped shirt more reminiscent of the Polish aristocratic Tadzio in Luchino Visconti's Thomas Mann adaptation *Morte a Venezia* (*Death in Venice,* 1971) than the other unkempt Romani figures in *Black Cat.* The second figure is the beautiful and exotic Ida (played by Branka Katić), whose sexualized femininity, especially when she is dancing to a western European pop video, recalls European fantasies of the exotic, seductive dancing Romani, who can be seen on the screen as early as in Stellan Rye and Hanns Heinz Ewers's *Der Student von Prag* (*The Student of Prague,* 1913). Notwithstanding the obvious visual difference between these two and the other Romani figures, the audience of *Black Cat* is lured into the imagined world of the fictional characters, which at the same time becomes a Felliniesque gangster musical and a Balkan version of Shakespeare's *A Midsummer Night's Dream. Black Cat* presents a world of its own, devaluing existing stereotypes of the Romani, while also operating as an important cinematic validation of eastern European settings and sounds.

Similar to Akın's distinct musical soundtrack that notably diversifies European cinema's sound, Kusturica's soundtrack provides an eccentric compilation of diegetic musical scenes. These include Romani musicians such as Dr. Nelle Karajlić, Dejan Sparavalo, Vjislav Aralica, Verisa Miloradović, Dejan Manidogić, Bokan Stanković. The soundtrack mixes lesser-known brass bands, Romani songs, and more popular Western musical sounds like ABBA's 1976 song "Money, Money, Money." By also disseminating the dance sound produced by Frank Farian's Europop, such as the 1996 No Mercy song "Where Do You Go?" (itself a cover of the popular 1994 La Bouche song of the same title), as well as Jim Steinman's 1984 film song "Nowhere Fast" performed by Fire Inc. for *Streets on Fire, Black Cat* juxtaposes a range of European sounds that have been adapted, remixed, and performed by a diversity of musical acts. Therefore, the musical performance of mixing, sampling, and covering—which, in a different context, has been attributed to Romani music as music that "steals"[27] from existing traditions—highlights musical permeability across European (popular) music. Aspects of mixing, sampling, and covering are also apparent in Akın's film soundtrack, as discussed in detail in chapter 3.

Finally, Kusturica's audiovisual depiction of travel, movement, and migration through the Balkans, like Akın's, creates an entry point into the "new" sights and sounds of European cinema for a larger European/global audience. While some scholars observe an invitation to Orientalize the Balkans through the depiction of the Romani and their music, as Szeman convincingly argues,[28] with their eastern European subjects (among others) such films also highlight a European connectivity and diversity, beyond the potentialities of overgeneralizing and Orientalizing. In juxtaposition with the Danube river and the seamless continuity of the Balkan landscapes, reaching far into central/eastern Europe and Turkey, the soundtrack invites an appreciation of the rich musical traditions of the Balkan regions. Even if it is offered only through a small selection of these traditions, the sounds travel to western Europe and around the globe via these cinematic imaginations. World-renowned, Sarajevo-born Croatian Serb Goran Bregović, a close collaborator of Kusturica's earlier films, such as *Time of the Gypsies* (1988), *Arizona Dream* (1993), and *Underground* (1995), offers an example of how Kusturica's films and soundtrack integrate musicians into the global market and normalize and popularize a version of an eastern European regional sound within European cinema.

Stephen Frears

The diversification and decentralization of European cinema is a phenomenon that appears in different European regional and national cinemas, including in northwestern Europe. By focusing on Stephen Frears's work, I begin this section with a British filmmaker who contributes to thematic and stylistic expansions of European cinema, and who frequently depicts protagonists stigmatized by mainstream societies. Frears has been known to engage in wide-reaching sociopolitical topics related to marginalized minority groups (based on race, ethnicity, gender, class), and representations of unconventional stories including sexually transgressive topics in his films. These range from love stories in nineteenth-century Paris, set in the life of courtesans and sex workers, outside of the Parisian bourgeois society (*Cheri*, 2009), to sexually transgressive (French) literary adaptations set in eighteenth-century France (*Dangerous Liaisons*, 1988); and from African American Muslim convert and professional boxer Muhammad Ali fighting against the US government's draft during the Vietnam War (*Muhammad Ali's Greatest Fight*, 2013), to films depicting critical perspectives of the contemporary multiethnic global city London (*My Beautiful Laundrette*, 1985; *Sammy and Rosie Get Laid*, 1987; and *Dirty Pretty Things*, 2002).

The last three are of particular interest for my discussion of contemporary European cinema's audiovisual dissemination of a decentralized and diversified Europe. These films are set in historically different—at that time contemporary—incarnations of London. Two take place in Thatcher's 1980s England, in which the films engage with the crisis of British white identity and the collapse of the social welfare state. That is, in the wake of a newly erupting understanding of Britain's multiethnicity in the backdrop of economic shifts and changes, these films subvert imaginings of a monolithic white nationalism in postwar (Thatcher) Britain. The third film is set in post–Cold War London, in which non-European im/migration and undocumented, exploited work meet with underworld criminality such as the organ mafia. These films, like Black British cinema in general, function as counter films to the so-called heritage films of England, which generally have a more "traditional image of the nation" and particularly about the "national past."[29] Frears and Kureishi reject the "nostalgic mode of heritage films" that reinforce a "pastoral identity and upper class culture."[30] Instead they replace such pastoral and fixed identities and settings with "urban and dynamic" ones, pairing them with Kureishi's understanding of British national identity as "fluid and shifting."[31] Frears's cinematic urbanity is in itself atypical for film. Uncommon cinematic perspectives on London, such as laundromats, indistinct streets, hotel basements, taxi driver break rooms, back doors of large urban hotels, and overcrowded residences of illegal immigrants, rather than the popular glamorous and touristic London sights such as Westminster Abbey, Buckingham Palace, Downing Street, Tower Bridge, or Trafalgar Square, form the main settings for the narrative in these socially critical depictions of multiethnic London.

Frears's collaborative work—either with writer Hanif Kureishi in the 1980s, who is known for his engagement with England's multiethnic citizenry in his literary work, or with Stephen Knight in 2002, who is known for his work on the game show *Who Wants to Be a Millionaire?*[32]—has a socially critical tone, but, at the same time, keeps a distinct humor and an aesthetic of heterogeneity. This is especially the case in *Sammy and Rosie*, which displays a mixed style: on the one hand, a social realist mode of filmmaking, typical for films of the time engaging with "real" people and their problems in Britain, and on the other, a highly stylized visualization of the riots and police actions on the streets.[33]

Produced with British production companies and sources (e.g., BBC Films, Celador Films, and Jones Company Productions for *Dirty Pretty Things*, and Working Title Films, SAF Productions, and Channel Four Films for *My Beautiful Laundrette*), these films are not multilateral European coproductions such as Akın's or Kusturica's films. Yet Frears's international cast and his collaborations are one way of seeing many of his films as having transnational aspects on the production side. In *Dirty Pretty Things*, for example, the multinational cast includes Catalan Sergi López, French Audrey Tautou, Nigerian-British Chiwetel Ejiofor, and Croatian Zlatko Buric, to name but a few. Thematically, these British-funded and British-produced works follow a London-based narrative; nevertheless they engage with larger European issues such as questions of postcolonialism, ethnicity, race, and class in a post–World War II and post–Cold War Europe.

My Beautiful Laundrette and *Sammy and Rosie Get Laid* are both set in postcolonial Britain in the 1980s. With "the decline of imperial power and the great influx of immigrants from the ex-colonies . . . , the seemingly stable ground on which this sense of Englishness was built [during British Imperialism and Industrialization] began shifting."[34] These racial and ethnic shifts and changes that threatened and challenged British identity merged with a renewed economic change in Margaret Thatcher's England. This era is associated with privatization, the reduction of social benefits, an increase in unemployment and poverty, and a reinforced divide between the classes. Both of Frears's collaborations with Kureishi are highly critical of Thatcherism, which enforced class divides and reinforced racist sentiments, especially among the white working class that was among those impacted by Thatcher's policies.[35] However, the principal characters (Omar and Johnny in *My Beautiful Laundrette* and Sammy, Rosie, and the lesbian couple in *Sammy and Rosie*) in both of the Frears-Kureishi collaborations trump the bleak times that are criticized. They might not all be "angelic protagonists," but as "more realistic and interesting"[36] characters, with their flaws, they in fact stand above a racist, xenophobic, and monolithic nationalism, and, compared to other characters in the film, neither are they antagonistic, callous capitalists—although they are complicit in it, in one way or another.[37] This is also true for the protagonists in Frears's later film *Dirty Pretty Things*.

Dirty Pretty Things is set in contemporary London (according to the year of production, this is post-9/11, yet prior to the 7/5 London bombings). The film portrays the lives of several (illegal) immigrants in London, who have different reasons for their permanent or transitory stay in Britain, and who have different legal statuses in Britain (coming from Turkey, Nigeria, Somalia, and China). Yet they are united in their desire to obtain (fake) EU citizenry in order to gain less limited access to "legal" work, travel, and quality of life. The place that connects the individual characters in the film is an unnamed London hotel, which provides the space for illegal employment (maid and nighttime receptionist), as well as illegal transactions that are of sexual (prostitution and forced sexual favors), surgical (organ transplantation), and economic (money for organs) nature. Besides the film's obvious criticism of global capitalism[38] and the exploitation of the poorest people (exposing the abuse of an undocumented group of people in London—the invisible ones, the "people you do not see"), the film also manages to provide and acknowledge, on a nonnarratological level, a sonic and visual diversity that has become a core element in all of European (urban) spaces, and therefore, an indispensable element in European cinema, as I argue.

That is, Frears's earlier multiethnic London classics, as well as his more recent *Dirty Pretty Things*, though expressing a diversity of criticism directed at Britain's and Europe's interior politics and global capitalism, help to compose an audio-visual depiction of London, and thereby of a metonymic European urban space. Such urbanity stands for transnational citizenship, for diversity and multiethnicity, in addition to the critique of socioeconomic inequalities associated with a globalized Europe. These films reconstruct and revise the sounds and sights of Europe. These elements of European film become extremely vital in today's Europe, especially considering the existing, and increasing, xenophobia in Europe of the new millennium. Most existing scholarship has engaged with a multitude of themes (Thatcherism, space and place, identity construction, national/British identity, occult economies and organ mafia, exploitation of immigrants, and so forth) that these films invite us to scrutinize. Some of that scholarship, even if indirectly, also foregrounds the issues of decentrality, multilocality, and diversity that I discuss in Akın's cinema and, above, in Kusturica's Balkan films.

Paired with the economic critique present in these films, and the filmic style in the complex narratives, I propose that Frears's characters diversify and ultimately highlight a multilocal and decentralized Europe. The characters, who represent a variety of political, philosophical, and lifestyle positions that at times overlap and at times stand opposed to each other (socialist, capitalist, entrepreneur, intellectual, homosexual, queer, heterosexual, patriarch, xenophobic, racist, middle-class, lower-class, white person, person of color, immigrant, legal citizen, undocumented person), help to diversify on a sonic level the soundscapes of London, and on a textual/narrative level, they continue to undermine the monolithic imagination of a national self, in this case of Britishness. Linguistically, English, for example, appears in a variety of forms, as do other languages from within and outside the traditional European language families. While the characters in *Dirty Pretty Things* state their perceived invisibility in Europe, within the film's narrative they make themselves visible and audible for the final economic transaction and for their eventual flight from London, even if using fake documentation. Frears's films not only make these previously invisible figures of European cinema visible and audible—affective portrayals that linger in the viewers' memory—but these films also forcefully revise xenophobic/hegemonic media images and stereotypical use of accent, skin color, and specific clothing, which the media have consistently foregrounded as a threatening and alienating Otherness.[39]

A look at Frears's depiction of multiethnic sexual relationships might result in similar observations about diversity. Discussing Omar and Jonny's relationship in *My Beautiful Laundrette*, Swamy notes that the protagonists are neither hiding their sexuality nor celebrating it, and therefore "their orientation becomes no more and no less than it deserves to be."[40] This simple yet stunning observation can be applied generally to the narrative strategies involving characters of different ethnicities, sexual orientations, and economic statuses. Like Frears, Akın uses a diversity of characters, whose diversity is part of the narrative, yet by neither "hiding" this diversity nor celebrating it for an ethnographic gaze, the films tell a variety of stories about love, intrigue, loss, family relationships, and so on, without misusing or overusing ethnic, racial, sexual, and economic differences. Thus, Frears's and Akın's multiethnic, multilingual, and otherwise diverse Europe becomes normalized for its audience. The cinematic diversity becomes the grid where life in Europe takes place. There are also films that actively engage with the topic of migration, race, and ethnicity, and those films even more directly elaborate on questions of European multiethnicity, mobility, and immobility, as I will discuss next.

Matthieu Kassovitz, Yamina Benguigui, and Philippe Lioret

Will Higbee states that over "the past twenty years, in France, as elsewhere in Europe, cinema has produced an increasing number of films that engage with the thematics of immigration (both legal and illegal)."[41] These characters often have a family history tied to previously (French) colonized places in the Maghreb (Algeria, Tunisia, and Morocco).[42] In French cinema, the depiction of these postcolonial immigrants, or of their offspring, has changed from an immigrant cinema in the 1970s, to the *beur* cinema of the 1980s (often filmed by filmmakers who have a migratory background themselves or who are the children of immigrants) and banlieue cinema of the 1990s (filmmakers who depict life in the banlieues) as discussed in detail by Carrie Tarr,[43] to a more diversified cinema of the 2000s. In the new millennium, French directors of North African origin have "begun adopting a broader range of modes of production and genres and now assume a greater variety of roles on both sides of the camera."[44] In this context, Sylvie Durmelat and Vinay Swamy's essay collection depicts the vast array of recent trends in cinema made by French directors of North African descent, notwithstanding some production and funding difficulties that remain for these (often still) nonmainstream French filmmakers.[45]

As discussed in my introduction, these trends, although slightly time-lapsed due to the immigration histories, are similar in the Turkish German contexts. A more varied mode of production, with broader themes and topics for the filmmakers and actors with and without a migratory background, becomes normalized across European cinema as the new millennium begins. Higbee links the growing range of ethnically diverse characters (including immigrant characters from a descent other than North Africa) in contemporary French cinema to the socioeconomic and cultural shifts and changes that have taken place in Europe and around the globe, where "neoliberal globalization" has led to "new waves of economic immigration" to the European Union.[46] This in turn has elicited state and European policymakers' anxieties about the outer European borders, as well their desire to control more than ever the influx of non-European trespassers. Philip Lioret's *Welcome* is a filmic representation of this problem, as I will discuss further below. Now, however, I will start my discussion of transnational French examples with the first banlieue film to gain global attention.

A film that has noticeably influenced Akın's *Short Sharp Shock*, Mathieu Kassovitz's *La Haine* (1995) is the first commercially successful banlieue film. The film depicts the friendship of three young Frenchmen of Jewish eastern European, North African, and sub-Saharan African descent (Vinz, Said, and Hubert, respectively). All three live in the banlieues, the outskirts of Paris. They share a glimpse into their lives, in the course of a twenty-four-hour window, as they are exposed to prejudice, inequality, and police violence.

Quite similar in genre, style, and tone to *Short Sharp Shock*, *La Haine* diversifies sights and sounds of European cinema. Interrogating the film from the perspective of a multiethnic and multilingual European cinema reveals that the film articulates such a diversification, highlighting fashion, music, vernacular, and popular culture as experienced and lived by the protagonists. However, as much as Kassovitz's film can be seen as a multiethnic urban thriller—by now a cult classic—with its very own noirish aesthetics, language, and sound, as Ginette Vincendeau has elaborated on,[47] it is as much a harsh critique of the past and present racism and xenophobia prevalent in the (un)employment and living conditions of the protagonists in (then-contemporary) 1990s Paris. This situation is marked as the result of a segregated, economically disadvantaged, and socially marginalized history of non-European (non-Catholic) migration to France, and the living situations of many of them in the banlieues in Parisian suburbia.

More than "4.4 million people live in the toughest parts of the banlieues classed as priority zones, where segregated along race and class lines, they face what [President] Hollande has called 'unbearable discrimination.'"[48] A 2015 article in *The Guardian*, entitled "'Nothing's Changed': 10 Years after French Riots, *Banlieues* Remain in Crisis," by Angelique Chrisafis, refers to the Parisian riots of 2005—which itself is already another ten years after Kassovitz's film—and points to the continuously bad living conditions of the inhabitants of the banlieues in Parisian high-rise suburbs such as La Grande Borne, Essone, or Gringy. In Essone, for example, general unemployment is double the national average at 22 percent, and if only counting youth, it is more than 40 percent, and three in five children live below the poverty line.[49] In addition, citizens of these neighborhoods are constantly discriminated against based on their skin color or the origins of their parents or grandparents. These neighborhoods lack services, education, hope, and respect, as the interviewees in the news article state. A woman from the banlieues said: "People here just want to be treated like normal citizens, not second-class citizens." Gringy's Communist mayor, Philippe Rio, specified: "We need more schools, more justice, better policing."

Discussing *La Haine*, Wayne criticizes the uncritical cultural advocates of Europe that promote a European diversity that is blind to economic inequalities. He reiterates the importance of class differences and economic inequalities that need to be addressed: "Trapped within a culturally hermetic discourse, the heterogeneity that the advocates of cultural plurality advocate, will reach no further than the middle class for whom the material conditions for the good life are already to some extent in place. Travel further down the social ladder and it is clear that a discourse about cultural heterogeneity must be articulated with a critique of the material conditions in which people live and culture is produced."[50]

Kassovitz began writing the script in 1993, the day a second-generation French man of North African origin died while in police custody.[51] Following this mysterious death, riots broke out in the banlieues; similarly, *La Haine*'s opening is marked by riots in the banlieues, which begin after the arrest and beating of a young French man of North African origin. In France, riots in the banlieues have been a reaction to a lasting phenomenon of police violence and continued discrimination. In 2005 renewed riots erupted in the banlieues following the death of two young boys who were hiding from police. The benevolent voices of Socialist politicians such as Hollande to end inequality and discrimination did not bring the desired change. Ten years after the 2005 riots, conditions had not improved much.[52] Twenty years after its release, *La Haine* stays valid as a controversial, social realist depiction of the lives of three ethnically diverse friends in the banlieues. At the same time, as Vincedeau reminds us, "*La haine* . . . captured a young generation on the brink, caught between French culture and that of their parents, and in love with American rap music and cinema. . . . *La haine* has social relevance, but it also possesses a raw energy and all the ingredients of a cult movie: a young director, attractive young stars, humor, violence, style—in one word, cool. *La haine* speaks of France but succeeds in transcending the national borders."[53]

In other words, it is transnational in its language and reach. The film is produced by French companies (Studio Image, Canal+, Cofinergie 6, Kasso Inc. Productions, Les Productions Lazennec, La Sept Cinéma) and by US and international companies such as Jodie Foster's Egg Pictures and the now-folded company Polygram Filmed Entertainment. Despite depicting a French setting and protagonists, its topic of violence, discrimination, and socioeconomic inequality finds resonance in other European cities as well as in the United States.[54]

In the French context, films such as *La Haine* have also been discussed as undermining a monolithic white French identity. Similar to John Kirk's discussion of Black British cinema, Guy Austin has pointed out that early beur cinema of the 1980s (made by French directors of North African descent), with its urban settings, staged counter images to the white French heritage films of the 1980s.[55] In her analysis of generational and gendered questions in French banlieue cinema, Cristina Johnston concludes that many banlieue films "demonstrate a far more pluralistic reality than the republican model is yet ready to admit. The hybridity which thus emerges can therefore be seen as leading towards a renegotiation of the French republican model . . . . The figure of 'the other' is no longer placed beyond the confines of the national in linguistic, social, or any other terms, but rather is firmly embedded within the national, modifying and challenging from within, and underlining the existence of a far more pluralistic and plurilingual reality."[56]

The "pluralistic and plurilingual reality" of *La Haine*—as well as its genre and noirish aesthetics of a crime movie, reminiscent of a Scorsese-esque New York gangster film of the 1970s, set in the outskirts of a European city—influenced Akın's first feature film, *Short Sharp Shock*. Even if *Short Sharp Shock* is not as openly a political film criticizing the socioeconomic situation of its protagonists, both films, similar in style and tone, help to popularize a new European genre: that of the European gangster movie. Clearly set in the multiethnic and multilingual context of European urbanity, these films help to diversify European cinema, its stories, genres, settings, casting, and soundtrack, while also depicting a milieu previously unknown in European cult classics.

Two decades later, the themes of the banlieue classic *La Haine* are revisited, and this time, new, perhaps even optimistic images, are disseminated from the French banlieues as seen in Abd Al Malik's *Qu'Allah bénisse la France* (*May Allah Bless France!*, 2015). While keeping the style of the archetypal predecessor, *May Allah Bless France!* circulates imaginings of possible ways forward by telling the autobiographical story of novelist and rapper Al Malik growing up in the projects of Strasbourg, France. Finally, the banlieues have even arrived in the mainstream shows of US streaming services: the Netflix original series *Marseille*, created by Dan Franck, is a much-criticized French crime show that depicts the city of Marseilles, including its banlieues near the city center, featuring Gérard Depardieu and Benoît Magimel as French politicians in the midst of Marseilles's mafia, banlieue criminality, and political conspiracy.[57]

Augmenting my categories of multiethnic and polyphonic diversity in European cinema, I read Yamina Benguigui's *Inch'Allah Dimanche* (Hopefully Sunday, 2001) as a creative, postmemory experience of migration. *Inch'Allah Dimanche* is different in style and content from *La Haine*, the first film to bring the banlieues to Film Festivals (e.g., to the Cannes Film Festival,1995). Benguigui's internationally acclaimed film (e.g., Critics Award at the Toronto International Film Festival), set in mid-1970s France, tells the story of migration and life in France, beginning in Algeria. It is a film about Zouina (Fejria Deliba), who together with her three children and her mother-in-law embarks on a ferry to reunite with her husband across the Mediterranean in France. The film gives a fictional narrative—focusing on an individual and her family—that refers to the historic moment in 1974 when foreign families, for example from Algeria, reunited in France due to the "*regroupement familial*" ("family reunion") laws that the French government issued for foreign workers.[58] With films such as *Inch'Allah Dimanche*, as well as Benguigui's earlier documentaries *Mémoires d'immgrés, l'héritage maghrébin* (Immigrant memories, Maghrebi heritage, 1997) about North African memories of immigration to France, French cinema opens up new approaches to history and the conception of home, inviting a broader viewing audience to participate in this history and "virtual home."[59] Referring to Benguigui's cinema, Isabelle McNeill states that Benguigui "highlights the missing foundations of her cultural identity in France: her parents' experiences of immigration, which were both silenced by her parents themselves and excluded from official discourses about the history of France and national debates about identity and ethnicity. . . . The reconstruction of these absent foundations through filmmaking can therefore be seen as a means of shaping a discursive and affective environment in order to foster a more stable relation between lived space and the subjective space of identity."[60]

While elaborating on the history of migration in her fictional and documentary work, Benguigui diversifies so-called French history, and by extension European history. The inclusion of a particular historic narrative and of items associated with the material culture of immigration in the mise-en-scène—the mixing of props, costumes, and sounds of actual families with nonpersonal props—personalizes and authenticates these textual and sonic elements within a European context, making them as much part of the filmic history of France and Europe, as of the history of the individuals and their offspring who migrated to or were born in France.

The soundtrack, in particular, consists of a mix of French, Algerian, and other Arabic music, which aurally diversifies the sonic memory of the 1970s. Musicians include, for example, French alternative and jazz musician Alain Blesing, the British instrumental rock musicians of The Shadows, and Berber Algerian musician Idir. These musicians provide a musical memory of 1970s France, which includes the diversity of sounds as experienced in the private and public spheres of immigration, making it a part of a more general soundtrack of the 1970s.

Such filmic memorialization of time, history, and sound, especially in relation to immigration, whether in the form of fiction or documentary, is also a strategy of Akın's filmmaking—especially if we consider his documentary

We Forgot to Return, which was a commissioned episode of the TV series *Denk ich an Deutschland* (When I think of Germany) by the German public TV station Westdeutscher Rundfunk (WDR). The first documentary of Akın, *We Forgot to Return* tells the story of his family's migration to Hamburg, thematically similar to Scorsese's 1974 documentary *Italianamerican*, where the American director interviews his parents in New York about their experiences living in New York as Italian Americans. Drawing a complicated web of familial, vocational, and friendship-related connections, Akın's film also includes conversations with his parents. Starting in Hamburg-Altona and moving to Istanbul and to the Turkish Black Sea Coast, the documentary foreshadows the travel that would come to determine the fictional *The Edge of Heaven* a few years later. As is typical for Akın, the film mixes musical, temporal, linguistic, and film-historical references to create a new history of migration, which is very personal, on the one hand (he interviews his family and friends), and very global on the other (by using global music of the 1970s, making intertextual references to Scorsese, and depicting the story of economic migration, the experiences of foreignness, bureaucratic and legal limitations of travel, and so on). In creating a cinematic memory of the 1970s, memorializing the migratory past as much as the sound of the time, which has a connection to contemporary life, Akın's documentary resembles Benguigui's fictional and documentary work. With these documentaries, both artists further augment a historical moment of their lives or of the lives of their parents' generation. They make it a part of, and in some cases challenge, existing narratives of national or regional histories, while at the same time expanding the genre of personal documentary and history film made in Europe.[61]

I turn to present-day France to conclude the section on France with Philippe Lioret's *Welcome* (2009)—a film that offers a narrative about a sympathetic refugee, similar to Akın's Ayten in *The Edge of Heaven*. This is a critically acclaimed and internationally awarded film that directly addresses and visualizes the physical act of contemporary migration into "Fortress Europe," and the challenges faced by non-European migrants without travel authorizations such as visas trying to reach Great Britain from the coast of France in Calais. The film narrates the friendship that develops between a middle-aged, sullen French man with marital problems, who is a swim instructor in a public pool, and a young Kurdish refugee in the camps in Calais, who is trying to reach England for a better life and to reunite with his girlfriend (he will try swimming across the channel by the end of the film). While the previously introduced films were more interested in the daily living situations and conditions of migrants and their offspring, *Welcome*, which also depicts the struggles and living conditions of illegal immigrants in transit in Calais, is about the impediments of legal movement and the pursuit of happiness as a nonwhite, non-European, non-Christian *sans papiers* (undocumented/illegal) im/migrant.

Will Higbee discusses *Welcome* with two other migration films, Merzak Allouache's Algerian-French *Harragas* (2009) and Tony Gatlif's *Indignados* (2012), which like *Welcome*, also portray young non-Europeans who try to move to and within Europe.[62] In this context, there are ever more films, especially documentaries, that deal directly with pressing questions of refugees, such as Gianfranco Rosi's award-winning Italian documentary *Fuocoammare* (*Fire at Sea*, 2016), which documents the refugee situation on the Italian island of Lampedusa, or Danish filmmakers Andreas Koefoed's *Et Hjem I Verden* (*At Home in the World*, 2015), about five refugee children in Denmark, and Michael Graversen's *Drømmen om Danmark* (*Dreaming of Denmark*, 2015), which follows the fate of a fifteen-year-old Afghan teenager and his travels through Denmark and Italy in search of a home. These documentaries offer a Mediterranean and a Nordic perspective on the discussion of refugees and their hardships during their travels in Europe.

In the French examples from above, all of the protagonists in the films ultimately face the at-times-fatal physical, psychological, and emotional borders of Fortress Europe. *Welcome*, like the other French co-productions, addresses a diversity of themes directly related to the topic of immigration and refugee migration (such as Fortress Europe; hardships, pains, dreams, and goals of refugees; reasons for leaving a home country; the criminalization of helping illegal immigrants in France; and so forth), but it is also a film about two love stories (Bilal and his girlfriend, and Simon and his wife Marion).[63] Perhaps it is through these love stories that the film achieves greater acknowledgement of these hardships within the broader public. By binding the political into the narrative of the amorous, the film perhaps even fruitfully—it was a commercial success—"continues the tradition of a return to political engagement in French cinema of the late 1990s that was guided by a sense of civic responsibility rather than partisan political dogma."[64]

In terms of my inquiry into the efforts to diversify European cinema, Lioret's film offers another example from a filmmaker without a traditional minority background. By telling a moving story that humanizes and generates empathy for the protagonist (an undocumented/illegal immigrant), *Welcome* brings the protagonist's sound and sight—that is, his name, his language, his accent, and his skin color—as unthreatening elements onto the "popular" cinematic screen of France and Europe. It was awarded the LUX Prize in 2009, two years after Akın's *The Edge of Heaven*, and both films use affect and love stories to lend a human dimension to illegal immigration, the impediments of travel for non-EU Europeans, and police surveillance. Thus, Ayten in *The Edge of Heaven* and Bilal in *Welcome* are both strong, likable, and attractive characters, who are humanized for a larger European audience. Thereby they become protagonists that invite audience identification and reject the stereotypical image of illegal immigrants as threatening. Ultimately, by awarding the LUX Prize to two films that represent "illegal" immigration via love stories within three years, the European Parliament shows self-reflexivity in immigration matters and foregrounds problematic aspects of the proverbial Fortress Europe and its travel regulations, which are shown to in fact cause human tragedies and inequalities.

Michael Haneke

Austrian auteur Michael Haneke's *Caché* intervenes in history writing within European cinema in similar ways as Benguigui did with *Inch'Allah Dimanche*, and Akın did with *We Forgot to Return*. German Austrian director Haneke is a true transnational filmmaker, who made critically acclaimed and award-winning films in German, such as *Der Siebte Kontinent* (*Seventh Continent*, 1987), *Benny's Video*, 1992, *Funny Games*, 1997, *Das weisse Band, eine deutsche Kindergeschichte* (*The White Ribbon*, 2009); in French, such as *La Pianiste* (*The Piano Teacher*, 2001) and *Caché* (2005); and in English, *Funny Games* (2007). In his films, whether set in contemporary Europe or in past periods, Haneke engages in a critical depiction of his subjects' living conditions in modern society, whether this is a sexually repressive, emotionally callous, or otherwise restrictive context. According to Fatima Naqvi, Haneke's films portray irrational violence and victimhood as possibly having "very rationally explicable roots in a Western European way of life."[65] Haneke himself sees this "Western European way of life" as marked by isolation, invisibility, alienation, and an obscenity of violence. Haneke's films expose these symptoms of this lifestyle, which eventually lead to an escalation of violence. In a different context, Naqvi writes, "Violence is a necessary defense mechanism against such willed invisibility."[66] In Haneke's films it is frequently the triangular bourgeois family that falls victim to these phenomena, as seen, for example, in *Benny's Video* or *Funny Games*.

The viewing experience of Haneke's films is often a painful one in contrast to the pleasurable entertainment frequently associated with the Hollywood mainstream cinema. In the DVD's extra features to *Funny Games* (1997), Haneke explains that his viewers can be actively involved in the cinematic experience. Especially with the DVD versions, this means that they can stop the film whenever they like, fast forward, or rewind the film. The painful viewing of the film is a choice the viewers make, and therefore they participate as audience members in deciding how much they would like to experience the film's violence.

Keeping the questions of this chapter in mind, I would like to concentrate on Haneke's French-language multinational coproduction *Caché*. Haneke's film is a prime example of a European transnational coproduction. It was coproduced by Austrian (Wega Films), German (Bavaria Film), French (Les Films du Losange), and Italian (BIM Distribuzione) companies, with further funds provided by

Eurimages (European cinema support fund), and ten other international companies, television channels, and film institutes. Filmed in French, set mainly in Paris, centering around a bourgeois, educated elite, the film does not represent its transnationalism of production on first sight; neither does one see right away its connection to France's Algerian war, France's colonialism, the Maghrebi massacre in Paris on October 17, 1961, and the feelings of personal or collective guilt that might have resulted from these events. Yet Haneke's film is all of this and more by building its narrative slowly and opening up, psychologically, to the protagonist's personal history, and to his (indirect) involvement in the nation's colonial and postcolonial history and present.

Caché tells the story of Georges and Majid, two men whose lives were entangled through the French-Algerian war. The film is set in contemporary France. Georges is married, has a son, and works as a host of a literary-review television show. Haunting videos received in the mail terrorize him and his family; these are surveillance-type videos that depict his house or his family. Slowly Georges finds out that these videos are linked to his past. As the narrative progresses, it is revealed that as a boy Georges was jealous of an orphaned Algerian boy, Majid, whose parents were killed in the Algerian War, and whom Georges's family wanted to adopt. Georges intervened, and because of his childish, yet malevolent intrigues, Majid was sent to an orphanage. Having lived a quite different life than Georges, Majid has a son, too. At the end of the film, Majid kills himself in front of Georges's eyes, cutting his own throat. When they were boys, Georges had forced Majid to kill a chicken similarly. The present suicidal cutting mirrors the past event, and thereby Majid renders visible the agony and sadness he lived through, brought to him by France and by Georges: France killed his parents in the war, and Georges prevented him from living with a new adopted French family. These events slowly trigger feelings of guilt on a personal and collective level regarding what happened to Majid's parents and how it affected him in the long term.

In the tradition of *Benny's Video* and *Funny Games*, *Caché* uses an individual who seemingly is the intruder (terrorizer/perpetrator) into the everyday order of a seemingly happy, affluent, bourgeois family in modern times. Yet such intruders in Haneke's films help to revisit questions of the complicated relationship between perpetrator and victim. In *Caché*'s case, the "intruder" is certainly linked to the Algerian war and the Paris Massacre of 1961, which through the film demand acknowledgment and responsibility. At the same time, the "intruder" brings to the foreground the personal wrongdoings of a boy, who caused further psychological damage to an orphaned child, denying him a second chance to live with a family.

In terms of diversification of European cinema, *Caché* elaborates and augments, similarly to Benguigui's *Inch'Allah Dimanche*, historical and personal narratives about the past and present. Haneke contributes to the diversification of French history by including the fictionalized, personalized story of two Algerian French destinies. Juxtaposing the lives of Georges and Majid (and their sons), he presents these as distinct perspectives on and outcomes of the same event. At the same time, Haneke forces, more than invites, his audience to recognize these aspects of cruelty within recent and not-so-recent French history. Neither of these events can be diminished in meaning, either by comparing it to the larger atrocities of the Holocaust,[67] or as the wrongdoings of a minor. Each event, personal and collective, has traumatic and fatal consequences for the characters involved.

While Haneke thus engages with the massacre in Paris in 1961 and the Algerian war through the intersecting story of Majid and Georges, Akın engages with the displacement and subsequent global migration of Armenians by following the story of one Armenian man and his daughters who separately escape from the Ottoman Empire during World War I. At best, Akın's film received mixed reviews for its treatment of the topic. As I will briefly discuss in this book's conclusion, I argue that the film deserves more credit for its aesthetic experimentation as a visualization of displacement, violence, and human suffering. Akın creatively engaged with a topic that frequently stirs emotions and evokes resistance in Turkey, where the topic is considered controversial. The different positions toward the issue are increasingly discussed in both public and academic settings. News magazines such as the Armenian Turkish *Agos*, as well as Turkish academics in the United States such as Taner Akçam and Fatma Müge Göçek, or in Turkey, such as Ayhan Akdar and US-educated scholar Yektan Türkyılmaz, engage with the Armenian-Ottoman relations and histories from a variety of disciplines and perspectives.[68]

Nuri Bilge Ceylan

Turkish cinema is part of European cinema. Turkish filmmaker Nuri Bilge Ceylan, like the previously mentioned European auteurs, contributes to the diversification of both its sights and sounds. Turkish cinema is a long-neglected aspect of European cinema. Iordonova, a scholar who truly works within a transnational framework and who has voiced her criticism against the lack of eastern and central European cinema scholarship within broader European cinema studies, includes, or at least mentions, Turkish cinema in her work, aligning it within the narrative of a broader European cinema scholarship. In her important book *24 Frames*, for example, Iordonova edited and compiled articles by scholars, film personnel, and critics, who introduce the cinema of the Balkans to a wider film-studies audience. Iordonova laments the exclusion of many directors, in particular of women filmmakers in this limited space; she also addresses the absence of Turkey's cinema specifically in her introduction. This is important because Turkish cinema, when discussed in terms of regional affiliations, is either grouped among Middle Eastern, North African, or, more recently, Balkan cinema, but rarely under the moniker of European cinema.[69] This is especially striking when considering that since the 1990s, and more so since 2001, Turkish cinema has profited from European funding structures for film, as Halle has pointed out.[70] There have been European coproductions with Germany, and Eurimages and MEDIA have supported the funding, distribution, and theatrical releases of Turkish cinematic works. Yet often these films are not promoted as examples of a European cinema but are framed and singled out as examples of Turkish cinema. These promotional strategies ultimately essentialize and even Orientalize Turkish content. However, as Halle states, often such Turkish European coproductions—such as the pro-Kurdish filmmaker Yeşim Ustaoğlu's *Güneşe Yolculuk* (*Journey to the Sun*, 1999)—are opposed to Turkish governmental positions, do not receive much Turkish funding, and do not actually represent any mainstream "Turkish" stance. Rather such films are stories supported and funded by the European Union.[71]

While Halle's criticism is justified and explains many of the different ways the production and marketing of films influence their reading inside and outside a particular nation-state, it is also important to note that films from any national context could be similarly diverse in their content and reception inside and outside national parameters. The critically acclaimed and certainly nonmainstream Ceylan, whose films are funded with sources form Turkey (TRT, NBC, Imaj, et al.) and Bosnia-Herzogovina (production 2006), and more recently also from Germany (Bredok Filmproduction) and France (Memento Films Production), should certainly not be regarded as a filmmaker whose films represent an essentialized notion of "Turkishness," or an Orientalizing of the Turkish Other, for a European audience. Ceylan's cinema is an art cinema that for a variety of audiences might have different entry points—perhaps Orientalizing for some, but existential, philosophizing, and simply aesthetically pleasing in its formal language for others.

Ceylan is an unusual filmmaker in Turkey. First a photographer, he became a filmmaker without formally studying film; his degree was in electrical engineering,[72] though he attended courses in photography and film while a student at Boğazici (Bosporus) University in Istanbul. Referring to his earlier work, Asuman Suner states that he prefers to work in small crews and performs multiple functions on his films, often producing, writing, directing, and acting in his work.[73] He thereby manages to keep directorial and authorial control over his films. Also unusual is his rejection of cinema. Ceylan states in an interview that he is not a cinephile, that, in fact, he does not really like films, even detests most (contemporary) films, including the ones from film festivals such as Cannes. He continues that he prefers reading and gets inspiration from literature. One main influence Ceylan names, especially in the context of *Bir zamanlar anadolu'da* (*Once Upon a Time in Anatolia*, 2012), is Russian writer Anton Chekhov.[74] Yet this noncinephile director is himself an acclaimed guest at the Cannes Film Festival, where he has won several awards for his films, including the Palme D'Or in 2014, the Best Director Award in 2008, the FIBRESCI Movie Critics award in 2006, and the Grand Jury Prize twice, in 2002 and 2011. Despite being celebrated at film festivals and in film circles in Turkey, his low-budget films remain little known in Turkey, far from being popular box-office hits. Nonetheless, they are an important contribution to and engage with diversifying contemporary European cinema. In the following section, I would like to give examples of Ceylan's cinema by briefly discussing *Once Upon a Time in Anatolia* and *Kış uykusu* (*Winter Sleep*, 2014).

Once Upon a Time is set in rural southeastern Turkey over the course of one night and one morning. A convoy of police officers, a federal prosecutor, a village physician, and some alleged murderers travel through the night across unlit and mountainous landscapes to locate a murder victim. In the morning hours, the body is found and brought to the village hospital for further autopsy, and the alleged murderers are escorted to prison. In the course of the calm film, many other universal themes such as friendship, rivalry, revenge, adultery, suicide, discrimination, unfulfilled life and love, unhappiness, depression, and urban/rural living are addressed via the various characters and their dialogues, monologues, and voice-overs. The 157-minute-long, slow-paced movie is driven by an abundance of initial long shots, few cuts, the interiority of its characters, and a special use of voice, which Rob White calls a "disassociating, isolating device."[75] Ceylan, who is interested in the inner world of the characters, states that he wanted the audience to be unsure if certain words are spoken or thought, an effect he creates by showing figures from the back, or by capturing the characters in close-ups or medium close ups not moving their lips as the voices continue their speech. He thereby tried to show the "inner psychology" of the characters.[76] Ceylan's films are generally marked by calm interiority and pensive existentialism. His characters are overcome with feelings of guilt and melancholy, and often face their own failed human interactions. An example for such a figure is the widowed prosecutor, who narrates his complicated relationship toward his deceased wife in *Once Upon a Time*: shortly after giving birth to their daughter, the prosecutor's beautiful wife, as the viewer and he himself find out in the course of the film, committed suicide as a form of revenge to her unfaithful husband. We learn about this event through the almost Socratic dialogue between the doctor and the prosecutor.

Often emotions and the interiority of thoughts are not verbalized or expressed; other times, when they are expressed vocally, they are not always understood and lead to miscommunications. This is also true of Ceylan's *Winter Sleep*. Similar in style, tone, and mood to *Once Upon a Time*, *Winter Sleep* also takes place in rural Turkey, yet this time it is a world heritage site, Cappadocia, a naturally rocky landscape honeycombed with systems of cave-like underground settlements filled with Byzantine art. As *National Geographic* states, in the

Göreme Valley, "thousands of years ago humans took a cue from Mother Nature and began carving an incredible chamber and tunnel complex into the soft rock. Beginning in the fourth century A.D., an urbanized—but underground—cultural landscape was created here."[77] Although the setting is a more touristic region than the Anatolian mountains in *Once Upon a Time*, the viewer experiences a similarly new façade of these settings. It is the cold, muddy, and gray winter season in the mountains. The setting invites the audience to experience the unhappy inner village lives of the poor, socioeconomically marginalized inhabitants who have difficulties paying their rent to the wealthy protagonists. The main figures are affluent, intellectual ex-urbanites (a middle-aged writer and ex–theater actor [Aydın] with his estranged younger wife [Nihal], and the writer's divorced sister [Necla]), who inherited the homes in these mountains, and who for personal reasons choose to live and work in the modernized Cappadocia caves turned into a hotel. All characters are faced with sadness. Their emotions, thoughts, and actions are at times as honeycombed as the landscape around them. Several of the characters, especially the women, share a feeling of boredom in these natural caves that frame their lives and seem to express their captivation.

How do Ceylan's artfully composed and narrated stories in *Once Upon a Time* and *Winter Sleep* contribute to the diversification of European cinema in the way that, for example, Akın, Kusturica, Frears, and Benguigui do? In fact, Ceylan's films, in many ways, augment and extend the category of European cinema similarly to the above-mentioned filmmakers. First of all, Ceylan masterfully mixes the art house cinema (commonly used as a category for his films) with the topic of rural, folkloric Turkey, which within the history of Turkish cinema can be attributed to Yeşilçam's mainstream melodramas, as well as the political, Leftist cinema of Yılmaz Güney.[78] Ceylan brings a new combination of theme and form without overt political implications, but with an aesthetic sensibility that foregrounds photography, color, and composition within the formal language of film, as well as psychology, philosophy, and the interiority of the characters within the narrative of the film. Second, by focusing on rural and Anatolian settings outside of the urban settings overused in films, such as Istanbul, Ceylan gives these newer localities and their people and landscapes a cinematic presence not previously experienced. Whether these localities foreground a "thematic preoccupation" with "homecoming, leaving home, getting settled, and making commitments to relationships," or whether "the trope of belonging is often connected to the question of provinciality,"[79] these Anatolian, nonurban settings enjoy a newly composed and aestheticized visuality in Ceylan's cinema.

Thereby, films such as *Once Upon a Time* and *Winter Sleep* regain an indirect political dimension, I argue. The visualization of the undesirable and often forgotten sides of southeastern Turkey as in *Once Upon a Time*—which is often stereotypically associated with terrorism; lesser-educated, underprivileged citizens;

underdeveloped villages and cities; and questions related to Kurdish sensibilities and life—elevates previously disregarded settings onto the global screens. Even the more touristic place in Cappadocia receives a new critical visuality, giving a glimpse into the socioeconomic difficulties as experienced in the village life, but also in the artful composition of landscape imageries that play out in Ceylan's long shots and carefully framed medium long shots, as in the scene depicting the married couple Nihal and Aydın. To give an example, in this scene, Nihal, like a captured princess, or the bird in the proverbial golden cage, is framed and fragmented by the wooden lattice window. She silently stares down from her room's window to the courtyard, where Aydın, her husband, stands, looking up at her. Aydin contemplates their relationship and his love silently, in his thoughts, which the audience hears in his voice-over, but Aydin knows and says that he will never express these thoughts to his wife directly, who looks at him during this voice-over. Furthermore, Ceylan's films engage with questions of female sexuality and gendered interaction. Even if these engagements are not at all times nonstereotypical (compared to the male leads, female figures seem less strong, and often still dependent on men), the director manages to address questions of Turkish femininities and sexualities as well as gender inequalities in the exclusively male-dominated worlds of *Once Upon a Time in Anatolia* as well as in his relationship films such as *Winter Sleep*.

It is this aspect of creating a new visuality for and sonic engagement with localities previously often excluded from art house cinema that reminds us in particular of Emir Kusturica and Akın, whose Romani settings and sounds expanded European cinema. Also similar to Akın, and in some ways to Frears and Benguigui, are the complex characters in Ceylan's movies, whether female or male. They help to undo stereotypes about Muslim and Turkish gender expectations. Whether this concerns patriarchal positions, secular urban, or nonsecular rural positions, sexual or other relationships between the genders, his characters portray a variety of opinions, philosophies, and lifestyles, and thereby help to undo one-dimensional stereotypes based on ethnicity, religion, and gender. Last but not least, the artistic contribution of Ceylan, whose films have been compared to Ingmar Bergman's cinema, and whose coloring and cinematic photography are praised for its artistry,[80] adds a new filmic language to European cinema. With his self-declared inspirations from Chekhov to Bergman,[81] Ceylan establishes a new school of filmmaking within European cinema.

The Ongoing Expansion of European Cinema

The small selection of films and filmmakers in this chapter does not do justice to the many other European films and filmmakers that have surfaced in recent years and that equally intriguingly engage in creative ways with questions of exile, migration, identity, and gender in Europe. There is, for example, Turkish French director Deniz Gamze Ergüven's debut feature *Mustang* (2015), which presents a completely new dimension of diversification within European cinema. The visually appealing film tells the story of five orphaned yet joyful sisters in rural Turkey, who increasingly experience the limitations of the patriarchal and dogmatic regulations imposed on them by their caregivers. The LUX Prize winner of 2015 and France's official selection and nominee for the Academy Awards in 2016, *Mustang* is set entirely in Turkey, at the Black Sea Coast, and has an all-Turkish cast and linguistic soundtrack (the original score is by Australian musician Warren Ellis and includes a song by Turkish psychedelic rock band Baba Zula, known from Akın's *Crossing the Bridge: The Sound of Istanbul*). The cast, set, and soundtrack of *Mustang* not only reflect the changes that the European soundtrack has undergone, but also what types of stories nowadays can become successful in national and international movie theaters. Even if one could criticize the film for the irregularities of dialects spoken by some figures in the village in terms of the soundtrack, and a privileged Westernized perspective on a dysfunctional, patriarchal Turkish family in terms of the plot, *Mustang* expands the scope of European filmmaking, and includes an empowering voice and perspective that contain a sensibility toward gender inequalities.

Other films absent from this chapter, but which equally should be mentioned, are the work of critically acclaimed Croatian Swiss director Andrea Štaka, whose 2006 *Das Fräulein* (*Fraulein*) as well as her 2014 *Cure: das Leben einer Andern* (*Cure: The Life of Another*) have not only brought questions of Balkan identity, language, exile, trauma, and mobility to the wider European screen, but have equally foregrounded a feminine experience of exile. Štaka's films are multilingual productions, with an international cast, predominantly from Croatia and Serbia, and they portray exile and identity at the crossroads of Balkan, Central European, and Swiss settings. There are also other films, such as Austrian Persian filmmaker Arash T. Hirahi's *Ein Augenblick Freiheit* (*For a Moment Freedom*, 2008), Belgian Olivier Masset-Sepasse's *Illégal*, 2010, or French Claire Denis's *Beau Travail* (1999), which contribute from various angles to the diversification of European cinema. They engage with questions of legal and illegal migration, racism, alienation, guilt, colonial history, and socioeconomic hardships in the past and present. Others present a happy cosmopolitanism of cultural hybridity such as British Damien O'Donnell's *East is East* (1999), Indian British Gurinder Chadha's *Bend It Like Beckham* (2002), or even Indian Mira Nair's multinational coproduction *Monsoon Wedding* (2001), which was coproduced with European and non-European funds. Analyzing in more detail these films and the ones briefly discussed in this chapter will produce a more complex, expanded, and differentiated perspective on European cinema and its visualization and sounding of an ever more diverse Europe.

Despite the limited selection of European films presented here, taken together they diversify our image of the European cinemascape in terms of its audiovisual output. The need for the important work that directors and writers do in sounding and visualizing difference—whether their films politicize, merely entertain, or perform a combination of both—increases as xenophobia, racism, and discrimination against the socioeconomically disadvantaged continues. That is, the films acoustically and visually react and adapt to an ever more diversifying notion of "Europe," however one might now define this geographic and cultural space called Europe. Having been at the forefront of this movement for more than two decades, Akın's films have continuously informed this cinematic project of diversification. Whether they tell a story of love, music, gentrification, or cross-generational family relationships, his films help to present an audiovisual imagination of an ethnically, linguistically, and socioeconomically diverse Europe on screen, much like Kusturica, Frears, Kassovitz, Benguigui, Lioret, Haneke, and Ceylan do in their cinematic work.

Notes

1. *Banlieue* is the French term referring to a prefab housing area as can be found, for example, in the suburbs of Paris. Stereotypically, banlieues are associated with lower income, crime, and underprivileged citizens, including migrants. The banlieues have also been used as settings for films in France and by now form a genre of its own.

2. Mica Nava, *Visceral Cosmopolitanism: Gender, Culture and the Normalization of Difference* (Oxford: Berg, 2007), 13, 162.

3. Thomas Elsaesser, "European Cinema and the Postheroic Narrative: Jean-Luc Nancy, Claire Denis, and Beau Travail," *New Literary History* 43 (2012): 703.

4. Thomas Elsaesser, *European Cinema: Face to Face with Hollywood* (Amsterdam: Amsterdam University Press, 2005), 13.

5. Rivi mentions Michael Haneke in this context as an example for such a "new hybrid and decentralized Europe." Luisa Rivi, *European Cinema after 1989: Cultural Identity and Transnational Production* (New York: Palgrave, 2007), 10.

6. The words Göktürk uses are "multilingual," "multilocal," and "European." Deniz Göktürk, "Mobilität und Stillstand im Weltkino digital," in *Kultur als Ereignis*, ed. Özkan Ezli (Bielefeld, Germany: Transcript), 35.

7. Mary P. Wood, *Contemporary European Cinema* (London: Hodder Arnold, 2007), xi; Katrin Sieg, *Choreographing the Global in European Cinema and Theater* (New York: Palgrave Macmillan, 2008), 31.

8. Jill Forbes and Sarah Street, *European Cinema: An Introduction* (Houndsmills, UK: Palgrave, 2000), 43; Jill Forbes, "La Haine," in *European Cinema: An Introduction* (Houndsmills, UK: Palgrave, 2000), 177.

9. Wendy Everett, introduction to *European Identity in Cinema*, ed. Wendy Everett (Bristol, UK: Intellect, 2005) 9, 14.

10. Rosalind Galt and Karl Schoonover, "Introduction: The Impurity of Art Cinema," in *Global Art Cinema: New Theories and Histories,* eds. Galt and Schoonover (Oxford: Oxford University Press, 2010), 4.

11. Rosalind Galt, *The New European Cinema: Redrawing the Map* (New York: Columbia University Press, 2006); Michael Gott and Todd Herzog, introduction to *East, West, and Centre: Reframing Post-1989 European Cinema*, eds. Michael Gott and Todd Herzog (Edinburgh, UK: Edinburgh University Press, 2015), 1–19; Randall Halle, *The Europeanization of Cinema: Interzones and Imaginative Communities* (Urbana: University of Illinois Press, 2014), 7–9, 33, 108; Dina Iordanova, *Cinema of Flames: Balkan Film, Culture, and the Media* (London: BFI, 2001); Kristine Kotecki, "Europeanizing the Balkans at the Sarajevo Film Festival," *Journal of Narrative Theory* 44, no. 3 (2014); Mike Wayne, *The Politics of Contemporary European Cinema* (Bristol, UK: Intellect, 2002), 27ff.

12. Daniel J. Goulding, review of *Emir Kusturica* by Dina Iordanova, *Slavic Review* 63, no. 2 (2004): 390.

13. Iordanova, *Cinema of Flames*, 121.

14. For a more detailed discussion of Kusturica's filmography and biography, see Dan Halpern, "The (Mis)Directions of Emir Kusturica," *New York Times* May 8, 2005, accessed November 24, 2015, http://www.nytimes.com/2005/05/08/magazine/the-misdirections-of-emir-kusturica.html?_r=0; Dina Iordanova, *Emir Kusturica* (London: BFI, 2002).

15. Dan Halpern, "The (Mis)Directions of Emir Kusturica."

16. *Underground* (1995) was heavily criticized despite winning the Palme d'Or at Cannes. Some critics, such as French intellectual Alain Finkielkraut, claimed *Underground*, a satire about Yugoslavia's political situation from World War II to the 1990s, to be Serbian propaganda, because it was also partially financed with Serbian funds. In contrast, Dina Iordanova speculates that the reason the Cannes jury selected the controversial film for a prize might have been purely aesthetically and formally motivated. For a contextualization of *Underground*, global reactions to the film, and a Finkielkraut quote, see Iordanova, *Cinema of Flames*, 117. For a brief discussion of Kusturica's reaction to the criticism on *Underground* and a film review of *Black Cat*, see Howard Feinstein, "'*Black Cat, White Cat*:' Kusturica Returns to the Gypsy Life," *New York Times*, September 5, 1999, accessed November 24, 2015, http://www.nytimes.com/library/film/090599film-cat.html. For further discussions of *Underground*, see Iordonova, *Cinema of Flames*, 215.

17. *Black Cat* is Kusturica's first film after his more overtly political allegory, *Underground* (1995). For a review of *Black Cat*, see Janet Maslin, "Black Cat, White Cat (1998) Film Festival Review; Take Gypsies, Add the Danube and Mix Well with Jubilation," *New York Times Book Review*, October 3, 1998, accessed November 24, 2015, http://www.nytimes.com/movie/review?res=9b05efde1338f930a35 753c1a96e 958260.

18. For a discussion on Balkan films on the Yugoslav war and for Kusturica and Paskaljevic's animosity, see Iordonova, *Cinema of Flames*, 10, 135.

19. Dina Iordanova, *Cinema of Flames*, 213.

20. Dina Iordonova, *Cinema of Flames*, 213, 214.

21. Dina Iordonova, *Cinema of Flames*, 215.

22. For a discussion of the discrimination of Roma and Sinti in Austria, see Ursula Hemetek, "Applied Ethnomusicology in the Process of the Political Recognition of a Minority: A Case Study of the Austrian Roma," *Yearbook for Traditional Music* 38 (2006): 42–43. For discrimination in the Balkans, see, for example, Ioana Szeman, "'Gypsy Music' and Deejays: Orientalism, Balkanism, and Romani Musicians," *TDR: The Drama Review* 53, no. 3 (2009): 101, 109.

23. Iordonova and anthropologist Marko Živković, whom Iordanova cites, make suggestions that Romani in Balkan cinema might often be used as metonomies, showing the relationships between the Balkans and the "gypsies," and between western Europe and the Balkans. Iordanova phrases it as "Balkans to Europe as Gypsies to us," and Živković is quoted as stating:

"If the Balkans are perceived as a pariah and at the bottom of European hierarchies, one can expect to see the demon of metonymic misrepresentation declare Balkanites to be the Gypsies of Europe." Iordanova, *Cinema of Flames*, 216–217. Iordonova further suggests that there is a "'projective identification' in Yugoslav Roma" cinema. She sees films like Kusturica's *Dom za vesanje* (*Time of the Gypsies*, 1988) and Slobodan Šijan's *Who Is Singing Out There* (1984), who treat "Roma heritage with respect and feature memorable musical scores," as revealing "elements of this same 'projective identification' found in more recent examples." Iordonova, *Cinema of Flames*, 220.

24. Szeman discusses the multiple influences in Romani music (such as traditional Romanian music, Ottoman music, and western European musical traditions). She further stresses the negative effect of Balkanism that results from generalizations on Romani music. Szeman, "'Gypsy Music,'" 102–103.

25. Szeman, "'Gypsy Music,'" 101.

26. For examples of Romani stereotypes, see Szeman, "'Gypsy Music,'" 101; and Hemetek, "Applied Ethnomusicology," 42.

27. Referring to a Kusturica interview, Ioana Szeman discusses the implied accusation that gypsy music consists of mixed, previously existing, musical traditions, which she interprets as stressing the stereotype of the stealing gypsy. She also mentions that in other contexts, such as with western European musicians, this phenomenon is transformed into sampling, and does not feature as "stealing." Szeman, "'Gypsy Music,'" 109.

28. Szeman, "'Gypsy Music,'" 100.

29. John Kirk, "Urban Narratives: Contesting Place and Space in Some British Cinema from the 1980s," *Journal of Narrative Theory* 31, no. 3 (2001): 364. In a different context, Mike Wayne states about this cinema that "Asian and Black British cinema, while not unproblematic, offers much from which the mainstream and independent wings of the film industry could learn in the way it combines a popular cinematic idiom with an address to the culture and lives of 'minorities.'" Wayne, *Politics of Contemporary European Cinema*, 21.

30. Kirk, "Urban Narratives," 365.

31. Kirk, "Urban Narratives," 365.

32. Shital Pravinchandra, "Hospitality for Sale, or *Dirty Pretty Things*," *Cultural Critique* 85 (2013): 39.

33. Kirk, "Urban Narrative," 365.

34. Vinay Swamy, "Politicizing the Sexual, Sexualizing the Political: The Crossing of Political and Sexual Orientation in Stephen Frears's and Hanif Kureishi's *My Beautiful Laundrette* (1986)," *Comparative Literature Studies* 40, no. 2 (2003): 145.

35. John Kirk also references Kureishi himself, who has linked racism and class. Kirk, "Urban Narratives," 366.

36. Swamy uses these terms referring to the characters Omar and Johnny in *My Beautiful Laundrette*. Swamy, "Politicizing the Sexual," 156.

37. Pravinchandra convincingly discusses this aspect of the characters in *Dirty Pretty Things*. Pravinchandra, "Hospitality for Sale," 38.

38. Pravinchandra discusses this criticism of capitalism, occult capitalism, and also the transactional nature of interpersonal relationships in *Dirty Pretty Things*. Pravinchandra, "Hospitality for Sale," 42ff, 52, 56.

39. Berna Gueneli, "Reframing Islam: The Decoupling of Ethnicity from Religion in Turkish German Media," in "Framing Islam: Faith, Fascination, and Fear in Twenty-First Century Culture," special issue, *Colloquia Germanica* 47, no. 1–2 (2014, publ. 2017), 61–62.

40. Swamy, "Politicizing the Sexual," 155.

41. Will Higbee, "Hope and Indignation in Fortress Europe: Immigration and Neoliberal Globalization in Contemporary French Cinema," *SubStance* 43, no.1 (2014): 26.
42. Higbee, "Hope and Indignation," 26.
43. According to Guy Austin, beur cinema is made by second-generation North African–French (Algerian) immigrants, who made films in the suburban banlieues. These were in particular opposed to the French white heritage films of the 1980s. Carrie Tarr has written about beur and banlieue cinema in order to discuss the alternative inquiries about identity and ethnicity in French cinema. Guy Austin, *Contemporary French Cinema: An Introduction* (Manchester, UK: Manchester University Press, 2008), 48; Carrie Tarr, introduction to *Reframing Difference: Beur and Banlieue Filmmaking in France* (Manchester, UK: Manchester University Press/Palgrave, 2005), 1–25.
44. Higbee, "Hope and Indignation," 26.
45. Sylvie Durmelat and Vinay Swamy, eds. *Screening Integration: Recasting Maghrebi Immigration in Contemporary France* (Lincoln: University of Nebraska Press, 2012). For the limited access to financial sources for many Maghrebi filmmakers, see their introduction, 2.
46. Higbee "Hope and Indignation," 27.
47. Ginette Vincendeau, *La Haine* (London: I.B. Tauris, 2005), 1.
48. Angelique Chrisafis, "'Nothing's Changed': 10 Years after French Riots, *Banlieues* Remain in Crisis," *Guardian*, October 22, 2015, accessed December 7, 2015. http://www.theguardian.com/world/2015/oct/22/nothings-changed-10-years-after-french-riots-banlieues-remain-in-crisis.
49. Chrisafis, "'Nothing's Changed.'"
50. Wayne, *Politics of Contemporary European Cinema*, 29.
51. Ginette Vincendeau, "*La Haine* and After: Arts, Politics, and the *Banlieue*," *The Criterion Collection*, May 8, 2012, accessed 7, 2015, http://www.criterion.com/current/posts/642-la-haine-and-after-arts-politics-and-the-banlieue; Vincendeau, *La Haine*.
52. Chrisafis, "'Nothing's Changed'"
53. Vincendeau, "*La Haine* and After."
54. *New York Times* reviewer Caryn James notes that the film could resonate with American viewers. She states: "Yet for American viewers, the eeriest part of Mr. Kassovitz's precise and troubling film is how easily it reflects our own social problems." Caryn James, "Movie Review—Hate—Film Festival Review; Crime, Violence and Pessimism," *New York Times*, October 12, 1995, accessed December 7, 2015, http://www.nytimes.com/movie/review?res=9E0DE5D81339F931A25753C1A96395826 0.
55. Austin, *Contemporary French Cinema*, 48.
56. Cristina Johnston, "Intergenerational Verbal Conflicts, Plurilingualism and *Banlieue* Cinema," in *Polyglot Cinema: Migration and Transcultural Narration in France, Italy, Portugal and Spain*, eds. Verena Breger and Kiya Komori (Münster, Germany: LIT, 2010), 97.
57. The theme song is Arabic and some of the actors and characters are of North African heritage. However, interesting in this regard is that, as some of the viewer comments at the IMDB website demonstrate, the Arabic connections, especially of the soundtrack, are still not discernible to all global viewers. "Soundtrack Is Abysmal," IMDB, accessed May 23, 2016, http://www.imdb.com/title/tt4003966/board/nest/ 256981982? ref_=tt_bd_5.
58. See, for example, Isabelle McNeill, "Virtual Homes: Space and Memory in the Work of Yamina Benguigui" *L'Esprit Créateur*, 51, no.1 (2011): 12; and Gaëlle Planchenault, "Displacement and Plurilingualism in *Inch'Allah Dimanche*: Appropriating the Other's Language in Order to Find One's Place," eds. Verena Breger and Kiya Komori, *Polyglot Cinema: Migration and Transcultural Narration in France, Italy, Portugal and Spain* (Münster, Germany: LIT, 2010), 99.

59. McNeill, "Virtual Homes," 13.

60. McNeill, "Virtual Homes," 15.

61. Similarly, Dagmar Brunow's book chapter on Akın's *We Forgot to Return*, which appeared during the final stages of the completion of my book, presents a detailed reading of *We Forgot* as countering essentialist and hegemonic national narratives about migration. Brunow uses Bhabha's theory of the Third Space to situate Akın's film. See Dagmar Brunow, "Remembering Turkish German Labor Migration (Fatih Akin's *We Forgot to Go Back/Wir haben vergessen zurückzukehren*)," in *Remediating Transcultural Memory: Documentary Filmmaking as Archival Intervention* (Berlin: De Gruyter, 2015).

62. Higbee, "Hope and Indignation," 26–43.

63. Higbee, "Hope and Indignation," 35.

64. Higbee also discusses the political affiliations of the director and the possible political outcome or effect of *Welcome*. Higbee, "Hope and Indignation," 34.

65. Fatima Naqvi, *The Literary and Cultural Rhetoric of Victimhood: Western Europe, 1970–2005* (New York: Palgrave Macmillan, 2007), 53.

66. In this quote Naqvi references Axel Honneth's discussion of Ralph Ellison's 1952 novel, *Invisible Man*, that employs similar strategies showing the effects of isolation. Naqvi, *Literary and Cultural Rhetoric*, 59; For more details on Naqvi's analysis of Haneke and my analysis of Züli Aladağ's *Wut* in that context, see Berna Gueneli, "*Wut*—Who is Enraged? Violence in the 'Victim Society,'" *Jugendbilder: Repräsentationen von Jugend in Medien und Politik, Türkisch-deutsche Studien, Jahrbuch 2013* , eds. Yasemin Dayioğlu-Yücel, Michael Hofmann, Seyda Ozil (Göttingen: V&R Unipress, 2014); and Naqvi, *Literary and Cultural Rhetoric*.

67. Alice Rice points to the earlier (pre-1997) French discourse on the Holocaust and to the Vichy government, which is generally recognized, while the Battle of Paris/Massacre of Paris has often been "overlooked." It was only with the Maurice Papon trial in 1997 that the French government as well as fictional works have more effectively and seriously engaged with the massacre. For a more detailed discussion of this see, Alice Rice, "Rehearsing October 17, 1961: The Role of Fiction in Remembering the Battle of Paris," *L'Esprit Créateur* 54, no. 4 (2014), 91–92.

68. For questions and discussions on the Ottoman-Armenian relations, see Taner Akçam, *The Young Turks' Crime Against Humanity: The Armenian Genocide and Ethnic Cleansing in the Ottoman Empire* (Princeton: Princeton UP, 2012); Fatma Müge Göçek, *A Question of Genocide: Armenians and Turks at the End of the Ottoman Empire* (Oxford: Oxford University Press, 2011); Michael Petrou, "A Turkish Scholar Discusses the Armenian Genocide," Macleans.ca. Macleans, May 31, 2012, accessed February 9, 2016. http://www.macleans.ca/authors/michael-petrou/a-turkish-scholar-discusses-the-armenian-genocide/; and Yektan Türkyılmaz, "Rethinking Genocide: Violence and Victimhood in Eastern Anatolia: 1913–1915," (PhD diss., Duke University, 2007). I thank Barış Ülker for discussing the Turkish media and academic discourse on the Armenian-Ottoman history with me.

69. The Middle Eastern Cinema Dictionary for example, includes non-Arab cinemas from Turkey, Iran, and Israel. Gönül Dönmez-Colin's book *Women, Islam and Cinema* and her edited volume *The Cinema of North African and the Middle East* both discuss Turkish cinema in the context of North African or Middle Eastern cinema. And Kotecki states that the Sarajevo Film festival includes films from the Balkans, Greece, and Turkey. See Terro Ginsberg and Chris Lippard, eds., *Historical Dictionary of Middle Eastern Cinema* (Lanham, MD: Scarecrow, 2010); Gönül Dönmez-Colin, *Women, Islam and Cinema* (London: Reaktion Books, 2004); Gönül Dönmez-Colin, ed., *The Cinema of North Africa and the Middle East* (London: Wallflower, 2007); and Kotecki, "Europeanizing the Balkans."

70. Halle discusses, among other things, European film funding in Turkey in his article on Orientalism and European film funding structures. Randall Halle, "Offering Tales They

Want to Hear: Transnational European Film Funding as Neo-Orientalism," in *New Theories and Histories: Global Art Cinema*, eds. Rosalind Galt and Karl Schoonover. (Oxford: Oxford University Press, 2010), 313ff.

71. Halle, "Offering Tales," 313–314.

72. Asuman Suner, *New Turkish Cinema: Belonging, Identity, and Memory* (New York: I.B. Tauris, 2010), 77.

73. Suner, *New Turkish Cinema*, 78.

74. Interview at the Cannes Film Festival 2011, extra features, DVD, *Once Upon a Time in Anatolia* (New York: Cinema Guild, 2012). See also Suner, *New Turkish Cinema*, 90; and Rob White, "Nuri Bilge Ceylan: An Introduction and Interview" *Film Quarterly* 65, no. 2 (2011): 65.

75. White, "Nuri Bilge Ceylan," 68.

76. White, "Nuri Bilge Ceylan," 69.

77. "Cappadocia—World Heritage Site—National Geographic," *National Geographic*, December 19, 2015, http://travel.nationalgeographic.com/travel/world-heritage/cappadocia/.

78. In the German context, such rural settings are more reminiscent of the German Heimatfilm genre ("homeland films") of the 1950s rather than the art cinema of urban Germany.

79. Suner, *New Turkish Cinema*, 83.

80. White, "Nuri Bilge Ceylan," 68.

81. White, "Nuri Bilge Ceylan," 71.

Conclusion

INTERTEXTUAL FILM–TRANSNATIONAL FILM–TRANSNATIONAL FILM HISTORY

Turkish German Entanglements

This project analyzed the aesthetic and thematic composition of Akın's Turkey-engaged cinema. Thereby, it has also clarified Akın's audiovisual arrangement of Europe and the changing configurations of European cinema. By close-reading Akın's *In July*, *Head-On*, and *The Edge of Heaven* in chapters 1 through 3, I have deciphered the sonic and visual display of multiethnicity and polyphony in these films. I have argued that Akın audiovisually aestheticizes European diversity and complicates existing notions of the continent, its history, and its cinema. My scrutiny of his cinematic narrative, mise-en-scène, and sound, has helped to foreground Akın's "aesthetic of heterogeneity"—a productive and creative interplay of diverse, transnational, and often intertextual audiovisual elements that are manifested in his choice of music, dialogue, setting, and cast, among other elements. To be sure, such analysis has foregrounded the politics of these aesthetic dimensions.

The study of his films has shown that Akın erodes boundaries of any sort and that his films establish a differentiated view on gender, ethnicity, and class. The linguistic abilities and flexibilities of his characters, as much as their physical, multidirectional mobility, help to construct a filmic visualization of a new millennial generation and their adaptable position in an expanding European Union of the 2000s. By projecting images and sounds of a normalized diversity—that is, of a normalized multiethnicity and multilingualism—that can include "Turkishness"—without celebrating, lamenting, or fearing it—Akın subtly counters racism and challenges existing, simplistic notions of a cosmopolitan

"New Europe" and a xenophobic "Fortress Europe," the latter of which has risen in the public sphere, especially with the increasing numbers of migrants and refugees originating from "non-European" regions.

Akın's cinema emerges as particularly *au courant* when comparing his films and their aesthetic of heterogeneity with that of other European filmmakers. Hence, I have foregrounded in chapter 4 that his films partake in a larger European trend of diversifying and expanding the scope of European cinema. The work of Matthieu Kassovitz, Emir Kusturica, Michael Haneke, Philippe Lioret, and Yamina Benguigui, for example, gives insights about the new aesthetics in European filmmaking that also incorporate North African, Balkan, Turkish, and other traditionally nonwestern European cinematic discourses. I have argued that this new aesthetic of heterogeneity facilitates the emergence of a decentralized, multilocal, multiethnic, and polyphonic European cinema. This cinema stages and embraces, at times critically and at times humorously, a heterogeneous Europe of the past and present—even if only as a matrix for other stories to be told. In Akın's oeuvre, for example, the audience is exposed to stories about interpersonal relationships, in which the protagonists experience universal feelings of love, hope, hate, and pain. These stories are contextualized within a Europe that in its experienced reality has often already accepted its complicated diversity, its heterogeneous, multiethnic, and polyphonic make-up.

Additionally, Akın's Turkey-engaged cinema raises important new questions especially in regard to Turkey. These films have especially embraced and publicized topics of which some are controversial or less represented in Turkey's mainstream media. These range from engagements with female emancipation and sexual liberation (*Short Sharp Shock*, *Head-On*, *The Edge of Heaven*), to questions about the status of minorities—such as the Kurdish and Romani peoples (*Crossing the Bridge*, *The Edge of Heaven*), to depictions of homosexuality and homoeroticism (*The Edge of Heaven*), to environmental concerns (*Polluting Paradise*. The final film from this period, *The Cut*, sets its story against the backdrop of the events of 1915. The film visualizes cruelties committed against Armenians, the circumstances of which have differing narratives in Turkey.

Ultimately, Akın's transnational cinema from his Turkish German entanglement period intervenes in existing conversations and launches new interrogations. That is, Akın's films expand the categories and themes of an audiovisually diverse Europe and European cinema, engage in a cinematic conversation about topics that are controversial in Turkey's mainstream media, and, additionally, promote a transnational understanding of film and film history. However, with his last Turkey-engaged film, *The Cut*, Akın's initial Turkish German entanglement period seemed to have been terminated, and a new phase has been emerging. Describing his changing relationship to Turkey during the completion of his trilogy, Akın himself states that he entered a state of "separation" from Turkey: "First there was disillusion, then frustration, and finally a certain distance. Now the time has come for separate paths, for a creative separation. It is like in a marriage, in which you still love your partner, but you simply cannot go on living together any longer. The topic is no longer fruitful . . . perhaps in ten years again . . . . This is frustrating, but it also has something liberating to it."[1]

Although Akın took a period of "creative separation" from Turkey after finishing his trilogy, he did not really separate from Turkish German and other diversity-related themes completely. While his 2016 film *Tschick* definitely marks a move away from Turkey, it still disseminates his signature aesthetics of heterogeneity. The film takes Akın back to his beloved genre of road movies, but this time it is a new route, a journey from Berlin through the former East Germany's rural landscapes. His teenage protagonists with a German and Russian German background reflect Akın's continued preference for a mixed and multiethnic cast. How much Akın will continue to elaborate on these questions, directions, and narratives of a cinematic Europe or perhaps raise new ones while telling engaging stories about human interactions remains to be seen in the upcoming years. Europe, like Turkey's role in Europe, is constantly changing. Akın's films are part of that change, and future research will show how this change will affect forthcoming cinematic elaborations on the continent, its people, its sound, and its challenges.

While the larger thematic and stylistic trends in Akın's next periods of filmmaking remain open, the films he made in the early transition period depict a clear regional focus. Hamburg-related narratives seemed to dominate those endeavors. These include his feature film about Kurdish German victims of Neo-Nazi (NSU) murders set in Hamburg *Aus dem Nichts* (*In the Fade*, 2017) with global celebrity Diane Krüger, and his music documentary on German rock musician Marius Müller-Westernhagen (*Westernhagen MTV Unplugged*, 2016), a local hero and national superstar who lived in Hamburg for more than forty years until his recent move to Berlin. In 2018 Akın began filming a novel adaptation—*Der goldene Handschuh* (The golden glove, 2016) by Hamburg-based author and comedian Heinz Strunk—about the real-life serial killer Fritz Honka from Hamburg-Altona.

However, in 2018, Akın also mentioned two further projects, that, notwithstanding the new directions, new settings, and different epochs for these upcoming projects, also reconnect to Turkish and German histories, texts, and contexts. His announcement to adopt the literary book by Turkish author Sabahattin Ali, *Die Madonna im Pelzmantel* (*Madonna in a Fur Coat*, 1943), a romance set in 1920s Berlin, suggests a return to Turkish themes and contexts that are linked to Germany of the past. At the same time, his plan to film a miniseries with actress Diane Krüger about movie star and singer Marlene Dietrich during the Nazi years, connects him to a German national icon who lived in exile for many years.

Additionally, possibly reaching a larger global audience, Akın further plans to remake a Stephen King film adaptation, *Firestarter* (1984).[2] Whichever cinematic direction Akın goes next, he remains one of the first European directors who has constantly engaged with unifying and progressive images of a diverse, multiethnic, and polyphonic Europe. He has transformed and transnationalized cinema made in Germany.

Intertextuality and Akın's Aesthetics of Heterogeneity

In the following I add more reflection on a key component of the methodology that undergirds the approach of this book, namely the process of intertextuality. Repeatedly throughout the book, I have emphasized Akın's own understanding of his films' referentiality to other canonical films and have compared his stylistic signature to those of other directors. Such an explicit method by the filmmaker finds its correlation in the academic study of intertextuality. Akın's method for the creation of entanglements and his films' aesthetic of heterogeneity is often, even if not exclusively, the result of his intertextual cinematic references, and these have far-reaching effects. To elaborate more on this aspect of Akın's cinema, I will briefly revisit my findings from the perspective of intertextuality.

Intertextuality is in itself an old method of the creative arts. However, although references and allusions to other texts and images that shape art works' meanings have been customary for a long period of time, it was only in the second half of the twentieth century, through Julia Kristeva and her reworking of Mikhail Bakhtin's writings, that a theory of intertextuality was formulated in the field of literature,[3] with other fields following shortly thereafter. The theories and practices of postmodern criticism seemed to find intertextuality particularly handy for interpreting a work of art with its multiple references to and doubling or adaptation of previously existing texts. In film studies, the concept of intertextuality has helped critics develop analyses of adaptations, remakes, parodies, and other forms of references. Additionally, being an audiovisual medium, film offers a plethora of new forms of intertextualities that might appear simultaneously, including textual, visual, and sonic intertextualities. As his cinema's discussions have shown, Akın, too, uses intertextuality in various forms in his filmmaking, most prominently in his casting, his composition of the mise-en-scène, and his use of stock figures, sounds, and genres, a small selection of which I will revisit below.

Intertextuality and Casting and Mise-en-Scène

Returning to Akın's use of casting and mise-en-scène from the perspective of intertextuality more clearly reveals the transnationalizing effect it has on his films and illustrates how intertextuality becomes an integral part of his transnational filmmaking practices. Akın's casting creates links to a diversity of film histories ranging from Turkish, German, Swedish, French, and US, to former Yugoslav film history. The casting in *In July* set the tone for multinational casting in Akın's cinema and began a transnational connection to contemporary film made in Europe. To give an example, with Branka Katić and Gábor Salinger, actors formerly known from Yugoslav and Hungarian cinema, Akın established a link to Balkan cinema, particularly to Emir Kusturica's cinema.

The German cinema landscape is widely referenced in Akın's oeuvre. The star personality of Moritz Bleibtreu, who appears in *In July* and *Soul Kitchen*, creates associations with contemporary mainstream German cinema. The casting of esteemed stage and film actor Monika Bleibtreu in *Soul Kitchen* and Hannah Schygulla in *The Edge of Heaven* establishes a connection to German art film and theater. In addition, Turkish German stage and film actor Baki Davrak, also cast in *The Edge of Heaven*, marks the linkage to Turkish German art cinema of the 1990s. These examples signal only a few nexuses of the diverse cast members of Akın's films.

Akın similarly establishes connections to contemporary Turkish theater, TV, and cinema trough the actors Tuncel Kurtiz, Nurgül Yeşilçay, and Erkan Can as well as through actor and media personality Meltem Cumbul, who are all cast in *The Edge of Heaven*. In *Crossing the Bridge: The Sound of Istanbul*, Akın further chose to incorporate film clips and archival footage of famous musicians and popular film stars from Turkish film history such as Sezen Aksu, Orhan Gencebay, Erkin Koray, and Müzzeyen Senar, in addition to the life recordings of these pop, folk, rock, and classical Turkish music performers. Given that each artist is inflected with a professional and political past and history—which often carries over into the film, its narrative, reception, and legacy—these casting and editing choices have far-reaching consequences and demonstrate Akın's film-historical intertextualities and sensibilities.

More particularly, such transnational intertextualities urge us to analyze the sociopolitical, aesthetic, and stylistic changes that, for example, certain themes, actors, directors, and film industries stand for, and to incorporate these into the analysis of a director's filmic work. For example, as Richard Dyer states, star images are created through a variety of media texts.[4] In *The Edge of Heaven*, Güney, Kurtiz, and Schygulla as stars bring their media images as discussed in the media of the 1970s into Akın's contemporary films. In his films, Akın establishes transnational synergies, bringing young and old actors of past and contemporary cinemas, especially from Turkish and German cinema, to the foreground. That is, through his casting choices, Akın, on the one hand, generates international recognition for his actors, who appear at prominent film festivals and receive global attention. In the case of *Head-On*, for example, Turkish German Sibel Kekilli, who was a first-time feature-film actor when she won the

Best Leading Actress Award at the German Film Awards in 2004, was discovered for future films in the global workplace. Ever since her successes with *Head-On*, Kekilli has won multiple awards and has become an international actor, playing in twenty episodes of the US series *Game of Thrones* as well as in the Turkish feature *Eve Dönüş* (The return home, 2006), in addition to German films and television shows. On the other hand, as is the case with his casting of Tuncel Kurtiz, our attention might shift to Kurtiz's pervious leftist work and even lead to a (re) discovery of the Turkish director Yılmaz Güney and his films. Thereby, Akın connects his own filmmaking to that of a Kurdish Turkish political filmmaker who had to escape into French exile. Ultimately, Akın's cinematic allusions create a convergence of cinema and music histories, linking, for example, different stages of Turkish film, theater, and television history with German film history.

Like casting, the mise-en-scène equally alludes to different film-historical contexts. In chapters 1 and 4, I discussed the outdoor Balkan scenes in Akın's *In July*, and how these, together with casting, props, and sound, recreate the cinematic look and feel of Balkan landscapes and country roads along the Danube as known from Kusturica's films such as *Black Cat* and *Time of the Gypsies*. Similar to Balkan cinema's influence on *In July*, Turkish cinema influences the look and feel of the "Meze in Istanbul" scene in *The Edge of Heaven*. This scene very much alludes to the iconography of grief as known from Turkish Yeşilçam cinema. That is, the casting of Schygulla and Davrak in combination with the mise-en-scène in "Meze in Istanbul" brings another layer of film-historical intertextualities. The specific urban setting, sound, and mood recall classic Turkish Yeşilçam films, thereby converging once more on German and Turkish cinema histories. Thus, Akın draws directly from this iconography of Turkish cinema for the mise-en-scène and mood of his film.

Intertextuality and Genre

A final reconsideration of genre further helps to reveal the transnational cinematic intertextualities in Akın's films. Genre is an important element that allows Akın to pay tribute to prominent figures from throughout film history, while systematically engaging with their filmmaking. To give specific examples, I will briefly revisit the genres of melodrama, gangster film, banlieue cinema, and personal documentary, and also introduce the genres of war atrocities. Each of these genres addresses themes, films, and filmmakers from different film-historical contexts and creates a web of linear and nonlinear, direct and indirect connectivity between them.

The genres of melodrama and gangster thriller have been previously addressed in Akın scholarship.[5] Melodrama,[6] a beloved genre within German, Hollywood, and Turkish film history, dates from the early years of cinema. It is through this genre that Akın manages, once again, to transgress national boundaries, and to bridge generations and film histories. He connects through his work (*Head-On*) to the Third Reich (*La Habanera*), Hollywood (*All That Heaven Allows*), West German (*Ali: Fear Eats the Soul*), and Turkish (Yeşilçam melodrama) cinema history.[7] This happens similarly with the genres of gangster and banlieue films if we consider the previously stated connections between Scorsese's auteurist Hollywood gangster film *Mean Streets*, Kassovitz's French banlieue film *La Haine*, and Akın's Turkish German gangster film *Short Sharp Shock*.[8] In this context, Özgür Yıldırım's *Chiko* (2008), produced by Akın's first production company Corazón International, provides another German gangster film that could be productively discussed together with the above-mentioned films that introduced a new genre and setting to filmmaking in Europe.

The genres of personal documentary and war-atrocities films have not been highlighted as much in the context of Akın's work.[9] Yet these two genres provide innovative and important additions to Akın scholarship in general and to Akın's contribution to transnational film, film history, and history, in particular. The genre of personal documentary, as discussed in my examples in chapter 4, highlights the migration and exile experiences of ethnic minorities in Europe, as much as it introduces a new historical narrative about those years. Akın's *We Forgot to Return* is a film about Akın's family and friends in Hamburg, Istanbul, and the Black Sea coast of Turkey. It partakes in the discourse of this genre across generations and continents. First of all, *We Forgot to Return* begins a transatlantic dialogue with Scorsese's *Italianamerican* (1974). *Italianamerican* tells the stories of Scorsese's parents, their lives in Little Italy in New York, their families' lives in Italy, and their experiences of war and migration, among other things. *We Forgot to Return* thereby creates an intertextual reference to the experiences of migration and multiethnicity as narrated in *Italianamerican*, and links Akın's personal documentary to the documentary made by his cinema mentor and role model, Scorsese. Even if the films are different in tone, aesthetics, and content, they connect on the level of genre.

Second, in a European context, Benguigui's films, juxtaposed with Akın's work, form contemporary intersecting tales of migration and experiences of ethnic minorities in central and western Europe. That is, *We Forgot to Return* similarly relates to French director Benguigui's work, especially her documentaries that tell the stories of North African migration to France such as *Immigrant Memories*, even if the films differ in other ways. These films further augment our historical and audiovisual understanding of a specific time in the past from the perspective of personal documentary. Additionally, within this genre, Akın's documentary connects to transatlantic and European films and filmmakers with a multiethnic background. A future analysis of Akın's film in this transnational context would deliver new insights on this genre and its intervention in filmic and historical narratives.

Opening up to the genre of war-atrocities films, Akın's final part of his Turkey-engaged trilogy, *The Cut*, is particularly important. The film is relevant not only for its engagement with the cinematic discourse on war, violence, and atrocities films, but also for the way it establishes images and sounds for narratives on such events, and for its writing of cinematic history in this context. With *The Cut*, Akın opened up a new genre within the German cinematic context as the first German filmmaker to explicitly take up this specific topic. There are hardly any German films that overtly visualize such events in their cinematography and mise-en-scène, with the early exception of East Germany's DEFA coproductions *Sterne* (*Stars*, 1959) and *Jakob, der Lügner* (*Jacob the Liar*, 1974) based on the novel by Jurek Becker by the same title, or Uwe Böll's controversial and gruesome, much-criticized feature on the Holocaust, *Auschwitz* (2011). However, *Stars* and *Jacob the Liar* had primarily antifascist narratives that carried the films and did not principally focus on a critical engagement with and visualization of the committed atrocities themselves.[10] While *Auschwitz* is said to explicitly engage with the Holocaust atrocities and visualize its brutality, among critics it is commonly considered an artistically and intellectually inferior endeavor, with very few exceptions.[11]

It is with Akın's film that a transnational conversation with this complex film genre begins in Germany. How can cinema visualize and narrate the effects of war and atrocities on humans? Hollywood or British films that engage with the Holocaust, or films about the genocides in Rwanda and Cambodia, as well as Balkan films on the Bosnian war, are all films that arguably form part of this genre.[12] In relation to the Armenian case, there are a few films that make explicit reference to the events of 1915, such as the Canadian *Ararat* (2002) by Atom Egoyan, and perhaps also Elia Kazan's *America America* (1963). Future research on *The Cut* in the context of these and related films could offer productive insights into the transnational cinematic elaboration on, and the aesthetic visualization and creation of, a catalogue of filmic images of war, violence, and human suffering.

My initial comparison with such films suggests that Akın's visual experimentation with the topic—especially considering the refugee camp scenes—his depiction of starvation, despair, and death, is stylistically and aesthetically different from the above-mentioned films depicting war and violence. Although there are similarities between some of these films, such as the depiction and narration of rape and other enactments of physical violence and cruelties, Akın includes novel images, too. His stylized stage-like setting, his use of bleak colors with stark light-dark contrasts, his work with shadows, and the refugee camps' general mise-en-scène and mood create a deeply existential setting. This sequence even reminds viewers of an expressionistic setting. In the context of war movies, I suggest, it is visually evoking select scenes from prisoner-of-war (POW) camp movies, especially Bryan Forbes's opening scene in *King Rat* (1965) and, to some extent, David Lean's *The Bridge on the River Kwai* (1957).

To give an example, *King Rat*, based on James Clavell's novel, is set in World War II, in a Japanese prisoner-of-war camp, in Changi prison, near Singapore. It is a film about British and American prisoners of war who try to survive the harsh conditions in Changi prison. The opening is dialogue free, the sound is of mosquitos and a chicken, and nondiegetic somber, classical music follows. The panning camera depicts medium long shots of quiet despair. More specifically, people in this sequence do not talk, close-ups show their sweating faces; wet, ragged clothes; and undernourished bodies. Some are shown in silent pain, lying, as if entombed, under mosquito nets. These are people who might not survive the harsh conditions of the prison. The dry landscape, the sweat of the people, and the sound and sight of mosquitoes surrounding the close-up of a shark being slit open foreshadow the severe conditions of the camp that will be thematized in the course of the film. The opening sequence of David Lean's *The Bridge on the River Kwai* presents similar imagery of despair. Here, a vulture circling over the jungle, wooden crosses near the train tracks, and disillusioned, exhausted, and malnourished soldiers digging new graves for the ones who did not survive the camp visualize the quiet despair of the prisoners.

While Akın seems to borrow from this type of cinematic imagery to find unique images for the Armenian suffering, he locates these images in a camp for displaced and expelled Armenian refugees during World War I. Many of these refugees are shown suffering, dying, or as wishing to die to end their suffering. This despair is dramatically depicted through Nazaret (Tahar Rahim) and his encounter with his sister-in-law in such a camp. In the camp scenes, Nazaret holds his sister-in-law in his arms, while she repeatedly begs to be killed. Eventually, Nazaret barehandedly, and under agony, strangles her to relieve her from her pain. The mise-en-scène, the quietness of the scene, the faint colors, and this extraordinary moment of torment and moral dilemma experienced by the protagonists, is a unique visualization of human anguish in the context of (German) films within this genre.

With *The Cut*, Akın not only opens up a new genre and the visualization and sounding of a particular topic in German and Turkish film, he also intervenes into a specific historical narrative and its global discourse. In the introduction to this book, I referenced Leslie Adelson, who stated that by analyzing "the literature of Turkish migration," we might focus on the "reconfigurations of the German national archive."[13] I come back to this quote to suggest that with Akın, Turkish history, texts, and contexts further extend and change perspectives of historical narratives in Germany and Europe. Adding a specific Armenian Turkish context and story into his filmic opus, Akın opens up a discourse, a history, a genre to be discussed, analyzed, and critically engaged with in Germany, Turkey, Europe, and beyond. With *The Cut*, Akın directly refers to the Armenian history in the Ottoman Empire, adding it to the long list of twentieth-century European human suffering.

The Cut, depending on our grouping of films and comparative analysis, does different things simultaneously. It invites us to see a cinematic extension of film-historical and historical discourses on a shared European past and memory that have not received much attention in mainstream media thus far, and it also invites us to analyze the visualization of war and violence committed in the name of nationalism in general. That is, if we group *The Cut* together with films and documentaries such as Haneke's *Caché*, Benguigui's *Immigrant Memories* and *Inch'allah Dimache*, and Akın's *We Forgot*, we automatically intervene in the discourse on European history and memory, as these films depict a perspective on the past that was nearly absent from previous media depictions and historic discourses. At the same time, *The Cut* also invites us to contextualize and compare filmic and historical discourses on human suffering caused by other humans in a wider European context. By juxtaposing the Armenian experience with the Holocaust, the Algerian war, the Paris Massacres of 1961, and the Bosnian war, these European sufferings—some of which are more, others less part of a European public memory—relate to each other. Such a grouping of films could be as diverse as Spielberg's *Schindler's List*, Claire Denis's *Beau Travail*, Haneke's *Caché*, and Akın's *The Cut*. These films together provide insights into the transnational history and the intertextual particularities of the visualization of war war, violence, and human suffering.

Transnational Film and Transnational Film History

After reexamining the abundance of references, allusions, and intertextualities to Turkish, and also to other cinematic contexts above, Akın's cinema emerges as a synthesis of different cinemas, especially the traditionally and carefully segregated cinemas of Europe and Turkey. That is, on the one hand, we are urged to read Turkish cinema as a part of European cinema; on the other hand, since Akın's oeuvre includes plenty of allusions to other cinemas in addition to Turkish cinema, scholars and audiences alike are urged to acknowledge his cinema's transnational composition.

In other words, by juxtaposing Turkish cinematic references and intertextualities—including classic Yeşilçam, political Young Turkish, and artistically ambitious contemporary New Turkish Cinema—with German, Turkish German, and other European and non-European film-historical references, Akın constructs a wide-reaching, inherently transnational film opus and film history. Such transnationalism also serves as an example of how film histories communicate with each other and how their synthesis generates something new. These intertextualities and transnational contexts have consequences for a film's content and for the reading of a film's content at a specific moment in time. Hence, we are forced to reconsider existing frameworks when discussing Akın's work. The intertextual and intermedial references to American, French, Balkan, and in particular Turkish film—what we might call Akın's transnational intertextualities—invite us to locate and analyze new elements of Akın's transnational filmmaking, a process that, ultimately, intervenes with national film and film histories. The transnationalism in Akın's work challenges our traditional perception of nationally categorized cinemas, and even film archives and museums. Transnational film and film history not only allow for understanding Akın's oeuvre thematically and stylistically from new angles, but they also request a different mode of commemoration and recognition of such films in museums and archives. That is, Akın's films might augment our perception of not only German national cinema, but also of cinema and cinema history in general.

Books and educational syllabi on national cinemas demonstrate that film histories often continue to be read in a national context, even if the film industry is by now generally understood as a transnational undertaking. However, transnational studies influence the study of film *and* film history. Akın and his work, as analyzed in the present study, contribute to this new understanding of transnational cinema. Ultimately, Akın's cinema gives national cinemas and film histories a new direction through transnational intertextualities. As my discussion of his cinema suggests, traditional categories have become too narrow for transnational filmmakers like Akın.

In the context of Turkish cinema studies, for example, Asuman Suner discusses Akın's films such as *Head-On* and *Crossing the Bridge* in her illuminating book on *New Turkish Cinema* because of their setting and thematic and sonic references to Istanbul. Although Suner does not classify Akın as a New Turkish Cinema director, she nevertheless discusses him as a contributor to New Turkish Cinema from a transnational angle, calling Akın's films "transnational Istanbul films."[14] That is, Akın's cinema can even be read as belonging to a particular category of Turkish films, depending on the questions asked and films analyzed.

This fact alone, that Akın's films are analyzed in a national Turkish cinema book, challenges nationally confined films and filmmaking, and it further shows that transnational filmmaking is multidirectional. By acknowledging the transnational intertextualities within Akın's work, we complicate the structure and content of his cinema. While I have scrutinized aesthetic and film-historical components that had not been sufficiently analyzed before, revealing transnational ties, which include intersections of different film histories and connections between contemporary cinemas, I hope that future scholarship will reach more deeply into the Turkish archive, finding other tools to investigate Akın's transnational cinematic opus to continuously decipher the multilayered aspects of his work. At the same time, such transnationalism of film and film history needs to be analyzed and discussed in the work of Akın's contemporaries, within and beyond a German national context

Notes

1. "Zuerst kam Ernüchterung, dann Frustration und schließlich ein gewisser Abstand. Jetzt kommt die Zeit für getrennte Wege, eine kreative Trennung. Es ist wie in einer Ehe, in der man den Partner noch liebt, aber einfach nicht mehr zusammenleben kann. Das Thema ist nicht mehr fruchtbar. Vielleicht in zehn Jahren wieder. Das ist frustrierend, hat aber auch etwas Befreiendes." "Heute fühle ich mich als Grieche," interview, Goethe Institut Athen, accessed 24 September 2016, https://www.goethe.de /de/uun/akt/20488257.html.

2. For reference to these projects, see "Fatih Akin Verfilmt den 'Goldenen Handschuh,'" *Zeit Online*, February 14, 2018, accessed February 14, 2018, https://www.zeit.de /news/201802/14/fatih-akin-verfilmt-den-goldenen-handschuh-180214-9965702; Justin Kroll, "'In the Fade' Director to Take on Stephen King's 'Forestarter' for Universal, Blumhouse (EXCLUSIVE)," *Variety*, June 28, 2018, accessed June 30, 2018, https://variety.com/2018/film /news/firestarter-fatih-akin-stephen-king-universal-blumhouse-1202852347/.

3. For Toril Moi's introduction to Kristeva's engagement with Bakhtin's ideas and a reprint of Kristeva's essay that introduced Bakhtin to a Western audience, see Julia Kristeva, "Word, Dialogue, and Novel," in *The Kristeva Reader*, ed. Toril Moi (New York: Columbia University Press, 1986).

4. Richard Dyer, *Stars* (London: BFI, 1998), 34.

5. Mennel discusses ghettocentrism, while Berghahn and particularly Çelik in her chapter on Akın refer to and discuss the genre of melodrama. Barbara Mennel, "Bruce Lee in Kreuzberg and Scarface in Altona: Transnational Auteurism and Ghettocentrism in Thomas Arslan's *Brothers and Sisters* and Fatih Akin's *Short Sharp Shock*," in "Postwall Cinema," special issue, *New German Critique* 87 (2002); Daniela Berghahn, *Head-On (Gegen die Wand)*, BFI Film Classics (New York: Palgrave/BFI, 2015); Ipek A. Çelik, *In Permanent Crisis: Ethnicity in Contemporary European Media and Cinema* (Ann Arbor: University of Michigan, 2016).

6. As a critical category in film studies, melodrama surfaces generally in the 1970s. In 1970s feminist film criticism, especially the melodramas of the 1940s and 1950s, were reexamined. John Mercer and Martin Shingler, *Melodrama: Genre, Style, Sensibility* (London: Wallflower, 2005). For a detailed discussion of the genre of melodrama in the context of Douglas Sirk's cinema, see Barbara Klinger, *Melodrama and Meaning: History, Culture, and the Films of Douglas Sirk* (Bloomington: Indiana University Press, 1994).

7. In the context of Germany, and later Hollywood, Douglas Sirk is one of the prominent filmmakers who brought the genre of melodrama to perfection. Already with his *La Habanera*, made in the Third Reich, Sirk experimented with lavish, excessive mise-en-scènes and counternarratives in creating the visual opulence that would become the trademark for his Hollywood melodramas, notwithstanding the racist ideology present in the narrative of his early work. His well-known Hollywood studio production *All That Heaven Allows* (1955), a melodramatic love story across generational and class lines, was taken up by Fassbinder. Fassbinder played his tribute to Sirk's sensually and colorfully stimulating melodrama with *Ali: Fear Eats the Soul*, a socially critical love story across generational, ethnic, and class lines set in Munich in the 1970s, where the remnants of the Nazi past were still in the air. Akın, as

a recipient of the Sirk award already linked symbolically to the fellow Hamburg filmmaker, connects both these filmmakers from Third Reich, German, and Hollywood film history with *Head-On*, a love story against all odds between two Turkish Germans, set in the local boroughs of contemporary Hamburg and Istanbul. Additionally, melodrama is a favorite genre of Yeşilçam cinema, and as such makes its way into Akın's cinema through music and the theme of unfulfilled love, among other elements. For a discussion of the genre of melodrama and the Sirk-Fassbinder-Akın connection, see also Berghahn, *Head-On*, 47–81. For a detailed work on Sirk and melodrama, see Klinger, *Melodrama and Meaning*.

8. In a different context, Berghahn references *La Haine* and *Short Sharp Shock* in the context of the American "hood film" from the early 1990s, which includes films such as John Singleton's *Boyz n the Hood* (1991) and Allan and Albert Hughes's *Menace II Society* (1993). Barbara Mennel makes references to these and other American films from the early 1990s, which are set in the urban ghettos and often depict racialized violence and aggressions, and discusses, among others, their new aesthetics. Daniela Berghahn, *Far-Flung Families in Film: The Diasporic Family in Contemporary European Cinema* (Edinburgh: Edinburgh University Press, 2014), 122; Barbara Mennel, *Cities and Cinema* (New York: Routledge, 2008), 155–163, 165.

9. An exception is the work of Dagmar Brunow, who discusses *We Forgot to Return* in one chapter of her book. Brunow's work presents an insightful addition and extension to my understanding of historical augmentation via cinema. Dagmar Brunow, "Remembering Turkish German Labor Migration (Fatih Akin's *We Forgot to Go Back/Wir haben vergessen zurückzukehren*)," in *Remediating Transcultural Memory: Documentary Filmmaking as Archival Intervention* (Berlin: de Gruyter, 2015), 53–71.

10. The latter was also remade by Hungarian-French director Peter Kassovitz (*Jakob the Liar*, 1999), father of Matthieu Kassovitz.

11. For a brief discussion and reception of Böll's *Auschwitz*, see Kate Connolly, "German Director's Holocaust Film Causes Outrage," *Guardian*, November 12, 2010, accessed May 10, 2016, http://www.theguardian.com/world/2010/nov/12/uwe-boll-auschwitz-film-causes-outrage; and Matthew Rozsa, " Uwe Boll a Master of Bad Movies Finally Makes a Winner with Auschwitz [Graphic Video]," *Mic*, June 28, 2012, accessed May 10, 2016, https://mic.com/articles/10370/uwe-boll-a-master-of-bad-movies-finally-makes-a-winner-with-auschwitz-graphic-video#.SNFmTIArB.

12. Exemplary films would be Steven Spielberg's *Schindler's List* (1993), Mark Herman's *The Boy in the Striped Pajamas* (2008), Terry George's *Hotel Rwanda* (2004), Alrick Brown's *Kinyardwanda* (2011), Roland Joffé's *The Killing Fields* (1984), Danis Tanivic's *No Man's Land* (2001), Srdan Golubovic's *Krugovi* (*Circles*, 2013), and Srdjan Dragojevic's *Lepa sela lepo gore* (*Pretty Village Pretty Flame*, 1996).

13. Leslie A. Adelson, *The Turkish Turn in Contemporary Turkish Literature* (New York: Palgrave Macmillan, 2005), 12.

14. Asuman Suner, *New Turkish Cinema: Belonging, Identity and Memory* (London: I.B. Tauris, 2010), 153..

Filmography/Discography, Bibliography, and Online Sources

Filmography and Selected Discography

40 qm Deutschland (40 Square Meters of Germany). Directed by Tevfik Başer. 1986. Berlin: Studiocanal GmbH, 2000. VHS.

300 Worte Deutsch (300 Words of German). Directed by Züli Aladağ. 2014. Berlin: DCM, 2015. DVD.

Abschied vom falschen Paradies (Farewell to a False Paradise). Directed by Tevfik Başer. Hamburg, Germany: Studio Hamburg, ZDF, Ottokar Runze Filmproduktion, 1988/1989.

All That Heaven Allows. Directed by Douglas Sirk. 1955. New York: The Criterion Collection, 2001. DVD.

Alles inklusive (All Inclusive). Directed by Dörris Dörrie. 2014. Munich: Constantin Film, 2014. DVD.

Almanya: Wilkommen in Deutschland. 2011. Directed by Yasemin Samdereli. Grünwald, Germany: Concorde Home Entertainment, 2011. DVD.

Angst essen Seele auf (*Ali: Fear Eats the Soul*). Directed by Rainer Werner Fassbinder. 1974. New York: Criterion Collection, 2003. DVD.

Aprilkinder (April children). Directed by Yüksel Yavuz. 1998. Fridolfing, Germany: Absolut Medien GmbH, 1999. DVD.

Arizona Dream. Directed by Emir Kusturica. 1992. Berlin: Studiocanal, 2003. DVD.

Auf der anderen Seite (*The Edge of Heaven*). Directed by Fatih Akın. 2007. Culver City, CA: Strand Releasing, 2008. DVD.

Auf Der Anderen Seite / Edge of Heaven. Essay Recordings, 2007. CD.

Beau Travail. Directed by Claire Denis. 1999. New York: New Yorker Video, 2002. DVD.

Bend It Like Beckham. Directed by Gurinder Chadha. 2002. New York: Fox, 2004. DVD.

Benny's Video. Directed by Michael Haneke. 1992. New York: Kino Video, 2006. DVD.
Berlin in Berlin. Directed by Sinan Çetin. 1993. Berlin and Istanbul: Plato Film and Çetin Filmproduktion, 1992/1993.
Bir zamanlar Anadolu'da (Once Upon a Time in Anatolia). Directed by Nuri Bilge Ceylan. 2011. New York: Cinema Guild, 2012. DVD.
Bullard, John. *Bach on the Banjo*. Albany Records, 2006. CD.
Bure baruta (Powder Keg). Directed by Goran Paskaljević. France: Canal (II), 1998.
Caché (Hidden). Directed by Michael Haneke. 2005. Culver City, CA: Sony Pictures Home Entertainment, 2006. DVD.
Chéri. Directed by Stephen Frears. 2009. Santa Monica, CA: Miramax Film, 2009. DVD.
Chiko. Directed by Özgür Yıldırım. 2008. Stuttgart, Germany: Ascot Elite Home Entertainment, 2008. DVD.
Code Inconnu (Code Unknown). Directed by Michael Haneke. 2000. New York: The Criterion Collection, 2015. DVD.
Crna macka, beli macor (Black Cat, White Cat/Schwarze Katze, weisser Kater). Directed by Emir Kusturica. 1998. Leipzig, Germany: Kinowelt Home Entertainment, 2011. DVD.
Crossing the Bridge: The Sound of Istanbul. Directed by Fatih Akın. 2005. Culver City, CA: Strand Releasing, 2006. DVD.
Cure: das Leben einer anderen (Cure: The Live of Another). Directed by Andrea Štaka. Switzerland: Okofilm Productions, 2014.
Dangerous Liaisons. Directed by Stephen Frears. 1988. Burbank, CA: Warner Home Video, 1997. DVD.
Das Fräulein (Fraulein). Directed by Andrea Štaka. 2006. New York: Film Movement, 2008. DVD.
Das Leben der anderen (Lives of Others). Directed by Christian Henckel von Donnersmarck. 2006. Culver City, CA: Sony Pictures Home Entertainment, 2007. DVD.
Das weisse Band, eine deusche Kindergeschichte (The White Ribbon). Directed by Michael Haneke. 2009. New York: Sony Pictures Classic, 2010. DVD.
Der blaue Engel (The Blue Angel). Directed by Josef von Sternberg. 1930. New York, NY: Kino Lorber Films, 2001. DVD.
Der Siebte Kontinent (The Seventh Continent). Directed by Michael Haneke. New York: Kino Video, 2006. DVD.
Der Student von Prag (The Student of Prague). Directed by Hanns Heinz Ewers and Stellan Rye. 1913. West Conshohocken, PA: Alpha Video, 2004. DVD.
Der Untergang (Downfall). Directed by Oliver Hirschbiegel. 2004. Culver City, CA: Sony Pictures Home Entertainment, 2005. DVD.
Die Feurzangenbowle. Directed by Helmut Weiss. 1944. Berlin, Germany: Studiocanal, 2009. DVD.
Die Fremde (When We Leave). Directed by Feo Aladağ. 2010. Chicago: Olive Films, 2011. DVD.
Dirty Pretty Things. Directed by Stephen Frears. 2002. Santa Monica, CA: Miramax Films, 2004. DVD.
Dom za vesanje (Time of the Gypsies). Directed by Emir Kusturica. 1988. Cologne, Germany: Alive-Vertrieb und Marketing, 2010. DVD.
Drømmen om Danmark (Dreaming of Denmark). Directed by Michael Graversen. Copenhagen, Denmark: Klassefilm, 2015.

East is East. Directed by Damien O'Donnell. 1999. Munich, Germany: Senator Home Entertainment (Vertrieb Universum Film), 2010. DVD.
Ein Augenblick Freiheit (For a Moment, Freedom). Directed by Arash T. Hiraki. 2008. Wien, Austria: Falter, 2010. DVD.
Einmal Hans mit scharfer Soße (Hans in hot sauce). Directed by Buket Alakuş. 2013. Ismaning, Germany: EuroVideo Medien GmbH, 2015. DVD.
Et Hjem I Verden (*At Home in the World*). Directed by Andreas Koefoed. Copenhagen, Denmark: Sonntag Pictures, 2015.
Fatih Akın—Tagebuch eines Filmreisenden (*Fatih Akin—Diary of a Film Traveler*). Directed by Monique Akın. 2007. Extra features in *The Edge of Heaven*. Culver City, CA: Strand Releasing, 2008. DVD.
"Feuerteufel (Fire devil)." *Tatort*, episode 872. Directed by Özgür Yıldırım. Hamburg, Germany: Wüste Medien for ARD, 2013.
Funny Games. Directed by Michael Haneke. 1997. New York: Fox Lorber, 1999. DVD.
Funny Games. Directed by Michael Haneke. 2007. Burbank, CA: Warner Home Video, 2008. DVD.
Fuocoammare (Fire at Sea). Directed by Gianfranco Rosi. France, Italy, et al.: Stemal Entertainment, 21 Unofilm, Les Films d'ici, et al., 2016.
Gegen die Wand (*Head-On*). Directed by Fatih Akın. 2004. Culver City, CA: Strand Releasing, 2005. DVD.
Getürkt (Turkified). Directed by Fatih Akın. Hamburg, Germany: Wüste Filmproduktion, 1996.
Go Trabi Go 1 + 2. Directed by Peter Timm. 1991. Ismaning, Germany: EuroVideo Medien GmbH, 2004. DVD.
Goodbye Lenin!. Directed by Wolfgang Becker. 2003. Culver City, CA: Sony Pictures Home Entertainment, 2004. DVD.
Gothika. Directed by Mathieu Kassovitz. 2003. Burbank, CA: Warner Home Video, 2004. DVD.
Güneşe Yolculuk (Journey to the Sun). Directed by Yeşim Ustaoğlu. 1999. Chicago: Facets, 2004. DVD.
Harragas. Directed by Merzak Allouache. Algeria and France: Librisfilms, Baya Films, et al., 2009.
High Fidelity. Directed by Stephen Frears. 2000. Burbank, CA: Touchstone Pictures, 2000. DVD.
Hotel Rwanda. Directed by Terry George. 2004. Beverly Hills: MGM, 2014. DVD.
Ich Chef, Du Turnschuh (*Me Boss, You Sneakers!*). Directed by Hussi Kutlucan. Stockholm, Sweden: Margarita Woskanian Filmproduktion, 1998.
Illégal (Illegal). Directed by Olivier Masset-Depasse. 2008. New York: Film Movement, 2011. DVD.
Im Juli (*In July*). Directed by Fatih Akın. 2000. New York: Koch Lorber Films, 2004. DVD.
Inch'Allah Dimanche. Directed by Yamina Benguigui. 2001. New York: Film Movement, 2005.
Indignados. Directed by Tony Gatlif. Paris: Arte France Développement, 2012.
Italianamerican. Directed by Martin Scorsese. 1974. New York: National Communications Foundation.

Kanak Attack. Directed by Lars Becker. 2000. Munich, Germany: Concorde Filmverleih, 2000. DVD.
Katzelmacher. Directed by Rainer Werner Fassbinder. 1969. Berlin: Studiocanal GmbH, 2009.
Kebab Connection. Directed by Anno Saul. 2004. Munich, Germany: Universum Film GmbH, 2005.
Kinyardwanda. Directed by Alrick Brown. 2011. Philadelphia: Breaking Glass Pictures, 2012. DVD.
Kış uykusu (Winter Sleep). Directed by Nuri Bilge Ceylan. 2014. Long Island City, NY: Adopt Films, 2015. DVD.
Knockin' on Heaven's Door. Directed by Thomas Jahn. 1997. Planegg, Germany: Koch Media GmbH, 2003. DVD.
Krugovi (Circles). Directed by Srdan Golubovic. 2013. Ascheffel and Hamburg, Germany: Barnsteiner/Lighthouse, 2015. DVD.
Kurz und schmerzlos (Short Sharp Shock). Directed by Fatih Akın. 1998. Hamburg, Germany: Wüste Filmproduktion. DVD.
La Habanera. Directed by Douglas Sirk. 1937. New York: Kino Lorber Films, 2004. DVD.
La Haine. Directed by Mathieu Kassovitz. 1995. New York: The Criterion Collection, 2010. DVD.
La Pianiste (The Piano Teacher). Directed by Michael Haneke. 2001. New York: Kino International, 2002. DVD.
Last Resort. Directed by Pawel Pawlikowski. 2000. BBC America. Amazon Video Streaming.
Lepa sela lepo gore (*Pretty Village Pretty Flame)*. Directed by Srdjan Dragojevic. 1996. New York: Fox Lorber, 1998. DVD.
Les rivières pourpres (The Crimson River). Directed by Mathieu Kassovitz. 2000. Culver City, CA: Sony Pictures Home Entertainment, 2001. DVD.
Lisbon Story. Directed by Wim Wenders. 1994. Santa Monica, CA: Lions Gate, 2007. DVD.
Lola and Bilidikid. Directed by Kutluğ Ataman. 1999. Fridolfing, Germany: Absolut Medien GmbH, 2002. DVD.
Lola rennt. Directed by Tom Tykwer. 1998. Culver City, CA: Sony Pictures Home Entertainment, 1999. DVD.
Man spricht deutsch (We Speak German). Directed by Hanns Christian Müller. 1988. Ismaning, Germany: EuroVideo Medien GmbH, 2011. DVD.
Marseilles. Directed by Dan Franck. 2015. TF 1 France. Netflix Original Series, 2016. Streaming.
Mémoires d'immgrés, l'héritage maghrébin (Immigrants' memories, Maghreb heritage). Directed by Yamina Benguigui. 1987. Brest, Nantes, et al, France: TF1 Video. 2008. DVD.
Mercedes mon amour (The Yellow Mercedes). Directed by Tunç Okan. 1993. Berlin: Salzgeber & Co. Medien GmbH, 1997. VHS.
Mission Backup Earth. Directed by Alexander Pfander. Berlin: Pfander Film. Webseries, 2013–present.
Monsoon Weddding. Directed by Mira Nair, 2001. Universal City, CA: Universal Studies Home Entertainment, 2002. DVD.

Muhammad Ali's Greatest Fight. Directed by Stephen Frears. 2013. Neenah, WI: Warner Archive Collection, 2013. DVD.
Mustang. Directed by Deniz Gamze Ergüven. 2015. Port Washington, NY: Entertainment One, 2016. DVD.
Morte a Venezia (Death in Venice). Directed by Luchino Visconti. 1971. Burbank, CA: Warner Home Video, 2010. DVD.
Müll im Garten Eden (Polluting Paradise). Directed by Fatih Akın. 2012. Cologne, Germany: Alive Vertrieb und Marketing, 2013. DVD.
My Beautiful Laundrette. Directed by Stephen Frears. 1985. New York: The Criterion Collection, 2015. DVD.
New York, I Love You. Directed by Fatih Akın et al. 2008. Universal City, CA: Vivendi Entertainment, 2010. DVD.
No Man's Land. Directed by Danis Tanivic. 2001. Beverly Hills, CA: MGM, 2002. DVD.
Polyglot. Directed by Amelia Umuhire. 2015. Web series.
Positive Sinking. Directed by Thomas Heinemann. 2015–present. Munich: superNeun Filmproduktions GmbH. Webseries.
Qu'Allah bénisse La France (May Allah Bless France!). Directed by Abd Al Malik. Culver City: CA, Strand Releasing, 2014.
Sadakat (Fidelity). Directed by Ilker Çatak. Abschlussfilm (graduation film). Hamburg, Germany: Hamburg Media School, 2014.
Sammy and Rosie Get Laid. Directed by Stephen Frears. 1987. Irvine, CA: Lorimar Home Video, 1988. VHS.
Schindler's List. Directed by Steven Spielberg. 1993. Universal City, CA: Universal Studios Home Entertainment, 2013. DVD.
Sensin, Du bist es. (Sensin—you are the one!). Directed by Fatih Akın. Hamburg, Germany: Wüste Filmproduktion, 1995.
Shirins Hochzeit (Shirin's Wedding). Directed by Helma Sanders-Brahms. 1976. Leipzig, Germany: Zeitausendeins edition 5/1976. DVD.
Soul Kitchen. Directed by Fatih Akın. 2009. New York, NY: Ifc Independent Film, 2010. DVD.
Süperseks. Directed by Throsten Wacker. 2004. Hamburg, Germany: Warner Home Video, 2005. DVD.
The Boy in the Striped Pajamas. Directed by Mark Herman. 2008. Santa Monica, CA: Miramax Lionsgate, 2011.
The Cut. Directed by Fatih Akın. 2014. Culver City, CA: Strand Releasing, 2016. DVD.
The Killing Fields. Directed by Roland Joffé. 1984. Burbank, CA: Warner Home Video, 2014. DVD.
The Queen. Directed by Stephen Frears. Santa Monica, CA: Lions Gate, 2006. DVD.
Töchter zweier Welten (Daughters of two worlds). Directed by Serap Berrakkarasu. 1991. Lübeck, Germany: Gülsen-Film, 1990/1991.
Tschick (Goodbye Berlin). Directed by Fatih Akın. Berlin, Germany: Lago Film GmbH, 2016.
Ummah unter Freunden (Ummah among friends). Directed by Cüneyt Kaya. 2013. Berlin, Germany: Wild Bunch, 2014. DVD.
Underground. Directed by Emir Kusturica. 1995. Cologne, Germany: Alive-Vertrieb und Marketing, 2013. DVD.

Welcome. Directed by Philippe Lioret. 2009. New York, NY: Film Movement, 2010. DVD.
Westernhagen MTV Unplugged. Directed by Fatih Akın. Berlin: Virgin Records (Universal Music), 2016.
Wie haben vergessen zurückzukehren (We Forgot to Return). Directed by Fatih Akın. Unterföhring, Germany: Megaherz, 2001. DVD.
Wut. Directed by Züli Aladağ. 2006. Hamburg, Germany: Edel Germany GmbH, 2013. DVD.
Yara (Wound). Directed by Arslan Yılmaz. Mannheim, Germany: Yılmaz Arslan Filmproduktion GmbH, 1999.
Yasemin. Directed by Hark Bohm. 1988. Leipzig, Germany: Zweitausendeins edition 3/1988. DVD.

Bibliography

Adelson, Leslie A. "Opposing Oppositions: Turkish-German Questions in Contemporary German Studies." *German Studies Review* 17, no. 2 (1994): 305–330.
———. *The Turkish Turn in Contemporary German Literature.* New York: Palgrave Macmillan, 2005.
Akçam, Taner. *The Young Turks' Crime Against Humanity: The Armenian Genocide and Ethnic Cleansing in the Ottoman Empire.* Princeton, NJ: Princeton University Press, 2012.
Andrew, Dudley. "Fatih Akin's Moral Geometry." In *Global Auteur,* edited by Jeong Seung-hoon, and Jeremi Szeniawski, 179–198. New York: Bloomsbury Academic, 2016.
Androutsopoulos, Jannis. "Networked Multilingualism: Some Language Practices on Facebook and Their Implications." *International Journal of Bilingualism* 19, no. 2 (2015): 185–206.
Austin, Guy. *Contemporary French Cinema: An Introduction.* Manchester, UK: Manchester University Press, 2008.
Baer, Marc. "Mistaken for Jews: Republican Turkish Accounts of Nazi Germany." Paper presented at the annual meeting of the German Studies Association, Kansas City, Missouri, September 18–21, 2014.
Ballesteros, Isolina. *Immigration Cinema in the New Europe.* Bristol, UK: Intellect, 2015.
Barham, Jeremy and Holly Rogers, eds. *The Music and Sound of Experimental Film.* New York: Oxford University Press, 2017.
Bayraktar, Nilgün. *Mobility and Migration in Film and Moving Image Art: Cinema Beyond Europe.* New York: Routledge, 2016.
Barthes, Roland. "The Death of the Author." In *The Book History Reader,* edited by David Finkelstein and Alistair McCleery, 221–224. London: Routledge, 2002.
Bazin, André. *What is Cinema?,* translated and edited by Hugh Grany. Berkeley: University of California Press, 1967.
Berger, Verena and Miya Komori, eds. *Polyglot Cinema: Migration and Transcultural Narration in France, Italy, Portugal and Spain.* Münster, Germany: LIT, 2010.
Berghahn, Daniela. *Gegen die Wand (Head-On).* BFI Classics. London: BFI/Palgrave Macmillan, 2015.
———. *Far-Flung Families in Film: The Diasporic Family in Contemporary European Cinema.* Edinburgh, UK: Edinburgh University Press, 2014.

———. "Introduction: Turkish-German Dialogue on Screen." *New Cinemas: Journal of Contemporary Film* 7, no. 1 (2009): 3–9.

———. "No Place like Home? Or Impossible Homecomings in the Films of Fatih Akin." *New Cinemas: Journal of Contemporary Film* 4, no. 3 (2006): 141–157.

———. "Seeing Everything with Different Eyes: The Diasporic Optic of Fatih Akin's *Head-On* (2004)." In *New Directions in German Cinema*, edited by Paul Cooke and Chris Homewood, 239–256. London: I.B. Tauris, 2011.

Berghahn, Daniela and Claudia Sternberg, eds. *European Cinema in Motion: Migrant and Diasporic Film in Contemporary Europe*. New York: Palgrave Macmillan, 2014.

Breger, Claudia. "Configuring Affect: Complex World Making in Fatih Akın's *Auf der anderen Seite* (*The Edge of Heaven*)." *Cinema Journal* 54, no. 1 (2014): 65–87.

Brown, William, Dina Iordanova, and Leshu Torchin. *Moving People, Moving Images: Cinema And Trafficking in the New Europe*. St. Andrews, UK: St. Andrews Film Studies, 2010.

Brown, William. "Negotiating the Invisible." In *Moving People, Moving Images: Cinema and Trafficking in the New Europe*, edited by William Brown, Dina Iordanova, and Leshu Torchin, 16–48. St. Andrews, UK: St. Andrews Film Studies, 2010.

Brunow, Dagmar. "Remembering Turkish-German Labor Migration (Fatih Akin's *We Forgot to Go Back/Wir haben vergessen zurückzukehren*)." In *Remediating Transcultural Memory: Documentary Filmmaking as Archival Intervention*, 53–71. Berlin: Walter De Gruyter, 2015.

Burnand, David and Miguel Mera, eds. *European Film Music*. Hampshire, UK: Ashgate, 2006.

Burns, Rob. "Images of Alterity: Second-Generation Turks in the Federal Republic." *The Modern Language Review* 94, no. 3 (July 1999): 744–757.

———. "On the Streets and on the Road: Identity in Transit in Turkish-German Travelogues on Screen." *New Cinemas: Journal of Contemporary Film* 7, no. 1 (2009): 11–26.

———. "Toward a Cinema of Cultural Hybridity: Turkish-German Filmmakers and the Representation of Alterity." *Debatte* 15, no. 1 (2007): 3–24.

———. "Turkish-German Cinema: From Cultural Resistance to Transnational Cinema?" In *German Cinema: Since Unification*, edited by David Clarke, 127–149. London: Continuum, 2006.

Çelik, Ipek A. *In Permanent Crisis: Ethnicity in Contemporary European Media and Cinema*. Ann Arbor: University of Michigan Press, 2015.

Cheesman, Tom. "Talking 'Kanak': Zaimoğlu contra Leitkultur." In "Multicultural Germany: Art, Performance and Media." Special issue, *New German Critique* 92 (2004): 82–99.

Chin, Rita. *The Guest Worker Question in Postwar Germany*. Cambridge: Cambridge University Press, 2007.

Chion, Michel. *Audiovision: Sound on Screen*. Edited and translated by Claudia Gorbman. New York: Columbia University Press, 1994.

———. *Film: A Sound Art*. Translated by Claudia Gorbman. New York: Columbia University Press, 2009.

Christie, Ian. "Where is National Cinema Today (and Do We Still Need It?)." *Film History: An International Journal* 25, no. 1–2 (2013): 19–30.

Clark, Christopher. "Transculturation, Transe Sexuality, and Turkish Germany: Kutluğ Ataman's Lola und Bilidikid." *German Life and Letters* 59, no. 4 (2006): 555– 572.
Clarke, David, ed. *German Cinema: Since Unification*. London: Continuum, 2006.
Cohan, Seven and Ian Rae Hark. Introduction to *The Road Movie Book*, edited by Steven Cohan and Ina Rae Hark, 1–14. London: Routledge, 1997.
Cooke, Mervyn. *A History of Film Music*. Cambridge: Cambridge University Press, 2008.
Cooke, Paul and Chris Homewood, eds. *New Directions in German Cinema*. London: I.B. Tauris, 2011.
Delanty, Gerard. "What Does It Mean to Be a 'European'?" *Innovation* 18, no. 1 (2005): 11–22.
Dickinson, Kay. *Movie Music: The Film Reader*. New York: Routledge, 2003.
Dickinson, Kristin. *Translation and the Experience of Modernity: A History of Turkish German Connectivity*. PhD diss., University of California, Berkeley, 2015.
Dönmez-Colin, Gönül. "Women in Turkish Cinema: Their Presence and Absence as Image and as Image-Makers." *Third Text* 24, no.1 (2010): 91–105.
———. *Women, Islam and Cinema*. London: Reaktion Books, 2004.
Dönmez-Colin, Gönül, ed. *The Cinema of North Africa and the Middle East*. London: Wallflower Press, 2007.
Durmelat, Sylvie and Vinay Swamy, eds. *Screening Integration: Recasting Maghrebi Immigration in Contemporary France*. Lincoln: University of Nebraska Press, 2012.
Dyer, Richard. *Stars*. London: BFI, 1998.
Ellinger, Ekkehard and Kerem Kayi. *Turkish Cinema: 1970–2007*. Frankfurt am Main, Germany: Peter Lang, 2008.
Elsaesser, Thomas. "European Cinema and the Postheroic Narrative: Jean-Luc Nancy, Claire Denis, and Beau Travail." *New Literary History* 43 (2012): 703–725.
———. *European Cinema: Face to Face with Hollywood*. Amsterdam: Amsterdam University Press, 2005.
———. "Real Location, Fantasy Space, Performative Place." In *European Film Theory*, edited by Temenuga Trifonova, 47–61. New York: Routledge, 2009.
El-Tayeb, Fatima. *European Others: Queering Ethnicity in Postnational Europe*. Minneapolis: University of Minnesota Press, 2011.
———. "'The Birth of a European Public:' Migration, Postnationality, and Race in the Uniting of Europe." *American Quarterly* 60, no 3 (2008): 649–670.
Erdoğan, Nezih. "Star Director as Symptom: Reflections on the Reception of Fatih Akin in the Turkish Media." *New Cinemas: Journal of Contemporary Film* 7, no. 1 (2009): 27–38.
Eren, Mine. "Cosmopolitan Filmmaking: Fatih Akin's *In July* and *Head-On*." In *Turkish German Cinema in the New Millennium: Sights, Sounds, and Screens*, edited by Sabine Hake and Barbara Mennel, 175–185. Oxford: Berghahn, 2012.
———. "The Antiheroine in Fatih Akin's *Head-On*." In *Muslim Women, Transnational Feminism and the Ethics of Pedagogy: Contested Imaginaries in Post-9/11 Cultural Practice*, edited by Lisa K. Taylor and Jasmin Zine, 82–109. New York: Routledge, 2014.
Esen, Adile. "Beyond 'In-Between,' Travels and Transformations in Contemporary Turkish-German Literature and Film." PhD diss., University of Michigan, 2009.
Everett, Wendy. Introduction to *European Identity in Cinema*, edited by Wendy Everett, 7–14. Bristol, UK: Intellect, 2005.
Ezli, Özkan. "Von der Identität zur Individuation: *Gegen die Wand* – eine Problematisierung kultureller Identitätszuschreibungen." In *Konfliktfeld Islam*

in Europa, edited by Monika Wohlrab-Sahr and Levent Tezcan, 283–301. Baden-Baden, Germany: Nomos, 2007.

———. "Von der interkulturellen zur kulturellen Kompetenz. Fatih Akın's globalisiertes Kino." In *Wider den Kulturenzwang: Migration, Kulturalisierung und Weltliteratur*, edited by Özkan Ezli, Dorothee Kimmich, and Annette Werberger, 207–230. Bielefeld, Germany: Transcript, 2009.

———. "Von Lücken, Grenzen und Räumen. Übersetzungsverhältnisse in Alejandro Gonzáles Iñarritus *Babel* und Fatih Akıns *Auf der anderen Seite*." In *Kultur als Ereignis*, edited by Özkan Ezli, 71–88. Bielefeld, Germany: Transcript, 2010.

Ezli, Özkan, ed. *Kultur als Ereignis. Fatih Akıns Film* Auf der anderen Seite *als transkulturelle Narration*. Bielefeld, Germany: Transcript, 2010.

Ezli, Özkan, Dorothee Kimmich, and Annette Werberger. "Vorwort." In *Wider den Kulturenzwang*, edited by Özkan Ezli, Dorothee Kimmich, and Annette Werberger, 9–19. Bielefeld, Germany: Transcript, 2009.

Fachinger, Petra. "A New Kind of Creative Energy: Yadé Kara's *Selam Berlin* and Fatih Akin's *Kurz und schmerzlos* and *Gegen die Wand*." *German Life and Letters* 60, no. 2 (2007): 243–260.

Feinstein, Howard. "'Black Cat, White Cat': Kusturica Returns to Gypsy Life." *The New York Times*, September 5, 1999. Accessed November 24, 2015. http://www.nytimes .com/ library/film/090599film-cat.html.

Fenner, Angelica. "Turkish Cinema in the New Europe: Visualizing Ethnic Conflict in Sinan Çetin's *Berlin in Berlin*." *Camera Obscura* 15, no. 2 (2000): 104–149.

Fenske, Michaela. *Marktkultur in der Frühen Neuzeit. Wirtschaft, Macht und Unterhaltung auf einem Städtischen Jahr- und Viehmarkt*. Cologne, Germany: Böhlau, 2006.

Fischer, Ralf Michael. "A Film-Historical Whirl of Love and Multimedia Criticism of Illusions in Museum Space—Runa Islam's 'Martha' Adaptation 'Tuin.'" In *Fassbinder Now: Film and Video Art*, 210–219. Frankfurt am Main, Germany: Deutsches Filminstitut Filmmuseum and Rainer Werner Fassbinder Foundation, 2013.

Fisher, Jaimey and Brad Prager. Introduction to *The Collapse of the Conventional: German Film and Its Politics at the Turn of the Twenty-First Century*, edited by Jaimey Fischer and Brad Prager, 1–38. Detroit: Wayne State University Press, 2010.

Forbes, Jill. "La Haine." In *European Cinema: An Introduction*, Jill Forbes and Sarah Street, 170–180. New York: Palgrave Macmillan, 2000.

Forbes, Jill and Sarah Street. *European Cinema: An Introduction*. New York: Palgrave Macmillan, 2000.

Foucault, Michel. "What is an Author?" In *The Book History Reader*, edited by David Finkelstein and Alistair McCleery, 225–230. London: Routledge, 2002.

Fowler, Catherine. Introduction to *The European Cinema Reader*, edited by Catherine Fowler, 1–10. New York: Routledge, 2002.

Franklin, James. *New German Cinema: From Oberhausen to Hamburg*. Boston: Twayne Publishers, 1983.

Gallagher, Jessica. "Der neue deutsche Film ist türkisch: Issues of Space, Identity and Stereotypes in Contemporary Turkish-German Cinema." PhD diss., University of Queensland, 2008.

Galt, Rosalind. *The New European Cinema: Redrawing the Map*. New York: Columbia University Press, 2006.

Galt, Rosalind and Karl Schoonover. "Introduction: The Impurity of Art Cinema." In *Global Art Cinema: New Theories and Histories*, edited by Rosalind Galt and Karl Schoonover, 3–27. Oxford: Oxford University Press, 2010.

Gardner-Chloros, Penelope and Daniel Weston. "Code-switching and Multilingualism in Literature." *Language and Literature* 24, no. 3 (2015): 182–193.

Gemünden, Gerd. "Hollywood in Altona: Minority Cinema and the Transnational Imagination." In *German Pop Culture: How "American" Is It?*, edited by Agnes C. Mueller, 180–190. Ann Arbor: University of Michigan Press, 2004.

Gerstenberger, Katharina. *Writing the New Berlin: The German Capital in Post-Wall Literature*. Rochester: Camden House, 2008.

Gezen, Ela. "Converging Realisms: Aras Ören, Nazım Hikmet, and Bertolt Brecht." *Colloquia Germanica* 45, no. 3–4 (2012, publ. 2015): 377–393.

———. "Brecht on the Turkish Stage: Adaptation, Experimentation, and Theater Aesthetics in Genco Erkal's *Dostlar Tiyatrosu*." *German Life and Letters* 69, no. 2 (2016): 269–284.

Gezen, Ela and Berna Gueneli. "Introduction: Turkish-German Studies: Past, Present, and Future." In *Turkish-German Studies: Past, Present, and Future*. Special volume, edited by Yasemin Dayioğlu-Yücel, Michael Hofmann, Şeyda Ozil. Guest edited by Ela Gezen and Berna Gueneli. *Türkisch-deutsche Studien, Jahrbuch* 2015, 9–13. Göttingen, Germany: V&R Unipress, 2015.

Gezen, Ela and Berna Gueneli, eds. "Transnational Hi/Stories: Turkish-German Texts and Contexts." Special issue, *Colloquia Germanica* 44, no. 4 (2011, publ. 2015).

———. *Turkish-German Studies: Past, Present, and Future*. Special volume, edited by Yasemin Dayioğlu-Yücel, Michael Hofmann, Şeyda Ozil. Guest edited by Ela Gezen and Berna Gueneli. *Türkisch-deutsche Studien, Jahrbuch* 2015, 9–13. Göttingen, Germany: V&R Unipress, 2015.

Ghaussy, Sohelia. "Das Vaterland verlassen: Nomadic Language and 'Feminine Writing' in Emine Sevgi Özdamar's *Das Leben ist eine Karawanserei*." *German Quarterly* 72, no. 1 (1999): 1–16.

Gibson, Lela. "The Ottoman Empire and Turkish-German Studies." Paper presented at the annual meeting of the *German Studies Association*, Kansas City, Missouri, September 18–21, 2014.

Ginsberg, Terro and Chris Lippard, eds. *Historical Dictionary of Middle Eastern Cinema* Lanham, MD: Scarecrow Press, 2010.

Göçek, Fatma Müge. *A Question of Genocide: Armenians and Turks at the End of the Ottoman Empire*. Oxford: Oxford University Press, 2011.

Göktürk, Deniz. "Beyond Paternalism: Turkish German Traffic in Cinema." In *The German Cinema Book*, edited by Tim Bergfelder, Erica Carter, and Deniz Göktürk, 248–256. Suffolk, UK: BFI, 2002.

———. "Migration und Kino: Subnationale Mitleidskultur oder Transnationale Rollenspiele?" In *Interkulturelle Literatur in Deutschland: ein Handbuch,* edited by Carmine Chiellino, 329–347. Stuttgart, Germany: Metzler, 2000.

———. "Mobilität und Stillstand im Weltkino digital." In *Kultur als Ereignis. Fatih Akıns Film* Auf der anderen Seite *als transkulturelle Narration*, edited by Özkan Ezli, 15–45. Bielefeld, Germany: Transcript, 2010.

———. "Sound Bridges and Travelling Tunes." In *Congress Book: XVIIth International Congress of Aesthetics*, edited by Jale Nejdet Erzen, 423–236. Ankara: Sanart, 2008.

———. "Sound Bridges: Transnational Mobility as Ironic Drama." In *Shifting Landscapes: Film and Media in European Context*, edited by Miyase Christensen and Nezih Erdoğan, 153–171. Newcastle, UK: Cambridge Scholars Publishing, 2008.

———. "Strangers in Disguise: Role-Play beyond Identity Politics in Anarchic Film Comedy." In "Multicultural Germany, Art, Performance and Media." Special issue, *New German Critique* 92, (2004): 100–122.

———. "Turkish Delight—German Fright. Unsettling Oppositions in Transnational Cinema." *EIPCP: European Institute for Progressive Cultural Policies*, October 2000. Accessed January 15, 2008. http://eipcp.net/transversal/0101/goektuerk/en.

———. "Turkish Women on German Streets: Closure and Exposure in Transnational Cinema." In *Spaces in European Cinema*, edited by Myrto Konstantarakos, 64–76. Exeter, UK: Intellect, 2000.

———. "World Cinema Goes Digital: Looking at Europe from the Other Shore." In *Turkish German Cinema in the New Millennium: Sites, Sounds, and Screens*, edited by Sabine Hake and Barbara Mennel, 198–211. Oxford: Berghahn, 2012.

Göktürk, Deniz, David Gramling, and Anton Kaes, eds. *Germany in Transit: Nation and Migration, 1955–2005*. Berkeley: University of California Press, 2007.

Göktürk, Deniz, and Barbara Wolbert. Introduction to "Multicultural Germany: Art, Performance and Media." Special issue, *New German Critique* 92 (2004): 3–4.

Goldberg, Andreas. "Medien der Migrant/Innen." In *Interkulturelle Literatur in Deutschland: ein Handbuch*, edited by Carmine Chiellino and Andreas Goldberg, 419–435. Stuttgart, Germany: Metzler, 2000.

Goldmark, Daniel, Lawrence Kramer, and Richard D. Leppert. "Introduction: Phonoplay: Recasting Film Music." In *Beyond the Soundtrack: Representing Music in Cinema*, edited by Daniel Goldmark, Lawrence Kramer, Richard D. Leppert, 1–9. Berkeley: University of California Press, 2007.

Gorbman Claudia. *Unheard Melodies*. Bloomington: Indiana University, 1987.

Gott, Michael. *French-Language Road Cinema: Borders, Diasporas, Migration and "New Europe."* Edinburgh, UK: Edinburgh University Press, 2016.

Gott, Michael and Todd Herzog. Introduction to *East, West, and Centre: Reframing Post-1989 European Cinema*, edited by Michael Gott and Todd Herzog, 1–19. Edinburgh, UK: Edinburgh University Press, 2015.

Goulding, Daniel J. Review of *Emir Kusturica*, by Dina Iordanova. *Slavic Review* 63, no. 2 (2004): 389–391.

Gramling, David. "On the Other Side of Monolingualism: Fatih Akın's Linguistic Turn." *The German Quarterly* 83, no. 3 (2010): 353–372.

Gueneli, Berna. "Challenging European Borders: Fatih Akın's Filmic Visions of Europe." PhD diss., University of Texas at Austin, 2011.

———. "Fatih Akın's Filmic Visions of a New Europe: Spatial and Aural Constructions of Europe in *Im Juli/In July* (2000)." In *East, West, and Centre: Reframing Post- 1989 European Cinema*, edited by Michael Gott and Todd Herzog, 79–93. Edinburgh, UK: Edinburgh University Press, 2015.

———. "Reframing Islam: The Decoupling of Ethnicity from Religion in Turkish-German Media." In "Framing Islam: Faith, Fascination, and Fear in Twenty-First

Century Culture." Special issue, *Colloquia Germanica* 47, no. 1–2 (2014, publ. 2017): 59–82.

———. "Remixing Film Histories: Fatih Akın and the Creation of a Transnational Film History." In "Transnational Hi/Stories: Turkish-German Texts and Contexts." Special issue, *Colloquia Germanica* 44, no. 4 (2011, publ. 2014): 451–467.

———. "The Sound of Fatih Akın's Cinema: Polyphony and the Aesthetics of Heterogeneity in *The Edge of Heaven.*" *German Studies Review* 37, no. 2 (2014): 337–356.

———. "*Wut*, Who Is Enraged? Violence in the 'Victim Society." In *Jugendbilder: Repräsentationen von Jugend in Medien und Politik; Türkisch-deutsche Studien, Jahrbuch 2013*, edited by Yasemin Dayioğlu-Yücel, Michael Hofmann, Seyda Ozil, 95–112. Göttingen: V&R Unipress, 2013.

Gupta, Akhil and James Ferguson. "Beyond 'Culture': Space, Identity, and the Politics of Difference." In *The Cultural Geography Reader*, edited by Timothy S. Oakes and Patricia L. Price, 60-67. Hoboken: Routledge, 2008.

Hake, Sabine. "German Cinema as European Cinema: Learning from Film History." *Film History: An International Journal* 25, no. 1 (2013): 110–117.

———. *German National Cinema*. 2nd ed. London: Routledge, 2008.

Hake, Sabine and Barbara Mennel, eds. *Turkish German Cinema in the New Millennium: Sites, Sounds, and Screens*. Oxford: Berghahn, 2012.

Halle, Randall. *Europeanization of Cinema: Interzones and Imaginative Communities*. Urbana: University of Illinois Press, 2014.

———. "The Europeanization of Turkish-German Cinema: Complex Connectivity and Imaginative Communities." In *Türkisch-deutsche Studien, Jahrbuch 2015*, edited by Yasemin Dayıoğlu-Yücel, Michael Hofmann, Seyda Ozil. Guest edited by Ela Gezen and Berna Gueneli, 15–38. Göttingen: V&R Unipress, 2015.

———. *German Film after Germany: Toward a Transnational Aesthetic*. Urbana: University of Illinois Press, 2008.

———. "Offering Tales They Want to Hear: Transnational European Film Funding as Neo-Orientalism." In *New Theories and Histories: Global Art Cinema*, edited by Rosalind Galt and Karl Schoonover, 303–319. Oxford: Oxford University Press, 2010. Hanson, Helen. *Hollywood Soundscapes: Film Sound Style, Craft & Production in the Classical Era*. London: Palgrave Macmillan, 2017.

Hemetek, Ursula. "Applied Ethnomusicology in the Process of the Political Recognition of a Minority: A Case Study of the Austrian Roma." *Yearbook for Traditional Music* 38 (2006): 35–57.

Herbert, Ulrich. *A History of Foreign Labor in Germany, 1880–1980*. Ann Arbor: University of Michigan Press, 1990.

Herzog, Amy. *Dreams of Difference, Songs of the Same*. Minneapolis: University of Minnesota Press, 2010.

Higbee, Will. "Hope and Indignation in Fortress Europe: Immigration and Neoliberal Globalization in Contemporary French Cinema." *SubStance* 43, no. 1 (2014): 26–43.

Higbee, Will and Song Hwee Lim. "Concepts of Transnational Cinema: Toward a Critical Transnationalism in Film Studies." *Transnational Cinemas* 1, no. 1 (2010): 7–21.

Hillman, Roger. *Unsettling Scores*. Bloomington: Indiana University Press, 2005.

Hillman, Roger and Vivien Silvey. "Remixing Hamburg: Transnationalism in Fatih Akın's *Soul Kitchen*." In *Turkish German Cinema in the New Millennium: Sites, Sounds, and Screens*, edited by Sabine Hake and Barbara Mennel, 186–197. Oxford: Berghahn, 2012.

Horrocks, David and Eva Kolinsky. "Introduction: Migrants or Citizens? Turks in Germany between Exclusion and Acceptance." In *Turkish Culture in German Society Today*, edited by David Horrocks and Eva Kolinsky, x–xxviii. Providence, RI: Berghahn Books, 1996.

Hudson, Ray. "One Europe or Many? Reflections on Becoming European." *Transactions of the Institute of British Geographers* 25, no. 4 (2000): 409–426.

Iordanova, Dina. *Cinema of the Other Europe: The Industry and Artistry of East Central European Film*. London: Wallflower Press, 2003.

———. *Cinema of Flames: Balkan Film, Culture, and the Media*. London: BFI, 2001.

———. *Emir Kusturica*. London: BFI, 2002.

Jäckel, Anne. *European Film Industries*. London: British Film Institute, 2003.

Jeong, Seung-hoon and Jeremi Szeniawski. Introduction to *Global Auteur*, edited by Seung-hoon Jeong and Jeremi Szeniawski, 1–19. New York: Bloomsbury Academic, 2016.

Johnston, Cristina. "Intergenerational Verbal Conflicts, Plurilingualism and *Banlieue* Cinema." In *Polyglot Cinema: Migration and Transcultural Narration in France, Italy, Portugal and Spain*, edited by Verena Breger and Kiya Komori, 89–98. Münster, Germany: LIT, 2010.

Johnston, Sheila. "The Author as Public Institution: The 'New" Cinema in the Federal Republic of Germany." In *The European Cinema Reader*, edited by Catherine Fowler, 121–131. London: Routledge, 2002.

Kalinak, Kathryn. *Sound: Dialogue, Music, and Effects*. New Brunswick, NJ: Rutgers University Press, 2015.

Kassabian, Anahid. *Hearing Film*. New York: Routledge, 2001.

Kaya Mutlu, Dilek. "Between Tradition and Modernity: Yeşilçam Melodrama, Its Stars, and Their Audiences." *Middle Eastern Studies* 46.3 (2010): 417–431.

Kirk, John. "Urban Narratives: Contesting Place and Space in Some British Cinema from the 1980s." *Journal of Narrative Theory* 31, no. 3 (2001): 353–379.

Klinger, Barbara. *Melodrama and Meaning: History, Culture, and the Films of Douglas Sirk*. Bloomington: Indiana University Press, 1994.

Knopp, Matthias. "Identitäten zwischen den Kulturen: Gegen die Wand." In *Kontext Film: Beiträge zu Film und Literatur*, edited by Michael Braun and Werner Kamp, 59–77. Berlin: Erich Schmidt, 2006.

Konuk, Kader. *East West Mimesis: Auerbach in Turkey*. Palo Alto, CA: Stanford University Press, 2010.

Korte, Barbara and Claudia Sternberg. *Bidding for the Mainstream? Black and Asian British Film since the 1990s*. Amsterdam: Rodopi, 2004.

Kosnick, Kira. *Migrant Media: Turkish Broadcasting and Multicultural Politics in Berlin*. Bloomington: Indiana University Press, 2007.

Kosta, Barbara. "Transnational Space and Music: Fatih Akın's *Crossing the Bridge: The Sound of Istanbul* (2005)." In *Spatial Turns: Space, Place, and Mobility in German Literary and Visual Culture*, edited by Jamey Fisher and Barbara Mennel, 343–360. Amsterdam: Rodopi, 2010.

Kotecki, Kristine. “Europeanizing the Balkans at the Sarajevo Film Festival.” *Journal of Narrative Theory* 44, no. 3 (2014): 344–366.

Kristeva, Julia. “Word, Dialogue, Novel.” In *The Kristeva Reader*, edited by Toril Moi, 34–61. New York: Columbia University Press, 1986.

Kuhn, Anna A. “Bourgeois Ideology and the (Mis)Reading of Günter Wallraff’s *Ganz Unten*.” In “Minorities in German Culture.” Special issue, *New German Critique* 46 (1989): 191–202.

Laderman, David. *Driving Visions: Exploring the Road Movie*. Austin: University of Texas Press, 2002.

Loshitzky, Yosefa. *Screening Strangers: Migration and Diaspora in Contemporary European Cinema*. Bloomington: Indiana University Press, 2010.

Ludewig, Alexandra. *Screening Nostalgia: 100 Years of German Heimat Film*. Bielefeld, Germany: Transcript, 2014.

Luna, David and Laura A. Peracchio. “Moderators of Language Effects in Advertising in Bilinguals: A Psycholinguistic Approach.” *Journal of Consumer Research* 28, no. 2 (2001): 284–295.

———. “Sociolingusitic Effects on Code-Switching Ads Targeting Bilingual Consumers.” *Journal of Advertising* 34, no. 2 (2005): 43–56.

Machtans, Karolin. “The Perception and Marketing of Fatih Akın in the German Press.” In *Turkish German Cinema in the New Millennium*, edited by Sabine Hake and Barbara Mennel, 149–160. Oxford: Berghahn, 2012.

Mackuth, Margaret. *Es geht um Freiheit. Interkulturelle Motive in den Spielfilmen Fatih Akins*. Saarbrücken, Germany: VDM Verlag Dr. Müller, 2007.

Mani, Venkat. *Cosmopolitical Claims: Turkish-German Literature from Nadolny to Pamuk*. Iowa City: University of Iowa Press, 2007.

Massey, Doreen. “A Global Sense of Place.” In *The Cultural Geography Reader*, edited by Tomothy Oakes and Patricia L. Price, 257–263. Hoboken, NJ: Routledge, 2008.

———. *For Space*. London: Sage, 2005.

Maule, Rosanna. *Beyond Auteurism: New Directions in Authorial Film Practices in France, Italy and Spain Since the 1980s*. Bristol, UK: Intellect, 2008.

Mazierska, Ewa and Laura Rascaroli. *Crossing New Europe: Postmodern Travel and the European Road Movie*. London: Wallflower, 2006.

McNeill, Isabelle. “Virtual Homes: Space and Memory in the Work of Yamina Benguigui.” *L'Esprit Créateur*, 51, no.1 (2011): 12–25.

Meehan, Elizabeth. “Rethinking the Path to European Citizenship.” In *Migration and Cultural Inclusion in the European City*, edited by J.V. William Neill and Uve-Hanns Schwedler, 17–32. New York: Palgrave Macmillan, 2007.

Mennel, Barbara. “Bruce Lee in Kreuzberg and Scarface in Altona: Transnational Auteurism and Ghettocentrism in Thomas Arslan’s *Brothers and Sisters* and Fatih Akin’s *Short Sharp Shock*.” *New German Critique* 87 (2002): 133–156.

———. *Cities and Cinema*. New York: Routledge, 2008.

———. “Criss-Crossing in Global Space and Time: Fatih Akın’s *The Edge of Heaven* (2007).” *TRANSIT* 5, no.1 (2009): 1–28. Accessed August 2, 2017 http://escholarship.org/uc/item/28x3x9r0.

———. “Überkreuzungen in globaler Zeit und globalem Raum in Fatih Akıns *Auf der anderen Seite*.” In *Kultur als Ereignis*, edited by Özkan Ezli, 95–118. Bielefeld, Germany: Transcript, 2010.

Mercer, John and Martin Shingler, *Melodrama: Genre, Style, Sensibility*. London: Wallflower, 2005.

Mills, Katie. *The Road Movie Story and the Rebel: Moving Through Film, Fiction, and Television*. Carbondale: Southern Illinois University Press, 2006.

Naficy, Hamid. *An Accented Cinema: Exilic and Diasporic Filmmaking*. Princeton, NJ: Princeton University Press, 2001.

———. "From Accented Cinema to Multiplex Cinema." In *Convergence Media History*, edited by Sabine Hake and Janet Staiger, 3–13. New York: Routledge, 2009.

Naqvi, Fatima. *The Literary and Cultural Rhetoric of Victimhood: Western Europe, 1970–2005*. New York: Palgrave Macmillan, 2007.

Nava, Mica. *Visceral Cosmopolitanism: Gender, Culture and the Normalization of Difference*. Oxford: Berg, 2007.

Neill, William J.V. and Hanns-Uve Schwedler, eds. *Migration and Cultural Inclusion in the European City*. New York: Palgrave Macmillan, 2007.

Neubauer, Jochen. *Türkische Deutsche, Kanakster und Deutschländer: Identität und Fremdwahrnehmung in Film und Literatur: Fatih Akin, Thomas Arslan, Emine Sevgi Özdamar, Zafer Şenocak und Feridun Zaimoğlu*. Würzburg, Germany: Königshausen & Neumann, 2011.

Neumeyer, David. *The Oxford Handbook of Film Music Studies*. New York: Oxford University Press, 2015.

Orgeron, Devin. *Road Movies: From Muybridge and Méliès to Lynch and Kiarostam*. Houndsmills, UK: Palgrave Macmillan, 2008.

Petek, Polona. "Enabling Collisions: Re-Thinking Multiculturalism through Fatih Akin's *Gegen die Wand/Head On*." *Studies in European Cinema* 4, no. 3 (2007): 177– 186.

Peukert, Brigitte. "Fassbinder Re-Framed." In *Fassbinder Now: Film and Video Art*, 42–56. Frankfurt am Main, Germany: Deutsches Filminstitut Filmmuseum and Rainer Werner Fassbinder Foundation, 2013.

Planchenault, Gaëlle. "Displacement and Plurilingualism in *Inch'Allah Dimanche*: Appropriating the Other's Language in Order to Find One's Place." In *Polyglot Cinema: Migration and Transcultural Narration in France, Italy, Portugal and Spain*, edited by Verena Breger and Kiya Komori, 99–110. Münster, Germany: LIT, 2010.

Pratt, Mary Louise. "Language and the Afterlife of Empire." *PMLA* 130, no. 2 (2015): 348–357.

Pratt Ewing, Katherine. "Between Cinema and Social Work: Diasporic Turkish Women and the (Dis)Pleasures of Hybridity." *Cultural Anthropology* 21.2 (2006): 265–94.

Pravinchandra, Shital. "Hospitality for Sale, or *Dirty Pretty Things*." *Cultural Critique* 85 (2013): 38–60.

Reisoğlu, Mert Bahadır. "From Poetry to Prose: Özdamar and the Ikinci Yeni Poetry Movement." In *Türkisch-deutsche Studien, Jahrbuch 2015*, edited by Yasemin Dayioğlu-Yücel Michael Hoffmann, and Seyda Ozil. Guest edited by Ela Gezen and Berna Gueneli, 97–115. Göttingen: V&R Unipress, 2015.

Rentschler, Eric. "From New German Cinema to the Post-Wall Cinema of Consensus." In *Cinema and Nation*, edited by Mette Hjort and Scott MacKenzie, 260–277. New York: Routledge, 2000.

———. "Postwall Prospects: An Introduction." In "Postwall Cinema." Special issue, *New German Critique* 87 (2002): 3–5.
Rice, Alice. "Rehearsing October 17, 1961: The Role of Fiction in Remembering the Battle of Paris," *L'Esprit Créateur* 54, no. 4 (2014): 90–102.
Rivi, Luisa. *European Cinema after 1989: Cultural Identity and Transnational Production*. New York: Palgrave Macmillan, 2007.
Rothberg, Michael. *Multidirectional Memory: Remembering the Holocaust in the Age of Decolonization*. Stanford, CA: Stanford University Press, 2009.
Savage, Mika, Gaynor Bagnall, and Brian Longhurst. *Globalization & Belonging*. London: Sage, 2005.
Sergi, Gianluca. *The Dolby Era: Film Sound in Contemporary Hollywood*. Manchester, UK: Manchester University Press, 2004.
Schäffler, Diana. *Deutscher Film mit türkischer Seele: Entwicklungen und Tendenzen der deutsch-türkischen Filme von den 70er Jahren bis zur Gegenwart*. Saarbrücken: VDM Verlag Dr. Müller, 2007.
Seyhan, Azade. "Lost in Translation: Re-Membering the Mother Tongue in Emine Sevgi Özdamar's *Das Leben ist eine Karawanserei*." In "Culture Studies." Special issue, *German Quarterly* 69, no. 4 (1996): 414–426.
———. *Writing Outside the Nation*. Princeton, NJ: Princeton University Press, 2000.
Sieg, Katrin. *Choreographing the Global in European Cinema and Theater*. New York: Palgrave Macmillan, 2008.
Sieglohr, Ulrike. "New German Cinema." In *World Cinema: Critical Approaches*, edited by John Hill and Pamela Church Gibson, 82–86. Oxford: Oxford University Press, 2000.
Siewert, Senta. "Soundtracks of Double Occupancy: Sampling Sounds and Cultures in Fatih Akin's *Head On*." In *Mind the Screen: Media Concepts According to Thomas Elsaesser*, edited by Jaap Kooijman, Patricia Pisters, and Wanda Strauven, 198–208. Amsterdam: Amsterdam University Press, 2008.
Squires, Michael. "Adam Bede and the Locus Amoenus." *Studies in English Literature, 1500–1900* 13, no. 4 (1973): 670–676.
Staiger, Janet. "Authorship Approaches." In *Authorship and Film*, edited by David A. Gerstner and Janet Staiger, 27–57. New York: Routledge, 2002.
Stehle, Maria. *Ghetto Voices in Contemporary German Culture: Textscapes, Filmcsapes, Soundscapes*. Rochester, NY: Camden House, 2012.
Suner, Asuman. "Dark Passion." *Sight & Sound* 15, no. 3 (March 2005): 18–21.
———. *New Turkish Cinema: Belonging, Identity and Memory*. London: I.B. Tauris, 2010.
Swamy, Vinay. "Politicizing the Sexual, Sexualizing the Political: The Crossing of Political and Sexual Orientation in Stephen Frears' and Hanif Kureishi's *My Beautiful Laundrette* (1986)." *Comparative Literature Studies* 40, no. 2 (2003): 142–158.
Szeman, Ioana. "'Gypsy Music' and Deejays: Orientalism, Balkanism, and Romani Musicians." *TDR: The Drama Review* 53, no. 3 (2009): 98–116.
Tarr, Carrie. *Reframing Difference: Beur and Banlieue Filmmaking in France*. Manchester, UK: Manchester University Press/Palgrave Macmillan, 2005.
Tawada, Yoko and Rachel McNichol. "From Mother Tongue to Linguistic Mother." *Manoa* 18, no. 1 (2006): 1139–143.

Tezcan, Levent. "Der Tod Diesseits von Kultur—Wie Fatih Akın den Großen Kulturdialog umgeht." In *Kultur als Ereignis*, edited by Özkan Ezli, 47–70. Bielefeld, Germany: Transcript, 2010.

Thom, Randy and Philip Brophy. "Randy Thom in Conversation: Designing a Movie for Sound." In *Cinesonic*, edited by Philip Brophy, 1–28. New South Wales, Australia: Southwood Press, 2000.

Tonkiss, Fran. "Aural Postcards: Sound, Memory and the City." In *The Auditory Culture Reader*, edited by Michael Bull and Les Back, 303–309. Oxford: Berg, 2003.

Torres, Lourdes. "In the Contact Zone: Code-Switching Strategies by Latino/a Writers." In "In the Contact Zone: Language, Race, Class, and Nation." Special issue, *Melus* 32, no. 1 (2007): 75–96.

Totten, Monika and Yoko Tawada. "Writing in Two Languages: A Conversation with Yoko Tawada." *Harvard Review* no. 17 (1999): 93–100.

Trifonova, Temenuga. Introduction to *European Film Theory*, edited by Trifonova Temenuga, xviii–xxxiv. London: Routledge, 2009.

Tunc Cox, Ayca. "Hyphenated Identities: The Reception of Turkish-German Cinema in the Turkish Daily Press." In *Turkish German Cinema in the New Millennium*, edited by Sabine Hake and Barbara Mennel, 161–174. Oxford: Berghahn, 2012.

Türkyılmaz, Yektan. "Rethinking Genocide: Violence and Victimhood in Eastern Anatolia: 1913–1915." PhD diss., Duke University, 2007.

Vincendeau, Ginette. "Issues in European Cinema." In *World Cinema: Critical Approaches*, edited by John Hill and Pamela Church Gibson, 56–64. Oxford: Oxford University Press, 2000.

———. *La Haine*. London: I.B. Tauris, 2005.

Volk, Stefan. "Von der Form zum Material: Fatih Akin's doppeltes Spiel mit dem Genrekino in *Gegen die Wand* und *Auf der anderen Seite*." In *Kultur as Ereignis*, edited by Özkan Ezli, 151–158. Bielefeld, Germany: Transcript, 2010.

Wayne, Mike. *The Politics of Contemporary European Cinema: Histories, Borders, Diasporas*. Bristol, UK: Intellect, 2002.

White, Rob. "Nuri Bilge Ceylan: An Introduction and Interview" *Film Quarterly* 65, no. 2 (2011): 64–72.

Wierzbicki, James. *Film Music: A History*. New York, Routledge, 2009.

Wood, Mary P. *Contemporary European Cinema*. London: Hodder Arnold, 2007.

Wright Wexman, Virginia. Introduction to *Film and Authorship*, edited by Wright Wexman, 1–18. New Brunswick, NJ: Rutgers University Press, 2003.

Yeşilada, Karen. *Poesie der Dritten Sprache*. Tübingen, Germany: Stauffenburg, 2012.

Yıldız, Yasemin. *Beyond the Mother Tongue: The Postmonolingual Condition*. New York: Fordham University Press, 2013.

———. "Kritisch 'Kanak': Gesellschaftskritik, Sprache und Kultur bei Feridun Zaimoglu." In *Wider den Kulturenzwang: Migration, Kulturalisierung, Weltliteratur*, edited by Özkan Ezli, Dorothee Kimmich, and Anette Werberger, 187–206. Bielefeld, Germany: Transcript, 2009.

———. "Political Trauma and Literal Translation: Emine Sevgi Özdamar's 'Mutterzunge'." *Gegenwartsliteratur* 7 (2008): 248–270.

Yılmaz, Ferruh. *How the Workers Became Muslims: Immigration, Culture, and Hegemonic Transformation in Europe*. Ann Arbor: University of Michigan Press, 2016.

Yurdakul, Gökçe. *From Guest Workers into Muslims: The Transformation of Turkish Immigrant Associations in Germany.* Newcastle, UK: Cambridge Scholars Publishing, 2009.

Online Sources

"48 FIC XiXÓn: Festival International de Cine de Gijón 19–28 Noviembre de 2009." *Gijon Film Festival.* Accessed on July 22, 2010. http://www.gijonfilmfestival.com/noticias.asp?idioma= 3&idmenu=2&idnoticias=73.

"66th Venice Film Festival—Fatih Akin—Moritz Bleibtreu." YouTube. Accessed April 1, 2010. http://www.youtube.com/watch?v=qtv5BcDn-AA&feature=youtube_gdata.

"Akin, Fatih." Hamburg.de. Accessed July 22, 2010. http://www.hamburg.de/magazin/8204/hamburg-von-a-d.html.

"And the LUX Prize for European cinema goes to... 'Auf der anderen Seite' ('On the Edge of Heaven')." European Parliament, press release. October 24, 2007. Accessed February 1, 2016. http://www.europarl.europa.eu/sides/getDoc.do?type=IM-PRESS&reference=20071023IPR12109&language=EN

ARD Mediathek. "Anne Will: Die Kanzlerin in der Flüchtlingskrise—Können wir es wirklich schaffen, Frau Merkel?" Accessed October 8, 2015. http://www.ardmediathek.de/tv/Anne-Will/Die-Kanzlerin-in-der-Fl%C3%BCchtlingskrise-/Das-Erste/Video?documentId=30981456&bcastId=32 8454.

Ataman, Ferda. "Studie zu Ehrenmorden: Was den Mord zum Ehrenmord macht." *Zeit Online.* December 7, 2009. Accessed December 14, 2009. http://www.zeit.de/gesellschaft/ generationen/2009-12/ehrenmord-studie.

Auswärtiges Amt Deutschland. "Law on Nationality." September 16, 2005. Accessed January 8, 2010. http://www.auswaertiges-amt.de/diplo/en/WillkommeninD/EinreiseUndAufenthalt/Staatsangehoerigkeitsrecht.html.

Auswärtiges Amt Deutschland. "Das Schengener Uebereinkommen und Schengener Durchführungsübereinkommen." December 11, 2008. Accessed January 30, 2009. http://www.auswaertiges-amt.de/en/WilkommeninD/EinreiseUndAufenthalt/StaatSangehoerigkeitsrecht.html.

Badt, Karin Luisa. "Fatih Akin 'The Other Side of Heaven.'" *Parisvoice.* Accessed March 20, 2014. http://www.parisvoice.com/movies/427-fatih-akin-qthe-other-side-of-heavenq.

Baydar, Yavuz. "Death of a Great Actor—Tuncel Kurtiz." *Today's Zaman.* September 29, 2013. Modified September 30, 2013. Accessed on February 5, 2016. http://en.dunyatimes.com/article/death-of-a-great-actor-tuncel-kurtiz-24135.html.

"Berlinale 2004: 'Gegen die Wand ('Head On"), by Fatih Akin, 2007." YouTube. Accessed April 1, 2010. http://www.youtube.com/watch?v=035FuRpfmbA&feature=youtube_gdata.

Brenner, Bernd. "Der Klang der deutschen Sprache—'Wie eine Schreibmaschine, die Alufolie frisst.'" Deutschlandfunk. December 26, 2014. Accessed September 18, 2015. http://www.deutschlandfunk.de/der-klang-der-deutschen-sprache-wie-eine-schreibmaschine.1184.de.html?dram:article_id=307163.

"Brooklyn Funk Essentials." Last.fm. Accessed August 9, 2010. http://www.last.fm/music/Brooklyn+Funk+Essentials.

"Cappadocia—World Heritage Site—National Geographic." *National Geographic*. December 19, 2015. http://travel.nationalgeographic.com/travel/world-heritage /cappadocia/.

Cartwright, Garth. "Awards for World Music: Winner 2006 DJ Shantel (Germany)." BBC Radio, February 2007. http://www.bbc.co.uk/radio3/worldmusic/a4wm2006 /a4wm_ shantel.shtml.

Chrisafis, Angelique. "'Nothing's changed': 10 years after French riots, *banlieues* remain in crisis." *The Guardian*, October 22, 2015. Accessed December 7, 2015. http://www.theguardian.com/world/2015/oct/22/nothings-changed-10-years -after-french-riots-banlieues-remain-in-crisis.

Connolly, Kate. "German director's Holocaust film causes outrage." *The Guardian*, November 12, 2010. Accessed May 10, 2016. http://www.theguardian.com/world /2010/nov/12/uwe-boll-auschwitz-film-causes-outrage.

"Dresdner Sinfoniker: Aghet Projektseite." Accessed May 19, 2016. http://www.aghet.eu /aghet-aktu-intervention/.

"Dresdner Sinfoniker: Offener Brief." May 10, 2016. http://www.aghet.eu/.

Eddy, Melissa. "Migrant Tide Bringing Out Europe's Best and Worst." *The New York Times*, September 9, 2015. Accessed September 11, 2015. http://www.nytimes.com /2015/09/10/world/europe/migrants-refugee-tensions-in-europe.html.

European Commission: Multilingualism. "EU Languages and Language Policy." Accessed February 9, 2011. http://ec.europa.eu/ education/languages/languages -of-europe/index_en.htm.

European Parliament. "LUX 07 Cinema Prize." Last Modified October 24, 2007. http:// www.lux-prize.eu/lux07/index_en.htm.

European Union. "EUROPA-Languages-Language Learning." February 4, 2008. Accessed April 1, 2010. http:// europa.eu/languages/en/chapter/14.

European Union. "EU administration." Updated August 25, 2015. Accessed September 10, 2015. http://europa.eu/about-eu/facts-figures/administration/index_en.htm.

"Fatih Akin: 'El cine y la cocina tienen muchos elementos en común.'" *El Mundo*. March 30, 2010. http://www.elmundo.es/elmundo/ 2010/03/29/cultura/1269861236.html.

"Fatih Akin: 'Me estaba oscureciendo a mí mismo con tanta tragedia.'" *La tercera*. March 29, 2010. Accessed July 22, 2010. http://latercera.com/contenido/1453 _237639_9.shtml.

Fatih Akın Best Director at Altın Portakal Film Festival, 2007. YouTube. Accessed April 1, 2010. http://www.youtube.com/watch?v=fOeTz4gdjD4&feature=youtube_gdata.

"Fatih Akin Verfilmt den 'Goldenen Handschuh.'" *Zeit Online*, February 14, 2018. Accessed February 14, 2018. https://www.zeit.de/news/2018-02/14/fatih-akin -verfilmt-den-goldenen-handschuh-180214-99-65702.

Feinstein, Howard. "'Black Cat, White Cat': Kusturica Returns to the Gypsy Life." *New York Times*, September 5, 1999. Accessed November 24, 2015. http://www.nytimes .com/ library/film/090599film-cat.html.

Filmfest Hamburg 2014. "Douglas-Sirk-Preis für Fatih Akın." Accessed July 31, 2014. http://www.filmfesthamburg.de/de/presse/2014/2014.07.25_SirkPreis.php.

Filmportal. "Sowohl als auch: das 'deutsch-türkische' Kino heute." Filmportal.de. Accessed April 9, 2011. http://www.filmportal.de/thema/sowohl-als-auch-das-deutsch-tuerkische-kino-heute.

Fischer, Sebastian. "Ich bin sehr froh, dass ich die Tat begangen habe." *Spiegel Online*. October 10, 2007. Accessed December 14, 2009. http://www.spiegel.de/panorama/justiz/0,1518,510671,00.html.

Gesell, Sina. "Ein gnadenloser Romantiker." *Nordbayersicher Kurier*. May 24, 2010. Accessed July 22, 2010. http://nordbayerischer-kurier.de/nachrichten/1290618/details_8.htm.

Goethe Institut. "Heute fühle ich mich als Grieche." Accessed September 24, 2015. https://www.goethe.de/de/uun/akt/20488257.html.

"Gülsüm wurde nach Abtreibung erschlagen." *Die Welt*. April 2, 2009. Accessed December 14, 2009. http://www.welt.de/vermischtes/article3491080/Guelsuem-wurde-nach-Abtreibung-erschlagen.html.

Halpern, Dan. "The (Mis)Directions of Emir Kusturica." *New York Times*, May 8, 2005. Accessed November 24, 2015. http://www.nytimes.com/2005/05/08/magazine/the-misdirections-of-emir-kusturica.html?_r=0.

"*Italianamerican*—1/5 Martin Scorsese." 1974. YouTube. Accessed April 19, 2016. http://www. youtube.com/watch?v=2tzKa1Lb4lM.

"*Italianamerican* 2/5—Martin Scorsese." 1974. YouTube. Accessed April 19, 2016. http://www.youtube.com/watch?v=MzVGuCUj4yY.

"*Italianamerican* 3/5—Martin Scorsese." 1974. YouTube. Accessed April 19, 2016. http://www.youtube.com/watch?v=3gonQKFbtec.

"*Italianamerican* 4/5—Martin Scorsese." 1974. YouTube. Accessed April 19, 2016. http://www.youtube.com/watch?v=l1BVeHlFsbE.

"*Italianamerican* 5/5—Martin Scorsese." YouTube. 1974. Accessed April 19, 2016. https://www.youtube.com/watch?v=5JZX71w2DOA.

James, Caryn. "Movie Review—Hate—Fil Festival Review; Crime, Violence and Pessimism." *New York Times*, October 12, 1995. Accessed December 7, 2015. http://www.nytimes.com/movie/review?res=9E0DE5D81339F931A25753C1A963958260.

"Junges Deutschland: Fatih Akin—Ein Regisseur der Globalisierung." *Stimme Russlands*. April 24, 2009. Accessed January 14, 2011. http://german.ruvr.ru/radio_broadcast/4001839/4001863.html.

Kenny, Alison. "Coming to Terms with Turkey through Films: *Yol*—by Yılmaz Güney." *Today's Zaman*, September 20, 2010. Accessed on April 12, 2014. http://www.todayszaman.com/news-222104-coming-to-terms-with-turkey-through-films-yol-by-yilmaz-guney.html.

Krischke, Wolfgang. "Sprache: 'Ich geh Schule.'" *Zeit Online*. June 29, 2006. Accessed January 7, 2010. http://www.zeit.de/2006/27/C-Kiezdeutsch.

Kroll, Justin. "'In the Fade' Director to Take on Stephen King's 'Forestarter' for Universal, Blumhouse (Exclusive)." *Variety*, June 28, 2018. Accessed June 30, 2018. https://variety.com/2018/film/news/firestarter-fatih-akin-stephen-king-universal-blumhouse-1202852347/.

Lux—Filmpreis gegen Sprachbarrieren im europäischen Film." Lux-Prize.eu, Informationen zur europäischen Filmproduktion. Accessed January 10, 2010. http://lux-prize.eu/.

Musharbash, Yassin. "Man lebte in Kreuzberg, aber wohl nicht in Deutschland." *Spiegel Online*. April 13, 2009. Accessed December 14, 2009. http://www.spiegel.de/panorama/justiz/0,1518, 411283,00.html.

Maslin, Janet. "Black Cat, White Cat (1998) Film Festival Review; Take Gypsies, Add the Danube and Mix Well with Jubilation." *New York Times Book Review.* October 3, 1998. Accessed November 24, 2015. http://www.nytimes.com/movie/review?res=9b 05efde1338f930a35753c1a96e958 260.

"Offener Brief: Fatih Akin boykottiert Filmpremiere in der Schweiz." *MIGAZIN: Migration in Germany.* 4 December 2009. http://www.migazin.de/2009/12/04 /fatih-akin-boykottiert-filmpremiere-in- der- schweiz/.

Osborne, Samuel. "Recep Tayyip Erdogan Slams 'Fascist and Cruel' Europe and Says Turkey May Review Ties after Powers Referendum." *Independent.* March 21, 2017. Accessed March 23, 2017. http://www.independent.co.uk/news/world /europe/recep-tayyip-erdogan-europe-facist-cruel-turkey-president-powers -referendum-a7641171.html.

Petrou, Michael. "A Turkish Scholar Discusses the Armenian Genocide." *Macleans.* May 31, 2012. Accessed February 9, 2016. http://www.macleans.ca/news/world /a-turkish-scholar-discusses-the-armenian-genocide/.

Rozsa, Matthew. "Uwe Boll a Master of Bad Movies Finally Makes a Winner with Auschwitz [Graphic Video]." *Mic.*, June 28, 2012. Accessed May 10, 2016. https:// mic.com/articles/10370/uwe-boll-a-master-of-bad-movies-finally-makes-a-winner -with-auschwitz-graphic-video#.SNFmTIArB.

"Sarkozy Launches Presidential Bid with Anti-Turkey Stance." *EU Observer.* January 15, 2007. Accessed February 1, 2016. http://euobserver.com/political/23251.

Statista. "Tourismus—Beliebteste Urlaubsziele der Deutschen 2015." Accessed September 18, 2015. http://de.statista.com/statistik/daten/studie/170822/umfrage /tourismus---beliebteste-urlaubsziele-der-letzten-12-monate/.

Schulte von Drach, Markus C. "Jugendsprache: Yalla, Lan! Bin ich Kino?" *Sueddeutsche Zeitung.* May 19, 2010. Accessed August 2, 2017. https://www.sueddeutsche.de /wissen/jugendsprache-yalla-lan-bin-ich-kino-1.911134.

Sommer, Theo. "Endet Europa am Bosporus." *Zeit Online.* April 3, 1992. Accessed January 10, 2010. http://www.zeit.de/1992/15/Endet-Europa-am-Bosporus?page=3.

Soundcloud. "Djipek." Accessed May 23, 2016. https://soundcloud.com/djipek.

"Soundtrack Is Abysmal." IMDB. http://www.imdb.com/title/tt4003 966/board/nest /256981982?ref_=tt_bd_5.

"Sowohl als auch: Das 'deutsch-türkische' Kino heute." Filmportal.de. Accessed March 1, 2014. https://www.filmportal.de/thema/sowohl-als-auch-das-deutsch -tuerkische-kino-heute.

"Studenten-Oscars 2015: Gold für İlker Çatak." *Sueddeutsche Zeitung.* September 18, 2015. Accessed September 22, 2015. http://www.sueddeutsche.de/kultur/nachwuchs -filmpreis-in-los-angeles-ilker-atak-gewinnt-goldenen-studenten-oscar-1.2653342.

Stimme Russlands. "Junges Russland: Fatih Akin—Ein Regisseur der Globalisierung." Last modified April 24, 2009. http://german.ruvr.ru/radio _broadcast/4001839/4001863.html.

Szewczyk, Daniel. "Warum Deutsch hart klingt—und Arabisch forsch." *Welt Online.* August 18th, 2013. Accessed September 18, 2015. http://www.welt.de/wissenschaft /article119098264/Warum-Deutsch-hart-klingt-und-Arabisch-forsch.html.

Traynor, Ian and Patrick Kingsley. "EU Governments Push Through Divisive Deal to Share 120,000 Refugees." *Guardian*, September 22, 2015. http://theguardian.com /world/2015/ep/22/eu-governments-divisive-quotas-deal-share-120000-refugees.

Vincendeau, Ginette. "*La Haine* and After: Arts, Politics, and the Banlieue," *The Criterion Collection*, May 8, 2012. Accessed December 7, 2015. http://www.criterion.com/current/posts/642-la-haine-and-after-arts-politics-and-the-banlieue.

von Bullion, Constanze. "In den Fängen einer türkischen Familie." *Sueddeutsche Zeitung*, February 25, 2005. Accessed December 14, 2009. http://www.sueddeutsche.de/politik/118/358943/text/.

Index

BERNA GUENELI

is Assistant Professor of German at the University of Georgia at Athens.

www.ingramcontent.com/pod-product-compliance
Lightning Source LLC
LaVergne TN
LVHW020432080826
844660LV00034B/1409
9780253024459